D1279312

Sex Role Changes

HQ
1075
.W48
1986

Sex Role Changes

Technology, Politics, and Policy

Marcia Lynn Whicker
and
Jennie Jacobs Kronenfeld

WITHDRAWN

PRAEGER

PRAEGER SPECIAL STUDIES • PRAEGER SCIENTIFIC

New York • Philadelphia • Eastbourne, UK
Toronto • Hong Kong • Tokyo • Sydney

368547
Tennessee Tech. Library
Cookeville, Tenn.

Library of Congress Cataloging-in-Publication Data

Whicker, Marcia Lynn.
  Sex role changes.

  Bibliography: p.
Includes indexes.
  1. Sex role. 2. Sexual division of labor.
3. Contraceptives. 4. Technology—Social aspects.
I. Kronenfeld, Jennie J. II. Title.
HQ1075.W48   1985   305.3   85-16763
ISBN 0-03-001293-7 (alk. paper)

Published in 1986 by Praeger Publishers
CBS Educational and Professional Publishing, a Division of CBS Inc.
521 Fifth Avenue, New York, NY 10175 USA

© 1986 by Praeger Publishers

All rights reserved

6789   052   987654321

Printed in the United States of America on acid-free paper

INTERNATIONAL OFFICES

Orders from outside the United States should be sent to the appropriate address listed below. Orders from areas not listed below should be placed through CBS International Publishing, 383 Madison Ave., New York, NY 10175 USA

Australia, New Zealand
Holt Saunders, Pty. Ltd., 9 Waltham St., Artarmon, N.S.W. 2064, Sydney, Australia

Canada
Holt, Rinehart & Winston of Canada, 55 Horner Ave., Toronto, Ontario, Canada M8Z 4X6

Europe, the Middle East, & Africa
Holt Saunders, Ltd., 1 St. Anne's Road, Eastbourne, East Sussex, England BN21 3UN

Japan
Holt Saunders, Ltd., Ichibancho Central Building, 22-1 Ichibancho, 3rd Floor, Chiyodaku, Tokyo, Japan

Hong Kong, Southeast Asia
Holt Saunders Asia, Ltd., 10 Fl, Intercontinental Plaza, 94 Granville Road, Tsim Sha Tsui East, Kowloon, Hong Kong

Manuscript submissions should be sent to the Editorial Director, Praeger Publishers, 521 Fifth Avenue, New York, NY 10175 USA

Acknowledgments

The author would like to thank many people for assistance in writing this book. Our department chairs, Charles W. Kegley of Government and International Studies and Roger Amidon of Health Administration, School of Public Health, provided graduate assistants, secretarial support for manuscript copying, and support for travel to professional meetings. Several graduate students from both departments, and especially Ruth Ann Strickland of Government and International Studies, helped collect materials. Several colleagues at the University of South Carolina loaned us material from their personal libraries, including Natalie Jane Hevener and Sue Tolleson Rinehart. Colleagues at professional meetings were helpful in responding to the proposed ideas. Particularly helpful were various members of Sociologists for Women in Society.

Other people influential in our lives inspired us to explore the ideas included in this book. We would like to thank feminist scholars who preceded us and focused attention of the various social sciences on the particular problems of women in society. We are particularly grateful to the women who gave us something to write about in both the first and second feminist movements. Their commitment and political activism resulted in improvements for all women and made our positions as academic scholars possible today.

We would also like to thank those politicians who had the courage to support women's rights, even when doing so was not popular. We are appreciative of men who are willing to challenge stereotypes and support equal rights for women, in personal practice as well as theory. Special thanks are due former teachers who encouraged us to pursue our academic careers with enthusiasm and excellence, including John Wanat, Malcolm Jewell, Michael Baer, Jim White, Tom Cronin, Peter Filene, Charles Goldsmid, Basil Zimmer, Albert Wesson, and Lois Monteiro.

Marcia would like to thank her mother, Ola Whicker, and acknowledge her now deceased father, Gilmer Whicker, for their emphasis upon equality within the family. They supported her challenges to often heard statements that "Women and girls don't do that." She also thanks her brother, Steve Whicker, for encouraging her to excel in all activities, inclusing those not traditionally open to girls. Additional appreciation goes to Terry Taylor, Marcia's ex-husband, for tolerating a nontraditional relationship and marriage for ten years. Marcia would also like to thank her many friends, both male and female, whose daily lives, problems, and joys stimulated many of the ideas included here.

Jennie would like to acknowledge the early help and support of both her deceased father, Harry Jacobs, and her mother, Bessie Jacobs. Her mother later not only provided intellectual stimulation and encouragement to pursue whatever dreams she had, but was a crucial role model for how women could simultaneously be a successful professional, wife, and mother. Jennie's husband, Michael Kronenfeld, has been supportive of feminism, both as an ideal and in his personal life. He has encouraged her professional career, including this book. Both Mike and Jennie's older son, Shaun Kronenfeld, were understanding and patient about the time constraints involved. Jennie's younger son, Jeffrey Kronenfeld, born during the writing of this book, was also patient and understanding, although he did not know it.

Contents

List of Tables

Introduction

Political and social scientists have long recognized the role of technology in explaining social change. This book presents a four-stage technology based theory of social change. We argue that technology defines the physically feasible, which in turn, defines social organization and personal interaction. First, technological innovations are developed and disseminated. Second, social norms and values change in adaptation to the expanded opportunities made possible by the technological innovation. Third, pressure from changing behavior and norms builds in the political system, creating political movements and interest group demands. Fourth, legal and policy changes may result. We apply this general theory of technology driven social change to the changing roles of women and changing male-female relationships. The two major factors relating to social change are birth control and production technologies.

Chapter 1 describes sex roles in recent history. The lack of procreation technology throughout much of history has divided daily work and aspirations of men and women along gender lines. Women have been primarily responsible for childbearing, child care, nurturing, and other home-based roles. Men traditionally have been expected to provide financial support in a provider role and have not been major participants in child care. This sex-based division of labor has contributed to economic, political, and social inequality.

Chapter 2 argues that current changes in sex roles are a specific case encompassed by a general technologically based theory of social change. The uniqueness of sex role changes lies not in the process, but rather in the pervasive and comprehensive impact of birth control on daily living. Production technologies also have an extensive impact on daily living, but are not the main causes of changes in sex roles and in male-female relationships.

Chapter 3 examines the development and dissemination of birth control technology, focusing particularly upon the nineteenth and twentieth centuries. As the 1800s drew to a close, barrier methods of birth control were being perfected and disseminated. In the 1960s, two birth control technologies emerged—the IUD and the oral contraceptive pill.

The four basic components of human relations are love, intimacy, sex, and marriage. In Chapter 4, each is defined and examined historically. Chapter 5 looks at developmental sequences of these components and argues that birth control technology significantly expanded possible sequences.

Chapter 6 discusses home production technologies, while Chapter 7 explores work production technologies and labor force participation of women. Both home and work technologies have influenced changes in sex roles, by intensifying the value changes precipitated by birth control.

Chapter 8 explores the interrelationships between birth control and production technologies and the two major organized feminist movements in the past 100 years. The first movement gained strength in the late 1800s and culminated in the nineteenth amendment to the U.S. Constitution giving women the right to vote. The second movement began in the early 1960s. It resulted in many policy changes short of achieving passage of the Equal Rights Amendment, which remains a goal of many feminists.

Chapters 9 and 10 examine an array of legal changes and policy outputs from both feminist movements. Changes include family related legislation, work-related legislation, and statutes designed to enhance economic opportunities for women. Chapter 11 explores the paradoxes of technology driven social change.

1 Sex Differences: Biology and Roles

Men and women are different, an indisputable observation. Men are often physically larger and stronger than are women. Men have facial hair, women do not. Men appear angular, hard, and sometimes muscular; women seem softer, more curvaceous. But the most critical difference is inescapably this: women have babies—men do not. The differential implications for men and women of childbearing are examined thoroughly in later chapters. This chapter explores the nature of differences between men and women. Are these differences based in nature or nurture? On what traits besides childbearing do experts agree that definite differences between men and women exist? What role does socialization play in sex-based differences? Evidence bearing on this question is explored.

THE NATURE ARGUMENT: BIOLOGICAL DIFFERENCES BETWEEN MEN AND WOMEN

Sexually Dimorphic Characteristics

Almost all human characteristics appear in both men and women, but there are many sex-based differences in most traits. A *sexually dimorphic characteristic* is a trait that occurs in different frequencies among male and female populations. For a sexually dimorphic trait, more individuals of one sex may manifest the characteristic than of the other sex.

An example of sexual dimorphism where the genetics are clearly understood to be sex related is color-blindness. Men are more likely to experience red-green color-blindness than are women. This characteristic is a single gene trait and is carried on the X chromosome, the female sex chromosome. Women have two X chromosomes, while normal men have

3

an X and Y chromosome. *Sex-linked characteristics* are transmitted on one or the other of the two sex genes. Color-blindness is a sex-linked recessive genetic characteristic. For an individual to manifest a *recessive characteristic*, the trait must be present on both genes of a pair, where one gene comes from the female parent and the second gene comes from the male parent. Since men have only one X chromosome, the presence of color-blindness on that chromosome makes the man color-blind. If a woman has only one X chromosome for color-blindness, her vision is normal. Men exhibit color-blindness more frequently than women.

Most traits are more complex genetically than color-blindness, with inherited codes for the trait being carried on multiple genes. The more complex the genetic transfer, the greater the difficulty of arriving at conclusions about the inheritability of sex-based traits. On many sex-related biological characteristics, men on average differ from women. Yet the variability across individuals of the same sex is great. Typically, the range of observed differences with one sex exceeds the average differences between men and women. Weight and height are examples of within sex variability exceeding differences across the sexes. While on average, men weigh more and are taller than women, any particular woman could be substantially heavier or taller than any particular man.

Some sex-related differences between men and women, including height and weight, may also be influenced by environmental factors. Men have more muscle mass per body weight than women, a factor which gives men greater physical strength. Yet men also have traditionally been more physically active and placed a higher value on muscle development, exacerbating initial biological differences.

Rossi (1984) argues that some differences between men and women are partially biologically determined. One difference is sensory sensitivity—sight, hearing, smell, and touch. Women have greater sensitivity to touch, sound, and odor. Women judge sounds to be twice as loud as men, and are six times more likely to sing in tune. Fine motor coordination and finger dexterity are greater among women. Men do excel in the sense modality of vision, showing greater sensitivity to light (Gove and Carpenter 1982; McGuiness 1976; Parsons 1980).

Sex-Related Brain Differences

Do the brains of men systematically differ from the brains of women? Some brain research has shown differences in the right and left hemispheres of the brain. Emotions, music, visual tasks, identification of spatial tasks, and facial recognition are dominant in the right hemisphere of the brain. Language skills dominate the left hemisphere (Kinsbourne 1978; Goy and McEwen 1980). Human males have greater and more rigid separation of function between the two brain hemispheres than do females. Some research indicates that a larger proportion of space in the right hemisphere of male brains is devoted to spatial tasks than in females (McGuiness 1976; Durden-Smith and deSimone 1983).

No agreement exists among experts as to which brain differences between men and women are biologically determined and which are environmentally determined. Rossi (1984) argues that mathematical and verbal differences between the sexes are partially grounded in the earlier neurological development of female children. Females are four to six weeks more mature neurologically than males at birth. This partially explains girls' earlier acquisition of language and verbal fluency.

Mathematical ability is often cited as an area where there are biologically based differences between men and women, yet many experts feel environmental influences are equally if not more important. Girls generally excel at mathematics as well as reading and writing up to high school (Maccoby 1966). In high school, girls' scholastic achievements do decline, particularly in mathematics (Fox, Fennema, and Sherman 1977). From this decline came the traditional notion that men are biologically superior at math. Rossi attributes the greater mathematical skill exhibition of males to differences in brain lateralization. Women approach mathematical problems through left hemisphere verbal means, while men rely on right hemisphere symbols.

Studies of mathematical ability have focused on analytical ability, defined narrowly as spatial perception—perceiving an object independently of its background. Girls are more field dependent (Richardson 1981). They have more trouble seeing an object independently of its context than do boys. Men are more able to rotate objects in their minds, to read maps, and to perform in mazes (Rossi 1984).

The evidence as to whether girls are inferior mathematically in skills such as computation, geometry, and algebra is unclear and contradictory. Generally studies do not support a biological difference in these areas (Fox, Fennema, and Sherman 1977; Ernest 1976). Nor do the findings of cross-cultural studies of non-western cultures support a biological difference (Berry 1971). Further evidence eroding the biological determinant hypothesis is that young male and female children do not show differential mathematical abilities (Maccoby and Jacklin 1974).

Some evidence supports an environmentally induced explanation for the difference in mathematical skills between the sexes. Differences in mathematical achievement are highly related to the number of math courses taken. Traditionally, by high school and college, boys take more math courses than do girls (Fox, Fennema, and Sherman 1977). The orientation of math problems may also affect differential achievement across the sexes. If word problems are based on traditionally male activities, such as hunting and woodworking, girls do more poorly than if the problems are based on traditionally female activities, such as cooking and gardening (Andersen 1983).

One study concluded that mathematical differences between boys and girls were partially biologically determined and that genetic differences enabled boys to demonstrate superior mathematical skills (Tobias 1982). The researchers based this conclusion on the higher participation rates of boys in a program at Johns Hopkins that identifies mathematically precocious youngsters. The math score on the Scholastic Aptitude Test (SAT) was among the methods used to identify program participants. Especially at the top of the SAT scale (scores between 600 and 800), boys outnumbered girls by two to one. Critiques of the conclusion of genetic differences include that fewer girls than boys volunteered for the program and that the SAT tests knowledge of techniques rather than the ability to reason mathematically. Scoring well is related to the amount of mathematics studied. Many boys with high scores had systematically studied math with a parent or teacher before entering the talent search (Tobias 1982).

Hormones and Aggression

Myth holds that men are more aggressive than women and that the difference is grounded in nature rather than nurture (Goldberg 1973). Male hormones are the supposed culprit in greater male aggression. Yet women also have male hormones. The three sex hormones—estrogen, progestin, and testosterone—are present in both men and women. The difference hormonally between the sexes is variation in levels of production and concentration of each hormone. Before puberty, there are few sex differences in the quantities of sex hormones. For children, all sex hormones are at very low levels. In adult males, there is greater production of testosterone due to stimulation by the testes. Adult females have higher levels of estrogens and progestins from the ovaries. After menopause, female levels of estrogens and progestins are reduced. Postmenopausal women have lower levels of these hormones than do males of the same age (Hoyenga and Hoyenga 1979; Tea et al. 1975).

If male aggression were driven by high levels of testosterone, there should be no observable difference between preadolescent boys and girls in aggression, since testosterone differences at that age are slight. Nor is the reverse behavior observed for older men and women. Older men have higher levels of female hormones than do postmenopausal women, yet they do not subsequently exhibit more feminine behavior. Further evidence of the weak link between levels of testosterone and aggressive behavior comes from studies focusing only on males. Changes in testosterone levels are not consistent predictors of changes in levels of aggressive behavior (Hoyenga and Hoyenga 1979).

Cross-cultural studies provide further evidence of the importance of cultural and environmental factors in levels of aggression and basic temperament. Margaret Mead's famous study of the relationship between sex and temperament in three primitive societies in New Guinea argues strongly for the role of cultural conditioning. In two of the three societies, men and women exhibited very similar temperaments. In one society, the Arapesh, both sexes were peaceful, cooperative, and passive, resembling traditional western female roles. In a second society, the Mundugamore, both sexes exhibited violent, competitive, and jealous behavior, resembling traditional western male roles. In the third society, the Tchambuli, strong sex-linked behavior quite opposite from that in western cultures was exhibited. Males were viewed as artistic, sensitive, nervous, and emotionally dependent. Females were viewed as efficient, competent, and the sexual aggressors (Mead 1969). The wide variety of temperament displayed for both men and women across the three cultures provides strong evidence of the role of environment in personality development, even if later researchers disagree on the exact distribution of personality traits in the three cultures examined.

Despite evidence of environmentally induced aggressive behavior, debate continues to rage that aggression is grounded in sex-linked hormonal differences. Studies among monkeys found that baby female monkeys whose mothers received male hormones prior to giving birth desplayed more rough and tumble play than normal females. These females exhibited as much chasing behavior as their male counterparts (Kruez and Rose 1971).

Recent debates about premenstrual syndrome in females are another example of hormones potentially resulting in behavior differences between men and women. Some women experience large variations in mood, based upon monthly menstrual cycles. Before menstruation, levels of both estrogen and progestin are low. Symptoms of this syndrome include depression, irritability, fatigue, hostility, and anxiety. At present, the number of women suffering from this syndrome is unclear.

That observed differences between men and women exist remains indisputable. Whether those differences are grounded predominantly in biology or in environment remains quite controversial. Owing to the complexity of the subject and the difficulty of scientific inquiry, no scientific studies have definitively resolved the nature-nurture issue. Yet some consensus has emerged from the raging debate over male-female differences on two topics. First, most characteristics are present in both sexes, with variability within gender exceeding the average differences between the sexes. Second, many differences appear to stem from different reproductive roles.

THE NURTURE ARGUMENT: SEX ROLE SOCIALIZATION

Sex Role Specialization

The sexes have differed in exhibited role behavior. As used by social scientists, the term *social roles* bears resemblance to the usage of the same word by an actor or playwright. Roles typically are defined in relationship to culture. *Culture* is "the set of definitions of reality held in common by people who share a distinctive way of life" (Kluckhohn 1962). Culture provides ways of thinking about what are appropriate behaviors and beliefs for the members of a particular society, cuing people how to act, think, behave, and feel. It influences mundane things such as daily dress and pleasantries, as well as significant life events.

Roles Are culturally prescribed rights, duties, and expectations which define the relationship between individuals in particular social positions. Being a daughter is a specific social role which includes a variety of expectations, rights, and duties at various stages of a person's life. While a child, the role of daughter includes the right to be cared for and loved by parents. Childhood duties and expectations include obeying parents, loving them, attending school, and learning skills necessary to function in an adult world. An adult daughter has fewer rights in that role but many expectations and duties. She is expected to care for aging parents and be sensitive to family needs. Most people play multiple roles in society. The adult daughter is likely also to be a wife, mother, and worker. Each of these roles has expectations, duties, and rights as well, creating a need to balance between sometimes competing roles.

Sex roles are expectations for behavior and attitudes that a particular culture defines as appropriate for men and women. Men and women learn their expected sex roles through the process of *sex role socialization*. This process has traditionally taught girls to particularly value being attractive, young, nonaggressive, nonathletic, emotionally expressive, tender, domestic, conciliatory, and nurturing. Through the same process, boys have been trained to value aggression, dominance, strength, emotional stoicism, adventure, athletic ability, achievement, goal attainment through conflict, and monetary success.

Chafetz (1974) identified six major groups of traits viewed differently for men and women, based on surveys of students enrolled in sociology courses. Physically, men are viewed as virile, athletic, strong, and brave. Women are seen as weak, helpless, nonathletic, dainty, and graceful. Functionally, men are expected to be breadwinners and providers. Women are expected to be domestic and maternal. Sexually, men are viewed as more aggressive and experienced, while women are seen as passive, uninterested, and inexperienced, or sometimes, seductive and flirtatious. Men are to be unemotional, stoical, and avoid crying. Women are emotional, sentimental, romantic, and are allowed to cry. Intellectually, men are supposedly logical, intellectual, rational, objective, practical, and mechanical. Women intellectually are supposedly scatter-brained, frivolous, shallow, intuitive, perceptive, and idealistic. Men in interpersonal relations are trained to be demanding, dominating, individualistic, independent, free. Women are often described as petty, gossipy, sneaky, overprotected, dependent, submissive, and refined.

Chesler (1971) found that 79 psychotherapists asked to identify the traits of a mentally healthy man listed the same characteristics that they did when merely asked to identify the traits of a mentally healthy adult. When asked the traits of a mentally healthy adult woman, the answers differed from their earlier responses to characteristics for both mentally healthy men and mentally healthy adults. This sample of psychotherapists perceived mentally healthy women to be submissive, emotional, excitable, conceited about appearance, dependent, and not very adventurous. Both male and female psychotherapists articulated this image of the mentally healthy woman, demonstrating the strength of sex role socialization.

Feminist scholars have noted that equal value is not placed on sex-related characteristics. The majority of the masculine descriptions are positive traits that are valued by the general culture. The majority of feminine descriptions are negative traits devalued by the general culture. A man is applauded among some cultures for a high level of sexual activity. An equally active woman is labeled a nymphomaniac—a term for which there is no male equivalent

Models of Sex Role Socialization

Socialization is the process through which people learn how to behave and what is expected of them in their own culture. *Sex role socialization* is more specialized, emphasizing the learning of sex roles and how different behaviors and attitudes are encouraged or discouraged. Socialization occurs through a variety of agents in modern society, including parents, extended family, peers, teachers, and the media. The first socialization of children typically begins in their own families. The family of birth constitutes a *primary group* characterized by intimate face-to-face association and cooperation (Cooley 1909). The birth family generally provides the first socializing experience, the most intense and complete experience of belonging, and has greater longevity and stability as a source of socialization that most other sources. Other primary groups influencing socialization of small children include play groups, friendships, day-care centers, and later, schools.

Three models of socialization are the *identification, social learning,* and *cognitive development* models. *Identification* theory argues that socialization occurs for children as they learn gender appropriate behaviors through identification with the same sex parent. The *psychoanalytic explanation* was developed by Freud (1974) as part of the *identification* model to explain sex role development. Freud uses the concept of sexuality rather than sex role. He posits that sexuality is central as the organizing principle for mental life. Additionally, Freud contends that childhood emotions and perceptions have an enduring impact on adult life, and the nuclear family is salient for psychological functioning and development.

Postulating the existence of strong sexual desire between child and parent, the psychoanalytic model of male development focuses on the shift from longing for the opposite sex parent to identification with the same sex parent. Boys under six years of age desire sexual union with their mothers. Between four and six, boys begin to experience guilt over these desires and fear of the father's retribution, creating castration anxiety. This anxiety causes tha boy to give up the mother as a sexual object and take the father as his role model for future sexual identification.

Freud's view of female development is more complicated, and is critiqued by many feminists. According to Freud, the girl's original love object is also the mother. Originally, the girl has no fear of castration but develops this fear when she recognizes she has no penis. Discovering that the mother also has no penis, the girl blames the mother for her own "castrated" status and "penis envy," and rejects the mother as love object, turning to the father. In Freudian theory, female passivity is based on a sense of biological inferiority.

Feminists and female psychologists counter that penis envy is a male concept, not reflective of female psychology (Horney 1926). Further Freud ignores male envy of the female capacity to bear children. Other criticisms include disagreement with Freud's emphasis on the biological origins of female traits and female inferiority. Freud also emphasizes vaginal female sexuality, a finding refuted by later sexual research. His argument of female passivity in sexuality was more reflective of the cultural influences of the Victorian era in which he lived than innate differences (Koedt 1973; Masters and Johnson 1966).

Chodorow (1978) challenges Freud's assumption that gender differences are grounded in innate psychoanalytic processes. While agreeing that sex role behavior is learned by identification with parents, Chodorow emphasizes the division of labor by sex within traditional family structures as the explanation for gender-based personality differences. In traditional U.S. families, an asymmetrical structure of parenting is based on women "mothering" while the father is physically absent and emotionally distant. Boys identify with their father. They form personalities that are more detached from others and emotionally repressed, based on their fathers' role in the family.

Social learning theorists are also critical of Freudian psychoanalysis, arguing that it was culture bound and reflected the patriarchy of western societies. Social learning theory emphasizes the environment as a major factor in sex role socialization. Children are positively reinforced by rewards for appropriate behavior and punished for inappropriate begavior. Behavior in this perspective is not fixed at an early stage in life. Learning continues throughout adulthood. In both feminist identification theory and social learning theory, boys and girls model their behavior on same sex parents. In the former, however, emotional identification with the same sex parent is necessary for modeling to occur. In the latter, behavioral reinforcement and the adoption of gender appropriate roles can occur in the absence of emotional identification. Social learning theorists also place less emphasis on the role of the parents, arguing that children receive learning cues from their entire environment (Frieze et al. 1978; Bandura and Walters 1963; Kagan 1958).

A third model of sex role socialization is *cognitive development theory*. This model is based on Piaget's stages of cognitive development. All children go through distinct stages of cognitive development, alternating between stages of equilibrium and of disequilibrium during which new development occurs. Kohlberg (1966) argues that children discover quickly that people are divided into two sexes. Next, they come to know their own sex, and to categorize other people. After this, children begin to categorize behaviors and objects as appropriate for one sex or the other. They further believe that sex role identity is unchanging. Before this notion of permanency is developed, children often hold the notion that wearing clothes or using objects typically associated with the opposite sex makes them become the opposite sex.

Both social learning and cognitive development models emphasize the role of culture in shaping sex role identity. In social learning theory, culture provides the model for sex roles and becomes the reinforcer of appropriate behaviors. Cognitive development theory gives the child a more active role in the process. It argues that children construct their own images of male and female sex roles by searching for patterns in the culture. Eventually, children come to view themselves as others see them, but through an interactive rather than a receptive process (Mead 1934).

The Impact of the Media on Sex Roles

The media are a powerful socializing influence and play a significant role in influencing cultural sex stereotypes. Tuchman (1978) argues that the media provide symbolic representation of existing sex-based ideals, as opposed to literal portraits. On television in the 1950s, most shows that portrayed families typically starred a mother, father, and two children who lived in an upper-class suburban house. Even in the 1950s, such homes were not the typical family, either in income or composition, but did represent a cultural ideal. This same idealized image of the family was present in children's readers.

Television is the dominant mass medium in U.S. life. Almost all U.S. homes have at least one TV and most have more. More U.S. homes have TV sets than have private bathrooms. Women have not been portrayed realistically in many shows. Nor have they been portrayed as frequently in television as their real life proportion of the population would indicate. In 1952, only 32 percent of prime time television characters were women. Those figures stayed approximately the same through the 1970s (Gerbner 1978).

Part of the underrepresentation of women in television images and shows may stem from a low proportion of women in decision-making roles in the television industry. In the 1950s, only 20 percent of the people working in paid employment in television were women. That figure had changed little through the 1970s, despite the fact that the proportion of women in the labor force had increased from one-third of all women in 1950 to 45 percent in 1975. By the early 1980s, over half of all women were labor force participants, but the image of women in television shows did not reflect this change. Increasingly, women in television shows have occupational as well as familial roles, but women working outside the home are frequently shown in subordinate positions.

Through stereotyping on television, the sex role socialization begins subtly in childhood. Even through the 1970s, advertisements on shows designed for children showed two men for every woman (Sternglanz and Serbin 1974). In the 1980s, this trend continued on popular children's shows, expecially cartoon shows. In the Smurf show, which portrays mythical blue creatures living in the woods in a Middle Ages setting, all of the Smurfs but one are male. The one female, Smurfette, portrays traditional negative female characteristics—a concern with neatness, beauty, and vanity over her appearance which often results in her being lured into trouble. Smurfette is frequently helpless, necessitating rescue by the male Smurfs. Smurfette also displays positive but stereotypically feminine characteristics, including nurturing and concern over the welfare of the other Smurfs.

In an older cartoon show, the Flintstones, stereotypical images are even more blatant. The setting is in a prehistorical era where humans lived in caves but magically have equivalents to most modern conveniences. The men go out to work. They are portrayed as bumbling and imcompetent but still dominant. The women stay at home. They are characterized as more competent but conniving, submissive, and manipulating the men from positions of weakness through feminine wiles rather than having overt decision-making power.

Actual television shows are only part of the socializing content of the medium. Much air time is devoted to television commercials which often include stereotypical sex roles. Many commercials use voiceovers, a disembodied voice out of the background which comments on the product being shown. Voiceovers represent authority on a commercial, providing details on the quality and attractiveness of a product. Male voices have been disproportionately used on voiceovers.

The sales pitch emphasized also varies by the gender of the person making the voiceover. In one study, 86 percent of male delivered commercials emphasized performance of the product, compared to 29 percent for female voiceovers (Chafetz 1974). Sales pitches delivered by females emphasized ease, comfort, and luxury of the item. Males were presented as practical, accurate, and knowledgeable, while the typical commercial image of women emerged as concerned with creature comforts. Some efforts to redress this imbalance in sexual images is being made as companies become more sensitive to the changing role of women in society.

Sex Role Socialization Across the Life Cycle

Sex role socialization begins shortly after birth. Parents quickly impose their differential expectations, based on gender differences, on their newborn offspring. Social psychologists have documented how early and how much parents treat girl and boy babies differently. First-time parents were asked to describe their baby only 24 hours after birth. Parents of girls reported their babies to be softer, smaller, and less attentive than did parents of boys. Physical examinations of the babies, however, found no objective differences (Rubin, Provenzano, and Luria 1974). Fathers were more likely to sex stereotype their infants than were mothers. Fathers more than mothers described their sons as larger, better coordinated, more alert, and stronger that girl babies.

Parents in the past have often reflected their different attitudes toward girl and boy babies in choice of clothing. Girls have been dressed in pink and ruffles; boys have been dressed in blue and sports-oriented outfits. Different colors reinforcing sex roles are found not only in clothes, but in items such as diaper pins, rattles, comforters, and cribs (Walum 1977).

Beyond clothing, are little girls treated differently by their parents from little boys? Studies are inconclusive. Some studies find that parents elicit motor behavior more from boys than girls. Less difference was found in the amount of affectionate contact between mother and child (Maccoby and Jacklin 1974). Some studies report that mothers look and talk to girls more than boys during the first six months of life, responding more quickly to girls crying (Gagnon 1977).

Contradictory studies report that during the first six months, boys receive more touching, holding, rocking, and kissing, a trend reversed by the age of one. One study found that by thirteen months, girls were more likely than boys to cling to, look at, and talk to their mothers (Goldberg and Lewis 1969). Two other attempts to replicate this were not successful (Coates, Anderson, and Hartup 1972; Jacklin, Maccoby, and Dick 1973). Fathers are more likely to mock wrestle with sons and play gently with daughters (Komarovsky 1953). Sons are weaned from physical contact at an earlier age. Both parents are generally more restrictive with daughters, creating more limits on acceptable behaviors.

The world of infant and toddler socialization was traditionally a female world. Through the early 1970s, research found that typical fathers spent less than 20 minutes a day with infants of either sex (Bronfenbrenner 1974; Bernard 1981). Women's images of sex appropriate behavior formed the basis for early childhood socialization. Sons were played with roughly and rewarded for rough and mischievous treatment. Girls were expected to be sweet and docile, often receiving more punishment for mischievous behavior (Gagnon 1977).

As infants become toddlers, sex role typing increases. Toys and games are a major way children practice and learn future adult roles. Toys for toddler girls have been different from toys for their male playmates. Traditionally, girls were given dolls. Boys were given trucks and building blocks. One observer of a kindergarten noted that girls were encouraged to play in the doll corner, while boys were encouraged to play in the corner with wheeled toys and building equipment (Bernard 1981). Many preschools and kindergartens reinforce this orientation.

By the preschool years, most children know with which toys their sex is supposed to play. The Sears Christmas catalog clearly presents different types of toys for girls and boys. Toys that prepare for spousehood and parenthood showed only girls 84 percent of the time. Construction set illustrations included only boys 75 percent of the time (Walum 1977). Not only were the sexes given different playthings, but adults imposed the labels of "sissies" to boys and "tomboys" to girls who played with sex inappropriate toys. Partially based on research that most two- to three-year-old boys are fond of dolls, toymakers began to produce dolls for boys. These dolls were clearly male, never female. Sex role typing has decreased but not disappeared.

Boys and girls in one study were asked about their favorite toys and play activities. Girls preferred dressing up dolls, playing school, jacks, hopscotch, sewing, and cartwheels. Boys preferred playing soldiers, bandits, cops and robbers, spacemen, and playing with trains, airplanes, and marbles. A higher proportion of girls preferred male toys than the proportion of boys preferring female toys. By the third to six grade, the age of children in this study, boys showed more aversion to opposite sex toys (Rosenberg and Sutton-Smith 1968). Another study confirmed that boys avoided attractive but sex inappropriate toys to a greater degree than girls, especially if an adult observer were present (DeLucia 1963). Boys were particularly sensitive about playing with girls' toys when adults of either sex were present.

In a study by Hartley and Hardesty (1964), boys and girls ages five, eight, and eleven were shown pictures of children engaged in various activities. These children already had clear norms about sex roles, assigning most objects and activities to one or the other sex. The pictures assigned to both sexes referred mostly to play locales, showing play at the beach, in a park, or on a playground. Both boys and girls agreed that only girls played with doll carriages, dishes, sewing machines, pocketbooks, and jump ropes. Only boys played with toy guns, trucks, soldiers, tools, and erector sets. The toy choices of working-class children were more sex typed than those of middle-class children (Rabban 1950; Kohn 1959; Hartley 1964). Middle-class girls were the least restrictive in their choices.

Not only do children choose different play objects but they also engage in different games and activities. Traditionally, young girls tended to play house or games that were relatively uncomplex with few rules, such as jump rope or hopscotch. These involved little team effort and were minimally competitive. Boys games are more typically team oriented, such as cops and robbers, war games, or cowboys and Indians. Boys also played sports games with elaborate rules and team competition, such as baseball, football, and basketball. Until legislative changes in the 1970s, competitive team sports were rarely available to girls, either in the neighborhood, or in school (Walum 1977; Lever 1976). The lack of team sports has made it harder for women to work cooperatively in team settings, a necessity in many business settings. Nor did women develop competitive norms encouraged by team sports, where winning becomes crucial.

In addition to the family and peer interaction, schools provide a powerful socializing influence for children. Schools still frequently separate children on the basis of sex, expecially in the early grades. Boys and girls may be lined up separately for assemblies and lunch, placed in sex-segregated reading groups, and assigned to different teams for spelling bees and other competition. Housekeeping tasks for the classroom are frequently sex specific, with girls being asked to pick up and dust, while boys rearrange furniture. At school parties, girls may serve the cookies and punch, while boys rearrange the room (Pogrebin 1972).

The curriculum material and textbooks in the elementary grades traditionally place greater emphasis on males and male achievement. Many elementary texts paid little attention to the roles of women in history and the sciences. Children's readers often portrayed sex stereotypical roles. Women have been shown in fewer occupations than men, and frequently in low-paying helpmate jobs. Boys in stories have been shown to be more active, while girls were more conforming (Richardson 1981). In general, boys are more frequently characters in stories than girls. Tarvis and Offir (1977) found a seven to two ratio of boy-centered stories to girl-centered stories.

Despite the emphasis in school books on males, the elementary school environment has been overwhelmingly female. Almost all elementary teachers are women. If men are present, they usually are principals, reinforcing the child's notion of greater power and prestige in the masculine role (Guttentag and Bray 1977). Women teachers often present subtle expectations of male- and female-typed behavior. Teachers respond more often to boys than to girls who misbehave. Boys in school receive more reprimands and physical restraint (Serbin et al. 1973). Teachers often assume that girls love reading and hate math and science, while assuming the opposite for boys (Chafetz 1974). Subtle cues have been communicated, even in progressive schools where deliberate attempts were made to avoid sex role stereotyping. A researcher in one such school found teachers complementing girls when they wore dresses but not pants, and seldom commenting on the way boys dressed.

In junior high and high school, the curriculum becomes more sex-linked. Although most school systems have now eliminated legally mandated sex segregated curricula, custom and school administrators still reinforce differences in many places. Teenage girls take cooking, sewing, and typing classes. Teenage boys take woodworking and mechanical drawing classes. In more academic subjects, boys are strongly encouraged to continue in math, even if they dislike it. Girls are not similarly encouraged. Career choices presented to students still reflect sex stereotypes. A girl good in science will be urged into high school science teaching or nursing. Her male counterpart is more generally directed to medicine or engineering (Walum 1977; Chafetz 1974).

In the past, sex differences continued into adulthood. Women have traditionally married in their early twenties, spending their twenties and thirties in nurturing and parenting roles. Men during their twenties and thirties have typically devoted their greatest energies to work and career building. Men and women have been on separate tracks. During midlife crises, these different paths sometimes clash. Women often decide to pursue greater individuality and forgone career goals, at the very time men may decide to place greater emphasis on family and interpersonal relations. This conflict often results in family turmoil and sometimes divorce (Sheehy 1974).

In the future, birth control and work technologies may result in new options to traditional sex stereotyping and life cycles. Given improved birth building, saving childbearing until their thirties, making the male and female tracks more similar. Changing work technologies deemphasize physical strength, reducing one basis for sex stereotyping. These technological innovations are driving changes in sex roles and are altering the dynamics of male-female relationships.

2 Technology and Social Change Throughout History

One explanation of social change is technological innovation. Many theoreticians contend that technological innovations precede changes in social relationships. Marx (Lichtheim 1961) argued that changes in the relationships of productions lagged behind changes in the means of production. Ogburn (1950) similarly emphasized the cultural lag occurring in social norms when human behavior is altered by technological change. This book draws upon the theories of technologically based social change to examine waves of the women's movement and subsequent policy changes.

A four-stage process of technologically based social change is identified. Technology first defines the physically feasible, which, in turn, defines social organization and interpersonal interaction. Second, social norms and values change in adaptation to the expanded opportunities made possible by the technological innovation. Third, pressure from changing behavior and norms builds up in the political system, creating political movements and interest group demands. Finally, legal and policy changes may occur.

Current changes in policy outputs affecting the status of women are a specific case encompassed by a general technologically based theory of social change. These policy outputs have, in turn, contributed to a redefinition of sex roles. The uniqueness of sex role changes lies not in the process, but rather in the pervasiveness and encompassing impact such changes imply for daily living. The two areas of technological change which have accelerated changes in sex roles are birth control and production technologies. Birth control is the main technology affecting relationships between the sexes, but sex roles have also been influenced to a lesser extent by production technologies.

TRADITIONAL EXPLANATIONS OF SEX-BASED
STATUS DIFFERENTIALS

The Male Conspiracy Explanation

Two alternative explanations to technology have been developed to explain sex role differences and historical sexual inequality: the conspiratorial theory and the innate biological differences theory. Under the male conspiratorial theory, men intentionally covertly scheme to keep females subservient in power and money, opposing social reforms to improve the status of women. Used to wielding power in the external world, men also use the same Machiavellian techniques to conquer and control their wives. The traditional patriarchial structure of families gave husbands petty power over their wives. Men appeared to benefit from the subordinate position of women (Andersen 1983; Eisenstein 1979; Harding 1981).

Another more Marxian version of the conspiracy theory holds that only elite men benefit from the subservient status of women, although all men perceive that they are better off when women are comparatively subordinate economically and politically. According to this argument, only males in the wealthy and ruling classes benefit from female inferiority. The unpaid household labor of women relieves the government from taking responsibility for the economic support of the very young and the old, lowering the total tax burden and saving the wealthy from taxes. Some women, however, either owing to being unmarried or to the very low wages of their husbands, do engage in paid labor. They represent a pool of reserved labor paid lower wages than men and move in and out of the labor force as needed (Leacock 1983).

Two versions of Marxian analysis exist. Classical Marxists view the oppression of women as stemming almost exclusively from capitalism and its definition of women as the property of men. Within capitalism, an accumulation of profit necessitates the exploitation of women's labor. Socialists, by contrast, criticize a classical Marxian approach for its overemphasis on capitalism. Drawing on historical and anthropological studies, socialists note that women were also oppressed in precapitalist and noncapitalist-based systems. The interaction of capitalism with patriarchy is the culprit in the low status of women, rather than capitalism acting along (Andersen 1983; Mitchell 1971; Rosaldo and Lamphere 1974; Elshtain 1974). Firestone (1970) extends the Marxian economic argument to advocate female control of the means of reproduction to eliminate sexual inequality. Only when artificial reproduction is available will total equality be achieved.

The Innate Patriarchy Explanation

The second explanation for the differential status of men and women contends that biologically innate diferences between the sexes make patriarchy inevitable (Goldberg 1973; Jaggar and Struhl 1978). Male hormones are the basis for male aggressiveness and dominance, contend proponents of the innate patriarchy argument. Male status is determined by testosterone. This perspective is opposed to a feminist perspective which holds that status differentials are predominantly social and not biological.

Opponents of the innate patriarchy explanation offer several critiques. Both males and females have all three major sex hormones in their bodies: estrogen, progestin, and testosterone. Only during part of the individual's lifespan do the levels of these sex hormones vary across sexes. Some studies find small correlations between the levels of testosterone and aggressive behavior, but only showing association. Other studies find that changing environmental conditions which create stress, fatigue, or fear change hormone levels, making it difficult to impute causality (Hoyenga and Hoyenga 1979).

Another criticism of the innate patriarchy explanation is that it fails to address the considerable variability within sexes. On most traits, variability within gender is greater than the mean differences across gender. Overlaps between men and women are evident in most traits except those anatomical characteristics directly involved in reproduction.

TECHNOLOGY DRIVEN SOCIAL CHANGE

Documenting and understanding changes in society, social roles, and social relationships have fascinated humans across the centuries. While numerous theories of social change exist, one major explanation is based in technology. According to some theories of social change, technological innovations precede changes in social relationships. Technology has been offered as an explanation of differentials in status by sex (Rothschild 1983 a and b; Huber 1976; Tarde 1912; Clark 1969; Ogburn 1950).

Human beings must perform two activities to continue to survive as a species: they must produce and reproduce. Production results in the foodstuffs and materials needed for living. Reproduction of offspring is necessary to assure that young and future generations will replace older and aging ones. Technological innovations which affect these two basic activities are particularly profound. Productive and reproductive technological innovations have a great impact upon social change. Stages of development in each of these activities may be separated by the appearance of major far-reaching innovations.

William Ogburn has been a leading proponent of the theory that technological innovation explains social change. He stressed the differences between material culture (technology) and adaptive culture. Changes in material culture forced changes in other types of culture, such as social organization and customs. Social organization and customs do not change as quickly as material, producing a cultural lag.

In explaining the cultural lag, Ogburn argued that the basic elements of the social process were invention, accumulation, diffusion, and adjustment. The real sources of progressive change were found in material inventions: tools, weapons, and technical processes. Invention can be mechanical or social, and results from three factors: mental activity, demand, and the presence of other cultural elements. When more elements are added to the cultural base than are lost, accumulation occurs. Similarly, adjustment occurs when an invention interacts with other cultural elements. Typically, lag occurs between material and nonmaterial adjustment.

Nimkoff (1934, 1947) applied Ogburn's theory of technologically driven social change to explain changes in the family. Under plow technology in agricultural society, the family experienced its greatest strength by merging and subsuming educational, economic, protective, and state functions. With the advent of the industrial revolution, many of these functions were transferred to industry and to the state, leading to an accent within the family on affection and happiness, rather than the comprehensive functions of preindustrial times. Nimkoff and Ogburn (1955) argued that a number of factors in industrial society, such as the use of contraceptives, the market for the purchase of goods, the effects of the standard of living, and religious sanctions operated in clusters to cause changes in the family.

PRODUCTION THROUGHOUT HISTORY

Hunting and Gathering Production

Productive technologies may be divided into four major periods, based on the predominant activities and tools of production: the Hunting and Gathering, Agricultural, Industrial, and Informational Eras. The beginning of hunting and gathering society is called the Paleolithic Era, which began between 100,000 and 50,000 B.C. During the Paleolithic Era, Neanderthals learned to control fire and to act in rough concert in social groupings. Prior to this, unorganized subhuman activities characterized human precursors. Hunting and gathering societies were predominantly nomadic, wandering across large spans of geographic terrain in search of food.

The predominant staple food supply in early hunting and gathering societies came from gathering, a traditionally female task. Meat and fish from hunting activities most typically undertaken by males supplemented the food supply obtained from gathering. When climatic conditions were favorable, hunting and gathering production left substantial leisure time for societal inhabitants. In one modern hunting and gathering society, Kung Bushmen, an adequate food supply for the week can be obtained during good years by the men hunting for four days and the women gathering for two and a half days (Lee and De Vore 1968).

One early transformation in the transition from subhuman to human was toolmaking, such as using spears in hunting, and digging sticks in gathering (Binford 1968). Toward the end of the Paleolithic Era, paving the way for the upcoming agricultural era, was an acceleration in the development of tools, storage containers, and structures. The construction of devices to contain food, such as pottery, baskets, and nets, are now recognized as important precursors of agriculture.

An important transition step between hunting and gathering societies and agricultural societies was the discovery of seeds as food—a realization credited to women (Boulding 1976). Seeds are abundant, nutritious, and easy to store once containers are available. Complete use of seeds requires grindstones to aid in processing as well as storage containers. Archeological evidence in both Europe and the Middle East indicates that grindstones and containers preceded the development of agriculture (Binford 1968). During the same time period, boats made water a resource rather than a barrier. Dogs were first domesticated and used for hunting. Bows began to appear.

Today, stable monogamous pairings exist among almost all remaining hunting and gathering societies, leading to assumptions that similar monogamous pairings existed during the hunting and gathering era (Lee and De Vore 1968; Bicchieri 1972). On the basis of archeological evidence, researchers of the period feel that relationships between men and women were characterized by comparatively high sexual equality, even though the sexes had different functional roles.

Agricultural Production

Several theories exist about the discovery of agriculture. In one, after the use of storage vessels and grindstones, einkorn, a type of wild wheat easily rooted, was gathered while growing wild and incorporated into the food supply. Seeds accidentally left at an old campsite sprouted and matured. Returning to the campsite during their nomadic wanderings, members of hunting and gathering societies discovered the growing wheat. Slowly, they began to realize that they could deliberately leave some seed to grow, rather than relying on accident (Leonard 1973). Most likely the development of agriculture was accelerated by population pressure. A growing hunting and gathering population placed increasing demands upon a limited supply of game and wild foodstuffs.

Disagreement exists over whether the domestication of animals preceded the domestication of plants, or vice versa. Most likely, both happened simultaneously. At some point, hunters and gatherers realized that if they could capture smaller animals alive, such as wild sheep, goats, and pigs, they could bring these animals home, allow them to reproduce, and be more assured of a meat supply. The domestication of both animals and plants created pressures toward the development of fixed settlements and undercut nomadic wandering. Transporting domesticated animals becomes cumbersome and domesticated plants may require on-going care. While possessions were a burden in nomadic society, they became an increasingly valuable asset in fixed agrarian settlements.

Evidence exists that men had more varied and diverse roles in early agricultural societies than did women. Archeological findings from the city of Jericho indicate that men were the traders going to the Dead Sea for sulphur and other minerals. Men engaged in early mining and quarry activities, continued to hunt, and to look after the cattle herds removed from the settlement, escaping the confines of the village (Leonard 1973).

Women's activities were more confined than those of men, focusing on the three areas of hearth, courtyard, and fields. Courtyard activities included cooking, baking, grinding, crafts, and organizing social events. Field activities included clearing, planting, and harvesting; gathering and collecting fruits and nuts; caring for smaller animals such as sheep and goats; and collecting fuel for fires and materials for buildings. A major focus of hearth activities was cooking, feeding, and care of small infants. Infants and small children dominated the female world. Women breastfed small infants and were responsible for child care. There is no evidence of any society where men performed the breeder-feeder role (Boulding 1976).

A second agricultural period developed from the technological innovation of the plow. Men were already specialized as traders of the villages and were responsible for keeping the cattle.

Once people conceived of animals dragging hoes, the idea followed to have animals drag bigger, more effectively designed implements. Since men controlled the cattle, they also did the plowing, leaving women with subsidiary tasks, such as weaving, and carrying water to the fields.

Across time many civilizations in antiquity and the Middle Ages became prosperous enough that major centers of urbanization accompanied by limited job specialization developed within a general agrarian society. Urban dwellers developed a somewhat different style of life. The more productive agriculture created classes within society, making it possible for elite and some middle-class groups to no longer be engaged in the direct production of food. Women were increasingly confined. In Roman culture, women living in cities frequently worked outside the home. By the sixteenth century middle-class women had withdrawn from productive activities outside the home, focusing on domestic obligations. Across time, boys were prepared for public roles, while women were prepared for private roles related to the house. Differential sex roles were maintained throughout the agricultural period.

Life in the agrarian period was indeed short, nasty, and brutish. Life expectancy was short and stresses were great, especially on women. Average life expectancy in England in 1690 was 32 (Laslett 1965). As women were increasingly confined in the home, they suffered from the stress of crowded living quarters. One outgrowth was brutal childrearing practices with much references in the period literature especially to daughter beating. Daughter beating most frequently occurred when a child was resistant to parental marital plans, as when Marguerite of Navarre beat her daughter for weeks to make her agree to a politically designed marriage choice (Bainton 1973). A more typical middle-class solution to crowded households and the violence crowding bred was to apprentice children to other economically similar families. While boys were apprenticed to learn crafts, girls were domestic workers (Boulding 1976).

Throughout the Middle Ages, a few women had been able to maintain independent mercantile and religious roles. Convents provided an important exit for women to lead scholarly and separate lives. An erosion of this limited independence began in the sixteenth century. The Protestant Reformation eliminated the convent option in non-Catholic countries. In affluent and middle-class artisan homes, women no longer worked outside, but became the unpaid domestic servants of their husbands.

For the urban working and lower classes, life became much harder. Men began to petition against women being given weaving work, fearing their competition as employment became more scarce. Women without husbands or families were forced into the grimmest type of prostitution. Poorer women were more likely to be arrested for vagrancy and were a substantial proportion of convicts shipped to the New World between 1717 and 1775 (Rusche and Kirchheimer 1968).

Industrial Production

Between 1650 and 1750, the seeds of industrialism were planted. Unlike the preceding agricultural period where most energy was supplied by humans, animals, or sun, wind, and water, industrial societies developed energy supplies from irreplaceable fossil fuels, especially coal, oil, and gas (Toffler 1980). The industrial era resulted from a basic shift in how goods were produced and distributed. From the agrarian system that emphasized hand and craft production often in small shops or the home, the industrial system emphasized production in factories later organized in assembly lines and the use of machines, often run by fossil fuels to enhance output.

Distribution in the agrarian society occurred when craftsmen and peddlers sold wares. Gradually, railroads, highways, and canals increased the flow of manufactured goods to disparate geographic areas, leading to networks of jobbers, wholesalers, and department stores. Over time, this grew into national and international retailing chains. Production and distribution in this era moved outside of the home.

The growth of mechanized production stimulated two new social institutions: schools and corporations. Mass education served two functions in the Industrial Era—first, to teach the skills included in the basic curriculum, and second, to instill values critical to the functioning of industrial society, such as punctuality, obedience, and a tolerance for repetitive work, into youth. The growth of corporations and their concomitant limited liability was also a crucial underpinning of industrial production. Industrial era technologies required vast amounts of capital, yet few proprietors or partners were willing to risk their entire personal fortunes. The corporate form of organization allowed an investor to risk and potentially lose only the money invested on that particular venture, not one's entire net worth (Toffler 1980).

In agricultural society, job specialization was limited. Success of peasants in one geographic area and even from one family to the next did not dramatically influence the success of others. In the industrial factories, coordination and integration became essential as task specialization increased and as production and distribution moved outside the home. The same centralization and coordination did not occur in largely decentralized activities involving biological reproduction, child rearing, and familial cultural transmission.

Social stratification by class accelerated during the Industrial Era. Among the wealthy and growing middle class, an ideal developed of a woman of leisure who stayed at home and engaged in artistic and later civic activities tangential to production. This ideal was not new, but had intermittently existed throughout history in cultures as geographically disparate from Europe as ancient China. There upper-class women had bound feet which made it difficult to walk as a sign of the family's financial ability to forego their potential contributions to productivity. Coincidentally, the physical disability of bound feet also made women subservient and unlikely to stray from or challenge their husbands.

While the industrial ideal of the woman of leisure did not include such visible permanent disfiguring as foot binding, it did include such physically painful and incapacitating apparel as corsets and hoop skirts. Hoop skirts, clearly designed for show at parties and social events, restricted mobility and made sitting difficult. More seriously, corsets, especially tight binding styles donned around puberty, could permanently damage the ribcage and provided a physiological explanation for the frequent fainting and swooning of upper middle-class women.

For working-class women of the Industrial Era, leisure was not possible. Where obtainable, work began as early as childhood and continued throughout life. In much of the working class, even time off for childbearing was not possible. The Industrial Era created an unbalance between the number of women seeking jobs and the number of jobs available. Traditional jobs, such as home-oriented piecework and crafts, disappeared faster than factory jobs appeared as an increased capital-labor ratio brought on by industrialism.

Only fortunate working-class women found industrial jobs. Heavy industry was dominated by men, restricting job availability for women. Textile factories predominantly hired young girls, with 50 percent of their work force being under 14 years old (Richards 1974). Factories did not like to hire married women, since it was cheaper to hire new younger girls and unmarried women. Only about a quarter of female factory workers were married (Boulding 1976). The next best situation to industrial employment was domestic employment especially in the homes of the wealthy. The remaining working-class women were forced into begging, odd jobs, and prostitution.

Later in the industrial era, around the beginning of the twentieth century, more and different jobs for women became available. The invention of the telephone and the typewriter increased the number of clerical jobs in business settings. Over time, most jobs answering the telephone and typing were defined as women's work. The distribution network underwent major changes from small Mom and Pop stores and peddlers to larger department stores and later retail chains. White-collar sales clerks were needed, positions often filled by women.

Information Production

The development of the early analog and soon thereafter digital computers heralded the beginning of a new era in human production—the Information Era. Unlike the Industrial Era where most of the labor force worked to produce physical goods, most workers in the new era are producing information, ideas, symbols, and data. The new era in production is marked by a shift away from electromechanically based industries such as coal, railroads, textiles, steel, automobiles, and machine tool manufacturing toward a new mix of scientific disciplines such as information theory, quantum mechanics, molecular biology, and nucleonics (Toffler 1980). The number of jobs in traditional heavy industries, especially steel and automobiles, is decreasing, partially from the incorporation of new electronic technology and robotics.

New jobs are being created in the production sector manufacturing microchips, integrated circuits, and other parts of computers and electronic equipment. Other jobs are being created in industries developing and producing lasers, fiber optics, and communication equipment. While production in developed countries in the Industrial Era was oriented toward high volume homogeneous mass markets, production in these same countries in the post-Industrial Era will fall into one of three categories. Precision products will require precision engineering, testing, and maintenance not easily available in developing countries. Custom products will be made in relatively small batches in close coordination with customers. Technology-driven products must evolve so fast that constant development is a necessity (Reich 1983). Just as in the preceding industrial shift, new production jobs are not currently being generated at a rate sufficient to replace disappearing old production jobs. Not only are there fewer jobs, but the new production jobs are often at lower wage scales than the jobs they are replacing.

The most rapid growth of new jobs in the Information Era is in service industries. Service jobs run the gamut in pay and prestige from high-paying medical jobs to low-paying work in fast-food restaurants. Workers directly involved with information processing include computer programmers, systems designers, and file managers in a variety of institutional settings. The predominant number of service sector jobs, however, are lower paid. Compared to other sectors, service sector jobs are disproportionately female. The growth in service sector jobs has been partially fueled by the increased participation of women in the labor force in the Information Era. Many tasks that used to be performed by women in the home such as meal preparation and childcare are now often performed external to the home in the service sector. Domestic tasks that were not previously centralized in the Industrial Era as was food production are beginning to be centralized.

REPRODUCTION THROUGHOUT HISTORY

Reproduction is a second major activity in which humans must engage to survive as a species. With human sexual reproduction, genes from two parents are contributed to and are present in the offspring. This contrasts with numerous other organisms that reproduce asexually by cell division, or have the option of switching from sexual to asexual modes of reproduction as environmental conditions change (Hapgood 1979). Like production, reproduction can be broken into major periods, defined by available technologies.

Limited Birth Control

In the first reproductive period, the period which has prevailed throughout most of human history, sex could not be reliably separated from procreation. Most of the norms that regulated male-female interaction and

TABLE 2-1.   Production Eras

Era	Major characteristics
Hunting and gathering	Nomadic
	Major food supply from gathering
	Supplemental food supply from hunting
	Production oriented toward securing basic needs
Agricultural	Fixed settlements
	Domestication of plants
	Domestication of animals
	Beginning urbanization and some surplus production
	Human and animal energy sources
Industrial	Mechanical energy replacing human muscle power
	Factory system of production
	Corporate organization
	National distrubution systems
	Fossil fuel energy sources
	Mass production of durable and consumer goods
Information	Growth of service industries
	Production of information and ideas
	Electronic energy replacing human mental energy

social relationships were grounded in that unalterable and undeniable reality. Both social norms and laws in all cultures restricted and clearly limited sexual interaction between men and women to reduce the probability of undesired procreation. A common assumption during this period was that sexual drives and desires were so strong that even nonexplicitly sexual interaction and relationships between men and women must also be restricted and clearly limited.

During this first reproductive period, there were attempts to control fertility and separate sex from procreation. The technologies to do so, however, were comparatively crude, limited, and unreliable. The major method was coitus interruptus, a male controlled method involving withdrawal of the penis from the vagina before orgasm. A second major method used to control fertility was abortion. This method did not separate sex from conception, but rather terminated undesired pregnancies. While some knowledge of folk methods of abortion are found in most cultures, until the twentieth century many abortion techniques were either unreliable or both painful and dangerous.

Widespread Birth Control

In the second reproductive period, sex may occur without procreation, but the reverse is not true—procreation may not occur without sex. Severing the linkage of conception and childbearing from sexual intercourse has the potential for fundamentally altered male-female interactions and relationships. The second reproductive era began in the later phases of the industrial productive era, at the end of the nineteenth century.

The first effective birth control methods disseminated on a wide scale were barrier methods. Although some crude barrier techniques were known in antiquity, and the precursors of the more modern barrier devices developed in the early 1800s, the second reproductive period did not begin until barrier techniques were more effective and more widespread. As with many technologies, improved barrier birth control devices were available first to the upper and middle classes and spread more slowly to the working and lower classes. A second spurt of improved reproductive technologies occurred in the post-World War II Era with development of the oral contraceptive pill and the intrauterine device.

Artificial Procreation

A third era in reproductive technology looms on the horizon, approaching with great rapidity. In this third era, the potential may exist to totally sever procreation from sex. Not only will birth control technologies allow sex to occur without procreation, but fertilization technologies will allow procreation to occur without sex. Artificial insemination is already both technically feasible and widely available. This technology involves the introduction of sperm, often from an anonymous donor, into the vagina of a fertile woman by means other than sex.

Another technique with current limited availability and success is *in vitro* fertilization. *In vitro* fertilization is the entry of a male sperm into the woman's egg outside of the body, producing "test tube" conception. The initial cases of *in vitro* fertilization involved reimplanting the externally fertilized egg in the womb of the woman who produced it. As yet ethical and legal issues may arise with the possibility of implanting a fertilized egg in a second woman's womb.

Additional technological breakthroughs in this third reproductive era read like a list of science fiction thrillers. Freezing eggs and embryos raises the issues of surrogate mothers and the selling of choice eggs and embryos.

Preselection of offspring on the basis of sex, intelligence, beauty, and other characteristics raises an additional set of issues. Will the world be over-populated by males, since parents often prefer boys to girls? Who will set the standard for genetic selection? Will the variability in the gene pool be reduced to such a narrow range that a shift in environmental conditions will render humans extinct? Cloning involves asexual reproduction by inducing cell division from a single cell from a single parent. The offspring is an exact genetic duplicate of the parent. Yet another third reproductive era technique is parthenogenesis, the production of an embryo from an egg without fer-tilization by a sperm, a reproductive technology resulting in all females. An artificial placenta would make possible the development of an embryo out-side a female body.

TABLE 2-2. Reproduction Eras

Era	Major characteristics
Limited birth control	Crude, limited, and unreliable birth control
	Procreation requires sexual intercourse
	Sexual intercourse may result in unintended procreation
Widespread birth control	Widely available and reliable birth control
	Procreation requires sexual intercourse
	Sexual intercourse may occur without procreation
Artifical procreation	Widely available and reliable birth control
	Procreation may occur without sexual inter-course
	Sexual intercourse may occur without procrea-tion

IMPACT OF HISTORICAL ERAS ON SEX ROLES

The first reproduction era lasted through several production eras. Limited birth control existed throughout the Hunting and Gathering, Agricultural, and most of the Industrial Eras. Only in the last part of the Industrial Era of pro-duction did reproduction technologies advance forward toward widespread birth control. One crucial constant difference between men and women during limited birth control was that women bore the children and were not able to control the numbers and timing of births.

A traditional stereotype of sex roles originated in the Hunting and Gathering era of production and has persisted until the modern era. Men and women differed on nurturing, geographic mobility, and risk taking. This stereotypical view has some basis in the biological reality of reproduction. Sex differences in nurturing, geographic mobility, and risk taking can predominantly be traced to pregnancy and childbearing. Women were responsible not only for carrying and bearing the children, but also for nurturing and breastfeeding them after birth. In early societies, the only method of keeping infants alive was by breastfeeding.

Once the women were tied down with pregnancy, birth, and breastfeeding for a period of several years, they assumed other feeding and nurturing responsibilities as well. These additional responsibilities included the feeding and care of older children and the feeding of adults. Women's productive roles were restricted and determined by their reproductive roles. Women became the gatherers. Not only could women perform this activity more easily when pregnant than hunting, but women could also gather fruits, nuts, and other foodstuffs while surrounded by young children.

Men became hunters. Hunting in primitive societies with limited tools and weapons required both speed and stamina. Pregnant women were slower and had less stamina than men. Women past puberty, given poor nutrition and extended breastfeeding, were likely to be pregnant every three or four years, significantly reducing the time they would have been effective hunters. Once specialized productive roles developed, skill, practice, and learning all contributed to maintaining these roles.

In the course of hunting, men were often required to range across substantial distances, often in small hunting parties separate from the main group. Traveling away from the main group increased the possibility of success in hunting, since animals may have been alerted, alarmed, or agitated by obvious human activity. Women were less geographically mobile. Owing to carrying infants and the slowness of accompanying small children, they were able to cover less ground in any given day.

Related to sex-based productive role differences in hunting and gathering were differences in risk taking. In a time of limited weapons, hunting was a risky activity, with high probabilities of humans being hurt or killed by the animals they stalked. Gathering, while also raising the possibility of harm from large animals, was less resky. Furthermore, the preservation of society required that young women with young infants stay alive to produce the next generation. The same was not true for young men.

Men, then, were less nurturing, more geographically mobile, and more likely to take risks. Women were more nurturing, less geographically mobile, and less likely to take risks in economic activities. While women confronted great risks of illness and death during childbirth, those risks were not associated with economic production. These sex role differences were based in limitations of reproductive technology and did not change rapidly as production technology changed.

In agricultural society, women were still more nurturing, less geographically mobile, and less likely to take risks. Throughout the Agricultural Era in most known societies, women were primarily responsible for domestic chores such as food and clothes preparation, child care, and the care of small animals. Men raised large animals and worked in the fields, especially after the development of plow technology. Depending on the season of the year, men, women, and children participated in harvest. Men continued to hunt, especially in the off-season from planting. When productive tasks were differentiated by geographic mobility and risk taking, women typically performed those tasks requiring less travel and less risk taking.

By the Industrial Era, these early biologically based differences had hardened into firm stereotypical roles and expectations. Especially among the upper classes, women were perceived as nurturing, homebound, and physically weak. In all classes, the house and the children were more the responsibility of women. Men left the home to work in factories and remained there throughout most of their working lives. Women who worked in factories often did so for a much briefer period of their lives, typically while young and unmarried. Poor women needing paid jobs most frequently found them in the domestic sector, working as servants, thus reinforcing the stereotypical differences between men and women. The image of men as more mobile and greater risk-takers resulted in the upper classes in greater educational opportunities for men but rarely for women. Since upper- and middle-class women were perceived as more nurturing, less mobile, and weak, it was inappropriate for them to work outside the home in economically productive activities or to be highly educated.

A major crack in the biologically based stereotype of appropriate male and female roles did not occur until innovations in birth control began to alter the potential for reproduction. With modern birth control, women were able for the first time in history to separate sexual activity from procreation. Women began to have greater control over their own bodies and the timing and number of children. Birth control enabled women to fulfill a wider range of productive roles without having to give up marriage and sex. Men had always had this freedom, but this expansion in choice began to be available to women in the late Industrial Era. After World War II, greater improvements in birth control technology expanded choices even further.

Innovations in reproductive technologies rather than innovations in production technologies have been the driving force behind crumbling of the traditional sex role stereotypes. Production technologies, especially those

TABLE 2-3. Stereotypical Male and Female Sex Roles Resulting from Differential Reproduction Roles

Male	Female
Production emphasized over nurturing	Nurturing emphasized over production
Geographically mobile	Less geographically mobile
Risk taking	Risk averse

substituting mechanical and electronic power for human work, were necessary in some realms for women to assume new productive roles. But these changes alone, without changes in birth control technology, were not sufficient to alter traditional male-female roles. The full impact of production innovations did not occur until improvements in reproductive technologies. Innovations in reproductive technologies occurred at a much slower rate than innovations in production technologies. The Hunting and Gathering, Agricultural, and most of the Industrial Eras of production coincided with the entire first era of reproduction with limited birth control. Humans were in the third major era of production technology before the second era of reproduction technology began.

3 Birth Control Development and Dissemination

Women have attempted to control the number and timing of births throughout history. These attempts may be divided historically into two periods. In the first period, birth control technology was neither well developed nor very effective. In the second or modern period, which began in the late nineteenth century, more effective techniques were developed and gradually became available. This chapter deals with each of these two eras.

The modern post-birth control era may also be divided into two waves. The initial wave of birth control technologies consisted of barrier or restraint methods. Included among these techniques are condoms, diaphragms, foams, jellies, and spermicides. This wave was well underway by the beginning of the twentieth century. The second wave of birth control technologies occurred much later in the early 1960s. This wave involved the more effective techniques of IUDs and the birth control pill. Each of these eras will be discussed in this chapter.

Legal availability and dissemination of birth control devices, in addition to technological innovation, are important factors in determining the access of the average woman to effective birth control. Legal availability and dissemination have often lagged behind technological development, and now, as in the past, continue to generate controversy.

TRADITIONAL ATTEMPTS TO CONTROL BIRTHS

Before the widespread availability, dissemination, and use of effective birth control techniques, the typical woman spent much of her child-bearing years pregnant, nursing, or with small children. Women spent even greater amounts of their lifespan involved in the child-bearing and rearing cycle. Women had little ability to plan the timing, sequence, or numbers of offspring that they bore. Given higher infant and maternal mortality rates, serious illness and death were a more likely outcome of pregnancy and birth than today. Each pregnancy incurred higher risk of undesired sickness or even death for the mother, as well as the trauma of an infant death.

Despite the limited understanding of the reproductive process, people attempted to limit the number of births. Evidence exists that women used homemade devices such as pessaries—vaginal barriers similar to diaphragms—and solutions such as douches for centuries. Abstinence and rhythm approaches to sexual intercourse were also employed. Extended breastfeeding of infants decreased the probability of ovulation, another method used to control the timing and number of births. Though frequently unsafe, abortions have also been used throughout history to end unwanted pregnancies. Male methods of limiting births, including both penile sheaths and withdrawal, were also used throughout history. Withdrawal was probably the most widely used and most effective of these primitive techniques.

Preliterate Society

The most common techniques to control birth in preliterate societies were not contraceptive practices, but rather abortion and infanticide. Depending on the preliterate society, controversy surrounded these non-contraceptive techniques. Attempted abortions were uniformly dangerous and often resulted in female deaths. Infanticide was most commonly practiced on baby girls, which not only lowered the immediate popultion but also lowered the potential number of adult women who could give birth.

Most primitive societies also attempted to control births through magical rites, formulas, and potions, but few of these were effective in any way. Douching was commonly used, but then, as now, was ineffective in preventing undesired births. Withdrawal, or coitus interruptus, was used in some preliterate societies, in which some understanding of the linkage between sperm and births had been made (Himes 1970).

Antiquity

Evidence in ancient Egyptian writings of the use of various preparations to be inserted into the vagina shows that birth control was attempted, although how widespread these attempts were remains unclear. Popular preparations were crocodile dung and honey. Most Egyptian birth control methods were female initiated.

From written evidence in the Bible, coitus interruptus was known and used by the ancient Hebrews. This method, however, was not sanctioned by the Rabbis who declared it a sin. According to a story in the Bible,

Onan, the brother of deceased Er, was supposed to engage in intercourse with his dead brother's wife so that she could bear children. While technically performing this duty, Onan resisted procreating with Tamar, the brother's widow, by engaging in coitus interruptus. Onan did want his children raised under his brother's name, but refused to acknowledge this intention publicly. In the story, God was displeased with Onan's behavior and slew him.

Why God slew him was controversial and unclear. If the sin were the act of coitus interruptus itself, the religious implication was that birth control was a mortal sin. This is the interpretation of the story to which eventually the Catholic Church adhered. This text from Genesis is still used by the Church as justification for declaring birth control to be a sin. If the reason for Onan's destruction by the wrath of God was his deception about his true intentions and his selfish unwillingness to help his brother's wife, then birth control and coitus interruptus were not sinful.

Partially in response to rabbinical interpretation that coitus interruptus specifically was sinful, the contraceptive sponge was developed in this era. An ineffective practice employed was twisting violently during the act of intercourse and making rapid movements in an attempt to remove semen from the body. Internal potions were also used (Himes 1970).

The Greeks and Romans made some advances in contraceptive practices. They discouraged magical solutions and amulets and especially emphasized both medicated suppositories and wool as a way to plug the vagina. Experts now feel that some of the Greek and Roman methods did change the alkaline content of the vagina, having a negative effect upon conception rates. The Greeks and Romans also understood the linkage between sperm and conception and the technique of withdrawal (Himes 1970).

Non-western cultures developed their own techniques of birth control and population limitation, apart from Greek and Roman contraceptive development. In ancient China, infanticide and potions were the two most common techniques of limiting the population. In Japan, there was some mention of the use of the tortoise shell or horn condom or sheath. Whether these were used for contraception or as devices that allowed the impotent to engage in intercourse remains unclear. From Sanskrit sources, ancient Indians used techniques that inserted substances such as salt and butter into the vagina, and smeared the vagina with honey and oil. The use of salt, in particular, was widespread and may have been more effective than other primitive techniques (Dickinson and Bryant 1931; Himes 1970).

The Middle Ages to the Industrial Era

During the Middle Ages, attitudes toward birth control varied widely. Unlike Catholicism, where birth control was forbidden, Islamic religious principles forbade neither birth control nor abortion. Islam did not consider the fetus a human until it assumed human characteristics, and therefore did not consider abortion a sin. During this period, Islamic medicine exceeded the level of medical practices in Europe. Islamic practices used the introduction of various substances into the vagina to prevent pregnancy. By contrast, European attempts to prevent pregnancy often involved magic.

In the Middle Ages, the opposition of the Catholic Church to birth control hardened. In the thirteenth century, St. Thomas Aquinas condemned birth control, saying that it was against nature and morally wrong, thus relegating contraception to folk medicine rather than officially condoned practice. The lack of official sanctioning of birth control attempts by the church did not remove either the desire to prevent births or common knowledge about how to achieve that. Folk medicine techniques were many and varied. These included a huge variety of potions to be drunk or inserted into the vagina, the use of magical objects, and rituals involving the fingers. One such ritual specified that sitting or laying down on a certain number of fingers, or placing fingers in a child's first bath water to indicate the desired number of pregnant free years would prevent births.

From the Middle Ages through most of the nineteenth century, withdrawal remained a major method of preventing undesired births. Early make sheaths or condoms were sometimes used, especially in houses of prostitution. Other ancient techniques, such as sponges, vaginal preparations, and potions were used, but there was scientific improvement in birth control technology during this period.

FIRST WAVE BIRTH CONTROL TECHNOLOGIES IN THE MODERN ERA

Male Barrier Methods

Condoms were among the earliest of modern birth control barrier technologies, and had been mentioned in the earliest of times. Condoms are a thin sheath enveloping the penis; there are worn during intercourse to prevent sperm from entering the vagina. In addition to their use for contraception, condoms have also been recommended at various times as a device to prevent the spread of venereal disease. Condoms were described in some scientific and literary sources in the seventeenth and eighteenth centuries. For example, writings about Casanova reveal that he was knowledgeable about the benefits of condoms (Turner 1717; Casanova, n.d.).

Condoms from animal skins became available in the eighteenth century, but were very expensive. Mass production of relatively cheap condoms from nonanimal sources was not able to occur until the vulcanization of rubber in 1843 and 1844 by Goodyear and Hancock. Vulcanization lowered the costs of condoms dramatically, making them more readily available to the average person. The trend of lowered costs continued in the 1930s, with the use of liquid latex and automatic machinery. Once the costs were lowered, every late nineteenth century manual on sex included a section on the purpose and use of condoms. Latex condoms had several advantages over their crepe rubber predecessors. They resisted aging and therefore had a longer shelf life. They were odorless and often thinner, as well as comparatively inexpensive. Condoms were also portable.

Once condoms became less expensive, their diffusion depended upon where they were sold. Initially they were available almost exclusively in pharmacies, and therefore required direct contact with the pharmacist, often a well-known and highly regarded member of the local community. By the 1920s, condoms were carried in many other places such as gas stations and small groceries, where contact was less personal. By the 1920s, condoms were sold in coin slot machines in Germany and Holland (Himes 1970).

Despite the dramatic improvement condoms represented over prior birth control methods or no birth control at all, they also had several disadvantages. Condoms required preparation for intercourse considerably in advance of the act itself. Individuals had to remember to go to the store and purchase them. Condoms are a male technique. The motivation of males to prevent pregnancy is often different from that of females, and may vary from one social setting to another. Users criticize condoms as interruptions of lovemaking. Some contend that condoms reduce sensitivity and sexual pleasure.

Female Barrier Methods and Spermicides

The first modern female barrier contraceptives were the diaphragm and the cervical cap, introduced in the nineteenth century. For centuries, women had tried vaginal methods of contraceptives such as sponges, homemade pastes, and various locally developed spermicides with limited success. The diaphragm is a dome-shaped rubber cup which is inserted into the vagina and blocks the cervix. Diaphragms are typically used with some type of spermicide to achieve maximum effectiveness. The cervical cap is a smaller rubber device also inserted into the vagina which fits more tightly over the cervix.

The first cervical cap (1838) and the first diaphragm (late 1800s) were both developed in Germany. Cervical caps had several disadvantages. In the beginning, they were usually individually molded since a tight fit was necessary, requiring greater experience in appropriately fitting a cap. They were also harder to insert and to remove. Both the diaphragm and the cervical cap required the woman to probe her own vagina, an activity strongly discouraged by Victorian mores. Inserting the diaphragms, however, required less touching and probing than inserting a cervical cap. The advantage of cervical caps over the diaphragm was that they could be left in place for longer periods of time, and therefore inserted earlier, prior to intercourse. Cervical caps can be left inside the woman for up to 24 hours. However, an odor often developed if the cap had been left in place for more than a day or two. Because of their tighter fit, they required less accompanying spermicides (Cappiello and Grainger-Harrison 1981; Hastings-Tolsma 1982).

While the cervical cap was difficult to use, diaphragms became popular in much of continental Europe and England during the late nineteenth century. Recognition and use of these methods in the United States, however, lagged behind (Sherris, Moore, and Fox 1984). By the 1920s, middle-class women in the United States were using diaphragms.

Concomitant with the use of barrier methods was the use of spermicides—creams, jellies, and foams with chemicals to kill sperms. Spermicides are intended to inactivate sperm in the vagina before they can move into the upper genital tract. Spermicides have two components, the active spermicidal agent, and the carrier. The agent kills the sperm, while the carrier is the substance used to introduce the agent into the body.

The first commercially available spermicides were made of cocoa butter and quinine sulfate in London in 1885. By 1900, there were widely available in many countries. Newer more effective preparations were developed in the 1920s and 1930s, using more potent spermicides, and often using carbon dioxide to create an effervescent foaming effect (Connell 1982). In the 1950s, a new type of spermicide using surface-active agents or surfactants was introduced. This new more powerful ingredient acts mainly by damaging the sperm-cell membrane (Tatum and Connell-Tatum 1981).

There are seven spermicide carriers available in various countries today: jellies, creams, foams, melting suppositories, foaming tablets, foaming suppositories, and soluble film. Jellies and creams are sometimes used alone but must be used with a diaphragm to kill the sperm not trapped by the barrier if the diaphragm is to be effective. Foams, jellies, and creams are the most common carriers used in the United States. These carriers require no waiting, contrasted with foaming tablets and suppositories, which require a ten-minute wait, and suppositories and film, which can take from five to thirty minutes, depending on the manufacturer (Jackson, Burger, and Keith 1981). The advantage of the carriers which require waiting is that they are less messy. Clinical tests indicate that jellies, creams, and foams are at full effectiveness for at least an hour, and at reasonable effectiveness for up to eight hours. Suppositories and tablets are fully effective for only an hour or less (Keith, Burger, and Jackson 1982).

Before the 1920s, diaphragms used in the United States were produced in Europe. The first U.S. company to produce diaphragms began production in 1923 (Sherris, Moore, and Fox 1984). The combination of barrier techniques and spermicides were the most commonly used methods of birth control up through the 1950s. In 1955, 25 percent of white married couples using contraceptives used diaphragms; 27 percent used condoms (Ryder and Westoff 1971).

Effectiveness Rates

Effectiveness may be judged both in terms of preventing unwanted pregnancies and providing women with control over their own bodies. Condoms are a male controlled method, but are one of the few methods besides spermicides which do not require a physician's prescription and interaction with the medical community. Among those who use the condom exactly as directed and with each act of intercourse, the failure rate is 3 pregnancies per 100 woman years (i.e., 100 women using this method for a year). In actual use, reported failure rates range from 15 to 20 failures per 100 woman years (Hatcher et al. 1982).

The actual failure rate for the condom is higher than the obtainable failure rate for three reasons. Some couples use the condom improperly, especially by pulling it on too tightly so that it breaks under pressure. The second reason is that the condom is not actually used in all instances of intercourse. A third less frequent reason for contraceptive failure is improper removal after intercourse, so that some sperm spills. The use effectiveness of the condom could be improved if a spermicide such as foam were used at the same time, but this dual usage is uncommon.

Both diaphragms used with creams or jellies and other spermicides used separately can be very effective when used appropriately. First-year failure rates when used properly at each act of intercourse for a diaphragm are between 2 and 3 per 100 woman years (Jackson, Burger, and Keith 1981; Lane, Arceo, and Sobrero 1976). A range of failure rates, including much higher failure rates, are reported in some studies, up to 23 percent during the first year of use in one large population-based U.S. study (Ryder 1973). Low failure rates are found in women highly motivated to prevent pregnancy, women with higher levels of education, older women, and women who have had instructional experience with vaginal methods (Connell 1982; Lane, Arceo, and Sobrero 1976; Oliva and Cobble 1979).

Reported failure rates for spermicide used alone vary even more. A few studies have found very low pregnancy rates of 2 or less per 100 woman years (Bushnell 1965; Squire, Burger, and Keith 1979). Most large studies, however, report higher first-year failure rates ranging from 11 to 31 percent, with some reported failure rates as high as 60 per 100 woman years (Schirm et al. 1982; Bernstein 1971; Connell 1982).

SECOND WAVE BIRTH CONTROL TECHNOLOGIES IN THE MODERN ERA

Intrauterine devices (IUDs) and oral contraceptives (the pill) were two new methods of birth control widely available in the United States and other developed countries during the 1960s. Both the IUD and the pill were designed to prevent conception without affecting long-term fertility. Sterilization in the forms of vasectomies and tubal ligations prevent pregnancy by permanently ending reproductive capacity. Postcoital techniques such as menstrual extraction and the morning after pill have been developed but are used with questionable safety. Abortion techniques have become safer and more widely used.

IUDs

Of more modern methods of birth control, scientific work began first on the IUD. The first published report on IUDs made from silkworm gut appeared in 1909. In that year, Grafenberg also began working on IUDs made of silkworm gut which he later adapted into a circle of gut held in shape by silver and copper wires (Huber 1975). Further developmental work occurred up through the 1930s. Between 1930 and 1960, improved IUDs were used in some countries, especially Israel and Japan. In 1959, the Marguilies Spiral was the first marketed IUD in the United States, followed shortly thereafter by the Lippes Loop and the Saf-T-Coil series (Hatcher et al. 1982; Davis 1971).

Modern intrauterine devices consist of plastic or wire inserted for long periods into the uterus. Some IUDs also release hormones. An IUD that releases progesterone, the Progestasert-T, was first marketed in the 1970s. The mechanism or action of IUDs is still not completely understood. Seven possible reasons why IUDs work have been presented (Hatcher et al. 1982).

(1) The presence of the local foreign body may cause an inflammatory response, which in turn creates lysis of the blastocysts (prevention of implantation of the fertilized egg).
(2) Increased local production of prostaglandins may inhibit implantation.
(3) Competition of copper with zinc may inhibit estrogen uptake or cause other intracellular effects on the endometrium.
(4) Disruption of proliferative secretory maturation processes may impair implantation.

(5) The implanted blastocyst may be mechanically dislodged.

(6) The motility of the ovum in the Fallopian tube may be increased.

(7) Sperm passing through the uterine cavity may be immobilized.

Under optimal conditions IUDs may be left in the body indefinitely. The major advantage of this method of birth control is that once in place, little care is required other than periodically checking the strings attached to the IUD to make sure that it has not been dislodged. No special preparation for intercourse is required, nor is any reduction in sensation experienced. For these reasons, this method of birth control is often used in Third World countries. Approximately 60 million women around the world were using IUDs in 1982. The Lippes Loop is the most widely used, except in China, where a tailess IUD similar to the original Grafenberg Ring is still used.

The disadvantages of IUDs are occasional complications, such as spotting, bleeding, and anemia. Other complications may include cramping and pain. In some instances, when the IUD is improperly inserted, perforation of the uterus and pelvic inflammatory disease (PID) may cause infertility. A recent review of world medical literature found the risk of PID to be three to five times greater for IUD users than for nonusers. Some studies have also found a higher risk of PID the longer the IUDs are used. Other research indicated particularly high risks (seven to nine times greater) for never pregnant women, a finding that is still controversial (IUD Users 1980). IUDs must be inserted by trained medical personnel. Incorrectly inserted IUDs may be painful and expelled, resulting in pregnancy. Not all women can use IUDs. Women who experience difficulty include those with small uteri, who have never been pregnant, or who have any active pelvic infection including gonorrhea.

The Pill

In the early 1930s, scientific knowledge about the menstrual cycle enabled researchers to understand when during the cycle the probability of fertilization was highest. Only at that point was the rhythm method of birth control developed. The rhythm method involved timing intercourse to coincide with periods during the cycle where the probability of inception was lower. This initial study of the menstrual cycle led to basic research on the interaction and role of hormones.

Early developmental work discovering the power of progesterone to inhibit ovulation occurred in the 1930s. In 1934, Corner and Beard isolated progesterone and established its structure. Makepeace in 1937 established that progesterone inhibited ovulation in rabbits. Further developmental work produced synthetic hormones that could be used in a contraceptive pill (Scrimshaw 1981).

Contraceptive research was too controversial to receive federal funding in the 1940s and 1950s. Margaret Sanger, a pioneer in the introduction and dissemination of birth control in the United States, was interested in the development of new birth control technologies to supplement the diaphragm and other barrier methods. She was instrumental in linking Gregory Pincus, an early endocrinologist working on hormones, with a wealthy woman who funded the development of the pill to the point of test marketing (Scrimshaw 1981).

By the mid to late 1950s, oral contraceptives were developed and test marketed in Puerto Rico. By 1960, Enovid, the first commercially available contraceptive pill, was marketed in the United States. Enovid was quickly followed by competitors, including Ortho-Novum, Norlestrin, Norinyl, Provest, and Oracon (Hatcher et al. 1982).

Initial contraceptive pills combined both estrogen and progestin. Each worked in somewhat different ways to inhibit contraception. Ovulation, the production of an egg, is inhibited by estrogen. Estrogen acts on the hypothalamus by suppressing pituitary follicle-stimulating hormone and leutenizing hormone. In newer pills, estrogen is 95 percent effective in suppressing contraception. Pills have a higher overall effectiveness rate, however, from the additional suppressing effect of progestins.

Progesterone normally prepares the endometrium for implantation of the ovum and maintains pregnancy. The contraceptive effects of progesterone include keeping the cervical mucus scanty and thick, thus hampering the transport of sperm. A second inhibiting effect of progesterone is capacitation, which changes the surface of the sperm, and results in decreased stability of plasma membrane around the ovum. Progesterone also decelerates ovum transport and may play a role in inhibiting implantation, when the progesterone, as in the pill, is administered prior to ovulation. Last, progesterone may play a subtle role in inhibiting ovulation itself (Morris 1973; Speroff, Glass, and Kase 1978).

Early birth control pills in the 1960s contained large amounts—50 to 100 mcg—of an estrogen and 1 to 10 mg of the progestin. By the late 1960s, it was determined that smaller dosages of the hormones were adequate contraceptives and had fewer side effects. The most serious side effects and many of the minor side effects were related to the high dosages of estrogen. Current combination pills generally contain 30 to 50 mcg of an estrogen and 1 mg or less of a progestin. Since 1973, mini-pills containing progestin have been marketed in the United States. In at least 80 countries of the world, excluding the United States, progestin contraceptive injections are used. These deter pregnancy for three to six months. These types of injections have not been approved for use in the United States because of potential safety problems. In some tests, breast tumors have developed in beagles. There are also concerns that the drugs may produce birth defects.

There are some subgroups of women who cannot take or are discouraged from taking the pill. Women with heart disease, such as thromboembolic disorder, cerebrovascular accident, or coronary artery disease should not take the pill. Women with impaired liver function, or malignancy of the breast or reproductive system also should not take the pill. Other groups of women who generally should not take the pill include those with severe headaches, hypertension, diabetes, or a strong family history of diabetes, and gall bladder disease. Women with a history of abnormal vaginal bleeding or irregular menses, smokers over age 35, and nonsmokers over age 40 are also discouraged from taking the pill.

Concern over the many side effects of the pill has led to some skepticism over pill usage. Serious side effects are related to cardiovascular problems. In studies in both the United States and Britain, heart attacks and strokes occur more often in women who use the pill than in women who do not (Layde, Beral, and Kay 1981). The most severe complications, however, occur only in a small segment of women who use the pill, such as women who smoke or who already have hypertension. Healthy young women who are nonsmokers have a much smaller risk of developing serious complications. The Royal College of General Practitioners Contraceptive Study found that women between 35 and 44 who used the pill had a 1 in 2,000 chance of dying if they smoked, and a 1 in 6,700 chance if they did not. For women younger than 35, smokers had a 1 in 10,000 chance while nonsmokers had a 1 in 77,000 chance (Petitti et al. 1979).

Other serious side effects are headaches, blurred vision, severe leg pains or chest pains, gall bladder disease, and hypertension. Irritating though generally not life threatening side effects include nausea, weight gain, fluid retention, spotting, mild headaches, yeast infections, depression, and mood changes. The mini-pill can be used by some patients who have estrogen-related side effects from the combined pill, especially headaches, hypertension, leg pain, weight gain, and nausea. The major side effects of the mini-pill are irregular menses, spotting, and amenorrhea.

The combined pill has the lowest theoretical failure rate of all nonsurgical contraceptive methods. Its effectiveness rate is close to 100 percent. In the Royal College of General Practitioners study, the actual failure rate was 0.34 pregnancies per 100 women years (Royal College of General Practitioners 1974). The effectiveness rate in practice is more difficult to determine and is predominantly caused by women who forget to take pills, or who drop out of pill use. Missing one pill, if the woman remembers to take both of them the next day, rarely leads to pregnancy. When women miss two or more pills, a backup method of contraception is usually recommended for that month.

There are high attrition rates among pill users. Only 50 to 70 percent of women who start birth control pills are using them after one year. Most discontinue for nonmedical reasons (Hatcher et al. 1982). The theoretical effectiveness of the mini-pill is lower than that of combined oral contraceptives. Depending on the specific pill, drug companies report failure rates from 1.1 to 1.25 pregnancies per 100 woman years. Pregnancy rates are highest in the first six months of mini-pill use. Backup methods are now recommended for the first two months.

Postcoital Techniques

A variety of postcoital techniques are being developed for couples who have infrequent intercourse. Unprotected mid-cycle intercourse (during the height of fertility) carries a risk of pregnancy from 2 to 30 percent. One technique is the use of combined birth control pills the morning after intercourse. This use of regular birth control pills the morning after intercourse has not been approved by the Food and Drug Administration. In one study of the use of Ovral, failure rates from 0.6 to 1.6 percent were reported, a substantial decline from rates during unprotected intercourse. Other modern approaches to postcoital contraception use high-dose oral estrogens, DES (diethylstilbestrol) and EE (ethinyl estradiol). One test of DES reported no pregnancies (Morris and Van Waganen 1967). Tests with EE showed a rate of 4 pregnancies out of 546 patients (Dixon et al. 1980).

Some researchers believe that morning after IUD insertion is an effective postcoital contraceptive strategy. There have been some tests of the copper-T or copper-7. Menstrual extraction, another technique, involves removing the contents of the uterus by vacuum, including the potential menstrual flow. This is generally done a day or two after a period is late, before pregnancy is confirmed, causing many potentially unnecessary procedures to be performed.

Sterilization

Sterilization involves surgical procedures to create permanent fertility control by removing part of the reproductive system of either the male or the female. For married couples over the age of 30, sterilization is the most commonly used method of fertility control (Westoff 1972). Over 11.8 million adults in the United States and 100 million people worldwide have been sterilized (Association for Voluntary Sterilization 1980).

Vasectomy is a sterilization operation for men, which blocks the vas deferens, preventing the passage of sperm. It is a simple procedure that can be performed on an outpatient basis. Most side effects are mild, such as swelling or discoloration. While intended to be a permanent method, recent success at reversing vasectomies ranges from 18 to 60 percent depending on the initial surgical procedure and the center performing the reversals.

The major method of permanent fertility control for women is tubal ligation, a procedure that blocks the Fallopian tube through ligation (cutting), coagulation (burning), and mechanical occlusion (clips, bands, or rings). The procedure may be performed either abdominally or vaginally. Tubal ligation is a more extensive surgical operation than vasectomy, usually requiring general anesthesia. Complication rates vary enormously, depending upon the skill of the surgeon. Surgeons who do fewer than 100 cases a year have a complication rate four times greater than surgeons performing it frequently (Phillipps et al. 1975). Failure rates are low—2.5 cases per 1,000 over a four-year period (Phillips et al. 1976). Coagulation has greater risk of complications and a poor chance of reversal. With ligation or occlusion, reversal rates vary from 50 to 70 percent, depending on the skill of the surgeon.

Hysterectomy involves removal of the uterus, and until recently, was the most common method of female surgical contraception. Most experts today do not advise hysterectomy for sterilization since the costs, time of recovery, and complication rates are much greater than for tubal ligation. Many Catholic women who have not wanted to overtly violate church prohibitions against birth control which include sterilization have undergone hysterectomies to achieve permanent fertility control.

Abortion

Abortion is an old technique, although only recently a safe one. Safety has improved as a result of both its legalization and improved technologies. First and second trimester abortions were legalized in the United States as part of the 1973 Supreme Court decisions, *Roe v. Wade* and *Doe v. Bolton*. Deaths from illegal abortions in the United States declined from 39 in 1972 before national legalization to 3 in 1976.

A range of surgical methods are used to terminate pregnancies. Vacuum curettage is the complete emptying of the uterus in a short time through a small surgical opening, often done using local anesthesia. This was a newer method of abortion introduced into the United States in 1967 and now widely used. Through 13 weeks of gestation, it can be done on an outpatient basis. Traditional dilatation and curettage (D and C) uses a sharp metal curette in place of the vacuum curettage. General anesthesia is typically used. As compared to vacuum curettage, it is often more painful, causes increased blood loss, and requires larger dilation. Its advantage is greater familiarity among obstetricians and gynecologists.

Dilatation and evacuation (D and E) is an extension of both the traditional D and C and vacuum techniques. It is especially appropriate for use in the thirteenth through sixteenth weeks of gestation, although many proponents use it past 20 weeks. Hysterotomy is a small cesarean section operation. It involves major abdominal surgery and general anesthesia. Its use is limited.

With intrauterine or medical methods, abortions are induced rather than surgically removing the fetus. Intrauterine methods are used in second trimester abortions where the fetus is too large for curettage techniques. These methods require the woman to physically deliver the aborted fetus. Three primary medications are used to induce abortion—prostaglandins, hypertonic saline, and urea. Prostaglandin injections and suppositories are both used. The injections have a more rapid administration to delivery time. Both prostaglandin methods are associated with gastrointestinal symptoms, cervical lacerations, and some potential for delivery of a live fetus.

Another method is saline abortion—the introduction of a hypertonic saline solution into the uterus. The advantages are that this method is inexpensive, readily available, and almost never results in the delivery of a live fetus. The disadvantages include a greater risk of clotting problems. If the saline solution is mistakenly infused directly into the circulatory system of the woman, major complications result, including cerebral edema. Hypertonic solutions of urea are generally not used alone because of their high failure rate, but are often combined with prostaglandins.

The risk of dying from a legal abortion is slight, but is linked to the length of gestation which, in turn, determines the type of procedure. There are 1.3 deaths per 100,000 abortions for curettage techniques, 12.5 for intrauterine installation, and 41.3 for hysterotomy and hysterectomy. Complication rates are higher for intrauterine abortions than for curettage abortions.

BIRTH CONTROL DISSEMINATION

Comparative Usage Rates

With the wide availability of oral contraceptives and IUDs in the 1960s, the use of barrier methods decreased rapidly. In 1955, over half of white married couples using contraception relied on barrier methods. By 1965, the proportion of contraceptive-using white married couples relying on the diaphragm had dropped to 10 percent as a result of the availability of the pill and IUDs; by 1976 that figure had declined further to 3 percent, despite the growing concern and publicity about the deleterious effects of the pill and IUDs (Ryder and Westoff 1971; Mosher 1981). Compared to the pill and IUD, barrier methods seem obtrusive, more awkward, and less convenient. Users feared that barrier methods were less reliable.

In the United States, decreases in the use of oral contraceptives tend to follow spurts of adverse publicity over the health consequences of use (Jones, Beniger, and Westoff 1980). During the 1970s, publicity over the side effects of both the pill and IUD reawakened interest in barrier methods among highly educated couples and contributed to a slowdown in the use of the newer techniques. Among younger women receiving first-time contraceptives at Planned Parenthood Clinics, 12.9 percent chose the diaphragm in 1980 compared to 5.7 percent in 1975 (Sherris, Moore, and Fox 1984). Among users of contraceptive services in state-funded clinics in California, diaphragm use increased from 7.1 percent in 1976 to 12.8 percent in 1979 (Aved 1981). Use of the pill particularly dropped among couples intending to delay births. Sales of oral contraceptives declined 21 percent between 1976 and 1978 (Mosher 1982).

Despite a slight increase in the use of barrier techniques in the 1970s, the pill remains the most popular and commonly used form of birth control for younger unmarried women. Its advantages are obvious: once a user is on the pill, its effectiveness does not require any preparation immediately preceding intercourse, enhancing spontaneity and romance. Nor does it affect sensation for either partner as would a condom. As long as the woman remembers to take the pill daily, it is an extremely effective method of birth control. Among first-time contraceptive users at Planned Parenthood Clinics, 79 percent chose the pill in 1975; 57 percent in 1980; and 64 percent in 1982 (Sherris, Moore, and Fox 1984). In the California clinic sample, use of oral contraceptives decreased somewhat from 1971 to 1979 from 71 to 61 percent.

For highly motivated and more experienced users, both the newer IUD and pill as well as older barrier methods can be highly effective in preventing unwanted pregnancies. For less motivated or less experienced users, the pill and IUD provide higher actual effectiveness rates. Higher effectiveness rates result in feelings of greater control for women, first over their own bodies, and second, over their own lives.

For older women who have completed childbearing, sterilization is an extremely effective alternative to less permanent birth control methods. Surgical sterilization has become the most popular method of contraception among married women. In 1976, 26 percent of currently married women were using the pill, and 19 percent relied on sterilization of either themselves or their husbands. By 1982, sterilization was relied on by 27 percent of currently married women and the pill was used by only 14 percent (NSFG 1982).

Legal Availability

The development of modern birth control technology does not necessarily imply social and legal availability. The dissemination of information about birth control was particularly restricted in the United States by the passage of the federal Comstock Law in 1873. It prohibited the dissemination of contraceptives and contraceptive information, closing the mails to this material. The restriction of contraceptive materials was strengthened in 1897 by the passage of another law prohibiting the deposit of contraceptive materials with a common carrier. As a result, magazine and journal editors of professional as well as general lay publications were afraid to publish articles on contraceptives for fear that the whole issue would be seized.

Margaret Sanger became an early pioneer in the dissemination of birth control information, eventually going to jail for operating a birth control clinic in Brooklyn. Anticontraceptive laws were rigorously enforced before the 1920s and sporadically enforced through the 1920s and early 1930s. While public support for restrictive contraceptive laws was declining, there was insufficient political strength for the dissemination of birth control to repeal the legal restrictions. They continued to inhibit the spread of birth control information and devices, especially for the poor (Dienes 1972). The federal Comstock Laws remained in effect until 1936 in the crucial decision of *United States v. One Package*. Availability to the poor increased after this decision. North Carolina incorporated birth control into its public health program shortly thereafter in 1937. South Carolina followed in 1939 (Sulloway 1959).

The right to practice birth control was only established recently under U.S. law. In 1965, *Griswold v. Connecticut* was the first constitutional precedent that the use of birth control was a right for married persons, not a crime. Not until 1972 were laws that prohibited the dispensing of contraceptives to unmarried persons, or by other than a physician or pharmacist, held to be unconstitutional. In *Eisenstadt v. Baird*, a package of vaginal foam was handed to an unmarried woman during a lecture on contraceptives at Boston University, thus violating a Massachusetts law prohibiting the distribution of nonprescribed contraceptives. The final U.S. Supreme Court ruling overturned the Massachusetts law, establishing legal access to birth control for unmarried as well as married people (Andersen 1983).

The right to use abortion as a technique to control births has long been a controversial issue in U.S. society. With the exception of a few states with very liberal laws, the right of women to abortion was not established until the 1973 Supreme Court decisions of *Roe v. Wade* and *Doe v. Bolton*. The original decision argued that three rights collided: the constitutional right to privacy, the right of the state to protect maternal health, and the right of the state to protect developing life.

The Court set up different restrictions in the trimesters of pregnancy, arguing that in the first trimester the woman's right to decide her future privately took precedence. In the second trimester, while the state could not deny abortion, it could insist on reasonable standards of medical procedure to protect the health of the mother. In the third trimester, abortion could be performed to preserve the life or health of the mother (Goldstein 1979). Today, a major political movement in the United States is striving to abolish the right to abortion. A number of states and cities have passed restrictive laws, although many have been overturned through court proceedings. As with other methods of birth control, the technical feasibility of abortion does not assure dissemination and legal access.

4   *Components of Personal Relationships*

In a rapidly changing modern social milieu, most people spend much of their lives either in families, couples, or looking for partners. In 1980, 61.1 percent of the U.S. population was married. An additional 7.4 percent was widowed, and 5.8 percent was divorced (Bureau of the Census 1981b). Twenty-five percent of the population was single. Those happy with singlehood still have the task of establishing friendships and alternative relationships to meet their personal needs.

While laws prohibiting sex-based discrimination in the public arena were passed in the 1960s and 1970s, legal reform does not necessarily imply a change in the way men and women relate on a daily interpersonal basis. Interpersonal relationships between men and women have nonetheless been changing dramatically during the same time period, often driven by technological change. The introduction and dissemination of modern birth control technology has particularly altered the dynamics of male-female relationships.

Male-female relationships may consist of four components: love, intimacy, sex, and marriage. In this chapter we will define and explain each of these components, examining them across time. (See Table 4-1.)

LOVE

Love is probably the theme of more songs throughout history than any other topic. Love may take many forms: the love of a parent for a child, the love of brothers, sisters, and friends for each other, or the love of an individual for a god or spirit. Between men and women, love is often romantic and erotic. Some research indicates that romance is an integral part of love. Davis (1985) defines love as consisting of three clusters of feelings,

TABLE 4-1. Characteristics of the Four Components of Male-Female Relationships

Components	Major characteristics
Love	Caring between love partners
	An identification with the love partner
	Often includes romance and eroticism
Intimacy	Friendship, tolerance, and trust
	Expression of total self
	No need to maintain separate public and private images
	Detailed knowledge of other person
	Ability to predict behavior of other person in wide variety of situations
Sex	Intimate physical contact intended to lead to erotic arousal
	Physical intercourse
Marriage	A legally binding institution
	Implies financial commitments
	Institution for sanctioned childbearing and childrearing

including a passion cluster, which involves fascination, exclusiveness, and sexual desire. A second cluster in love relationships is friendship which includes enjoyment, acceptance, trust, respect, mutual assistance, confiding, understanding, and spontaneity. The third cluster is caring, including giving the utmost and being a champion or advocate of each other's interest. In one recent survey, a majority of respondents believe that romance is the first stage of love and that love springs from romance. In relationships, a majority of both men and women reported seeking love above romance, companionship, or sex (Rubinstein 1983).

Romanticism is a complex of feelings and attitudes which orient people to seek perfection, both in themselves and in others. The stereotypical image of a romantic situation involves an ideal woman meeting an ideal man. Also part of the romantic stereotype is the notion of a magical quality that makes life ecstatic, that overcomes all obstacles, and goes on forever in an unchanging fashion (Wells 1984). Romanticism is not a part of all cultures, but is particularly common in western cultures, including the United States

(Elliott and Merrill 1941). Parts of romanticism include notions of "love at first sight," and "falling in love."

One illustration of unbridled romanticism common to all European cultures is the mythical story of Cinderella. The Cinderella story involves four typical romantic assumptions which are fallacies when judged against the yardstick of reality. The first romantic notion is that anyone under the cover of a low status could assume a high-status position, such as that of princess. The second is that social and cultural differences, including great disparity in social status or family background, could be easily overcome with "true love." The third is that true lovers are always able to find each other and triumph, despite the opposition of family and friends. Last is the assumption that love conquers all problems and difficulties, resulting in living happily ever after (Mowrer 1927).

Several negative social consequences result from romanticism. One negative consequence is the double standard. Romanticism emphasizes reverence and worship for women, and thus the notion that women should be more pure and virtuous than men. Two aspects of the double standard stemming from this differential view are more freedom for men to engage in sexual experimentation, and the division of women into the "madonna" and "whore" categories. The hypothetical madonna is pure and virtuous, abstaining from sex until marriage, while fallen women experiment with sex. A second negative consequence are quickie marriages, where the engagement period is short, and youthful marriages, both initiated during the early bloom of romance. In each case, divorce is more likely than in other marriages, so that the younger the partners and the shorter the engagement period, the higher the probability of divorce (Nye and Berardo 1973; Goode 1959).

When marriage is based on romantic passion and nothing more, little foundation exists for subsequently building a solid marriage. Furthermore, romantic passion may encourage initial oversight of later crucial differences in background attitudes toward money, jobs, children, religion, and values. Romantic attractions are often based on physical appearance and attraction and foster unrealistic expectations about sexual gratification. Wells argues that realistically, there is little relationship between physical appearance and sexual responsiveness. Romanticism interjects confusion since it is often strongly based on physical appearance, leading to disappointment since physical attractiveness is not always synonymous with sexual responsiveness (Wells 1984).

Male-female love involves caring between the love partners, as well as an identification with the love partner. People tend to choose love partners who reinforce a positive image of themselves. In healthy love relationships, the reinforced image is good for both the individual and the larger society. A love partner who is strong and successful in a particular area may reinforce the mate's image of success in the same area, at least vicariously if not directly (Solomon 1981). In sociopathic love relationships, the reinforced image may include antisocial aspects. Romantic male-female love does not have to be reciprocal, but the probability of drastically one-sided love persisting for a long time is remote.

Safilios-Rothschild (1977) discusses five different types of male-female love. Adventuresome love is oriented toward pleasure, enjoyment, and fun, involving little commitment and responsibility. Friendship love is usually asexual and frequently occurs after a more passionate love has ended. This kind of love is usually neither possessive nor exclusive. Passionate or romantic love is often "exclusive" and involves a total sense of giving everything and expecting everything. Affectionate love involves constancy and predictability, often a major part of marriage. It includes sexual attraction, friendship, intellectual exchange, tenderness, understanding, and mutual concern. Mature love, the last type, is rare and involves willful control rather than unbridled emotional expression.

Safilios-Rothschild argues that people in the United States often treat love as a zero-sum game in which there is a fixed quantity to be distributed. This notion aggravates jealous feelings, so that a person who perceives his or her partner loving others, often even a parent or child, may feel threatened, jealous, and cheated. A romantic relationship with a member of the opposite sex is even more threatening.

Reiss (1960b) argues that there are four stages or cycles in the development of a love relationship. The first stage is rapport, which develops out of mutual attraction. If two people are able to establish a common ground for communication and relate in a mutually meaningful way, then rapport exists. After rapport exists, a couple can move to the second stage, self-revelation. Here couples discuss more serious topics, such as life values and goals. This stage is usually gradual, with first one partner revealing information, and then the other responding. Mutual dependency is a third stage which grows out of the previous disclosure of inner feelings. People desire praise or reinforcement from each other on a regular basis. Disclosure of personal feelings brings a sense of dependency upon each other. The fourth stage is personality need fulfillment. Each person feels he or she can meet the other's emotional, physical, and psychological needs. Couples at this point usually end up being both publicly and privately committed to loving each other.

INTIMACY

Intimacy involves friendship. It allows for the expression of the total self and presumes a special type of tolerance and trust. Within intimate relationships, the need to maintain a public image separate from the private self declines. Intimacy provides social support for the private self and is based on tolerance, trust, and deep affection (Bensman and Lilienfeld 1979).

Intimacy involves the acquisition of detailed knowledge of the other person, including an ability to predict his or her future behavior. Normally this detailed knowledge is built through a lengthy interactive process which slowly instills trust in each intimate partner, including an element of reciprocity (Lowenthal, Thurner, and Chiriboga 1975; Powers and Bultena 1976). Failure to engage in such a process of slowly revealing ever more personal details, which if misused could make the revealer vulnerable, may undercut trust in the relationship. A person who prematurely reveals personal details may inhibit the further development of an intimate relationship.

All of a person's intimate relationships are not necessarily romantic love relationships. Good same-sex friendships, relations between siblings, or even some male-female relationships may involve intimacy but not romantic erotic love. Nor are all love relationships necessarily intimate, especially short-term infatuations or the early stages of a budding romantic love. Traditionally, a major source of intimate relationships was the family.

Two types of intimacy are physical and affective. The chief component of physical intimacy is touching, both sexual and nonsexual. Sexual touching is intended to arouse erotically, while nonsexual touching involves physical contact between individuals that conveys physical and emotional attachment, not erotic interest. One traditional source of nonsexual touching is the family, where the incest taboo ordinarily prevents the connotative transition from affective to sexual. Outside of the family, opposite-sex adults often have difficulty engaging in affectionate touching without developing either the appearance or the reality of sexual touching. Same-sex affectionate touching may occur, but concerns about homosexuality limit this type of expression. These limits and fears are typically stronger for men than for women (Wells 1984).

Affectionate intimacy includes rapport and self-disclosure of one's private and personal self to another. Intellectual, personal, and social closeness are part of affective intimacy. Unlike physical intimacy, where there are strong norms regulating behavior, affective intimacy could possibly develop from almost any social situation involving verbal interchange. The greater possibilities for affective intimacy are especially true for cross-sex friendships outside of a family structure.

Rather than rigid social norms, a primary limit on the development of affective intimacy is the willingness of individuals to undertake the risk of self-exposure. People with high self-esteem who are self-confident are more likely to develop a number of intimate friendships. Persons with lower self-esteem and less self-confidence may perceive intimacy as a threat to their private selves.

The development of intimacy may be affected by the social setting. Intimacy is more likely to occur in primary groups, such as the family, work groups at the office or factory, living groups in a college or collective living arrangement, and play groups. Within primary groups, there is a sense of "we-ness" and a feeling of being an integral part of a group (Cooley 1909).

The conventional wisdom holds that women have valued intimacy more than men. One rationale for this difference has been the greater awareness women have exhibited of their own emotions and feelings. Women have been both more in touch with their emotions and more willing to talk about them to others. Female intimacy has also typically revolved around talking and verbal communication. Male intimacy has been less verbal. A man has been more likely to perceive just being together and spending time together as intimate, even in the absence of verbal communications about emotions and significant personal events (Rubinstein 1983).

The absence of rigid social norms about the development of appropriate levels of intimacy applies to love relationships as well as friendships and familial relationships. Daily contact may not occur in the early stages of a love relationship, allowing differences in perceptions about the meaning of intimacy to remain obscure. Once a relationship evolves into marriage or living together with substantial daily contact, the differences between men and women in definitions of intimacy may become a problem. Children may further mask these differences, since the couple must talk about the children and their activities.

While some long-term relationships manage to overcome different perceptions of intimacy, some marriages never become intimate. In some ethnic groups and social classes, intimacy comes from same-sex friendship groups rather than marriage. This pattern has been more common in working-class marriages and among certain ethnic groups where the couple lives within a cohesive ethnic neighborhood with many extended family relationships (Adams 1968).

The different life cycles of men and women in traditional marriages may further inhibit the development of intimacy. Many men during their 20s and 30s put most of their energies into career development and building financial success. By age 40, many men have plateaued in their careers, and begin to place more emphasis on the family and marriage. If the woman left the labor force to stay home and raise children in her 20s and 30s, she is frequently ready to reenter the labor force and possibly develop a new career by her early 40s. Perhaps frustrated by her earlier attempts to develop intimacy with her husband, she becomes less concerned with marriage and developing intimacy within it during the same time the man is becoming more focused on personal relationships. If the differences in life goals are sufficiently strong, divorce may result (Sheehy 1974).

Experts disagree about the role of conflict and fighting in intimate relationships (Landis and Landis 1977; Straus 1974). One position argues that fighting is inevitable in an intimate relationship and that quarreling and making up are the hallmarks of true intimacy (Bach and Wyden 1968). Quarreling episodes provide a means of venting anger and frustration and release negative feelings. The emotional catharsis is viewed as healthier than suppressing anger and frustration. Others view conflict as essentially harmful. They argue that disagreeing in a contained way, regulated by a carefully laid down set of rules, is not really fighting, but rather approaches a rational discussion (Mace 1976). Both positions agree that patterns of combative and continual conflict are destructive.

SEX

Sex is the third component of male-female relationships. Sex is one of the basic human drives, although a drive that has been subjected to strong social controls. Sex implies physical intercourse, but may also include other physical activities. Reiss (1960a, 1967) has described three different levels of sexual activity: kissing, petting, and coitus.

Several theories exist as to why most species, including humans, reproduce sexually. One theory holds that sex is an advantage because it speeds evolution through gene mixing. Another view holds that sexual reproduction slows down evolution by preventing too restrictive a biological adaptation to local transient conditions. Yet others argue sex repairs and rejuvenates genes. Some feel that the second set of genes received from the second parent serve as a "backup," enhancing versatility and resilience. One broader interpretation is that sexual reproduction allows an individual to leave behind a set of offspring with a wider range of specialized skills, increasing the possibility that at least some of those offspring will survive (Hapgood 1979).

Most sexual activity occurs between members of the opposite sex, although homosexuality also exists. Until 1961, when efforts to decriminalize homosexuality in the United States began, this type of sexual activity was illegal. Only rough estimates exist as to the prevalence of homosexuality. One estimate is that 3 to 4 percent of adult males in the United States are largely or exclusively homosexual (Gagnon 1977). More men have had some homosexual experience (Gagnon 1977; Kensey, Pomeroy, and Martin 1948). In Kinsey's studies, 37 percent of men had homosexual encounters. Many people feel this figure is too high, since Kinsey's sample included a disproportionate number of men who had been in prison or who were from poverty stricken homes. Many male homosexual experiences occur among young men. In the Kinsey data, 16 percent of the men had experienced a homosexual act only between puberty and age 16.

Estimates are that 2 to 3 percent of the female population may be exclusively homosexual, and an additional 2 to 3 percent frequently have mixed sexual experiences (Gagnon 1977). Kinsey's data on females did not have the biases present in the male data. His female data show that 2 percent of women had a homosexual experience and orgasm by age 12. The percent having a homosexual experience increased to about 10 percent by age 20. The percent experiencing an orgasm from a homosexual experience stabilized at 6 to 8 percent by age 20 (Kinsey et al. 1953).

While homosexuality refers to an erotic interest in the same sex, bisexuality refers to an erotic interest in either sex. The estimates of the prevalence of bisexuality are even rougher. Bisexuality can only be inferred from the Kinsey data. In these data from 1948 to 1953, three to four times as many single females as males were not sexually active. Removing those individuals from the sample, 75 to 85 percent of men and 80 to 90 percent of women ages 15 to 25 were exclusively heterosexual. Since Kinsey estimated 2 percent of women and 4 percent of men were exclusively homosexual, about 15 percent of men and 10 percent of women had mixed histories and might be bisexual.

In most traditional societies, male-female sex was legitimate only in the context of marriage, especially for women. Sex drive was presumed to be a current underlying all male-female relationships, even those that were not overtly sexual. Male-female friendships have been historically constrained and at times even discouraged as a result of the presumption of sexual overtones.

Not only were all male-female relationships presumed to have covert if not overt sexual overtones, but the converse was also true: same-sex friendships were rarely presumed to have sexual overtones. In nineteenth century United States, women in particular developed strong same-sex intimate friendships (Smith-Rosenberg 1975). In these friendships, women often used language and engaged in behavior which would be interpreted as sexual today. In that context, only heterosexual relationships were even suspected of carrying a sexual component, since heterosexuality was the only legitimate form of sexual expression.

Despite the difficulty of precisely ascertaining the prevalence of homosexuality and bisexuality, consensus exists that heterosexuality is the dominant form of sexual expression. Earlier norms that sex should occur only within marriage have not prevented premarital sexual expression. Reiss (1967) distinguishes among four broad categories of premarital sexual norms or standards. The first level is abstinence from intercourse, in which premarital coitus is considered inappropriate for both males and females. Within this category, various degrees of the other two levels of physical intimacy—kissing and petting—are acceptable. The most rigid would allow kissing only with affection present in the relationship. The next would allow kissing without affection. Two more lenient standards are petting with affection present and petting without affection present.

The second level of premarital sexual norms is the double standard in which intercourse is inappropriate for females but allowable for males. Two versions of the double standard are the orthodox and the transitional. In the orthodox version, intercourse is forbidden for all females, and women who engage in premarital intercourse are "whores" and "fallen women." For men, intercourse is allowed without moral condemnation, and frequently approved or even encouraged as a way to gain initial sexual experience. This standard assumes class differences. Boys gained sexual experience with women from a lower social class than themselves whom they would never consider to be suitable marriage partners. Wives-to-be were expected to be virgins. Examples of this are white males experimenting sexually with black slave women in the antebellum south. Upper and upper middle-class boys were often encouraged to sow "wild oats" with lower-class women before settling down into marriage.

In the transitional double standard, premarital intercourse is allowed for women who are in love or engaged, although males are still given greater freedom. The bachelor party for grooms on the eve of marriage vows is a carryover of this transitional double standard, where the male is expected to take advantage of one last chance to enjoy unfettered companionship with women hired to entertain. No such tradition exists for brides. Rather brides have showers to receive presents to prepare them for duties as wives and housekeepers.

Permissiveness with affection is the third level of premarital sexual morality. Here, premarital intercourse is allowed for both men and women in a stable relationship in which affection is present. In one version, the couple needs to be in love or engaged as a prerequisite for intercourse. In the other version, there must be some feelings of affection stronger than infatuation for coitus to be present, but these feelings do not necessarily imply long-term commitment.

The most lenient standard is permissiveness without affection. Intercourse is allowed in a relationship without affection for both males and females. Two versions of this standard are the sophisticated and the orgiastic. In the sophisticated version, although the pleasure of premarital intercourse is stressed, precautions are taken by both males and females about potential venereal disease and the possibility of pregnancy. In the orgiastic version, the pleasure of premarital coitus is paramount and little concern is placed on potential venereal disease, pregnancy, or their impact on the other person (Reiss 1967).

Some empirical studies have been conducted to explore the prevalence of these various premarital sexual norms. In 1960, over one-half of the females and one-quarter of the males surveyed in high schools and colleges held the abstinence standard. Only 2 percent of women and 13 percent of men supported the norm of permissiveness without affection (Reiss 1967). Variables such as the size and location of the school affected responses. More recent studies continue to reveal variability in findings, but generally have found a decline in abstinence and the double standard, replaced by broader acceptance of the two more permissive norms (King et al. 1977).

Another study using two panel surveys found an orthodox double standard in both attitude and behavior in 1967 through 1971 among single white college students in an introductory sociology class at a large midwestern university. In the second panel of similar students from 1970 through 1974, both men and women held an attitude supporting a more permissive standard for both men and women although male-female differences in self-reported coitus were greater in the second panel than in the first. These findings provide evidence of a maintenance in the double standard in behavior, although not in attitude (Ferrell, Tolone, and Walsh 1977).

Data from undergraduates at the University of Georgia in the 1970s indicate the development of a new double standard. Throughout the 1970s, the proportion of both men and women who believed that premarital sex is immoral steadily declined. At the same time, the proportion of both sexes engaging in premarital sex was increasing. Beginning in 1980, the proportion of men and women reporting that sex before marriage was immoral began to rise again. However, the proportion engaging in premarital sex also continued to rise. Robinson and Jedlicka (1982) interpret this as the beginning of a new form of double standard. Under a traditional double standard, both men and women set stricter standards of sexual behavior for women than for men. Under the new standard, both sexes now expect stricter morality of the opposite sex than of their own, explaining the difference between the belief that premarital sex is wrong while simultaneously engaging in it.

Traditionally, men have been the sexual aggressors while women have played a more passive role in initiating sex. A recent survey finds that among couples initiation is still more likely to be the husband's prerogative and refusal the role of the wife (Blumstein and Schwartz 1983). Women particularly hesitate to initiate sex when they perceive their partner to be feeling vulnerable. Traditionally, women have been more likely to refuse sex, because refusal was the major method available to them to demonstrate power.

Men are also more likely to place a sexual interpretation on behavior than are women. In an experimental study, Abbey (1982) split 72 men and 72 women into groups of four where each group was comprised of two male-female pairs. In each group, one couple became the actors who conversed for five minutes on an assigned topic, while the other couple observed the actors through a one-way window. All four students then completed questionnaires describing their perceptions of the actors' behavior. The women interpreted the behavior of the women as "friendly," while the male participants saw them as "seductive" and "promiscuous." The men interpreted both their own and the women's behavior as more sexually oriented than did the women. The sexual attraction of male actors to their female partners was greater than that of female actors to their male partners. Similarly, the interest of male observers in dating the female actors was greater than the interest of female observers in dating the male actors. Abbey argues that these differences are related to cultural stereotypes portraying men as more interested in sex than women. Many young men share these images, and in a situation of ambiguous information, are more likely to draw sexual conclusions.

In addition to cross-sex differences, attitudes toward more liberal sexual behavior are also influenced by the size of communities in which people previously and currently live. Using national opinion survey data collected between 1972 and 1976, attitudes toward homosexuality, extramarital sex, premarital sex, and pornography were assessed. Intolerant attitudes are related both to the size of the city in which the person currently lived and to the size of the city in which the person lived at age 16. In general, people who come from or live in small communities or rural areas are less tolerant. The size of the city in which people lived at age 16 was more strongly related to intolerance than the size of the city in which they lived as adults (Stephan and McMullin 1982).

MARRIAGE

Marriage is the fourth component of relationships between men and women. Marriage is an old institution, common throughout most of the civilized world for most of history. As a legally binding commitment, marriage implies an array of financial and social commitments as well as the sanctioning of sexual activities, especially for the purpose of procreation. Traditionally, marriage was more than the linkage of two individuals. Marriage involved two sets of extended families and mutually agreeable economic exchanges.

Through marriage, a husband committed to the future support of not only his wife and children, but also sometimes to needy members of the wife's family. A wife brought economic resources to the husband's family through the institution of dowries—payments made by the bride's family to the husband's family to compensate for the extra burden of caring for the wife.

The production of heirs was also an expected part of the marriage contract for the wife. Wives who failed to produce suitable heirs in some cultures could be divorced and returned to their original families to allow their husbands to find fertile mates. In traditional marriages, unlike the importance placed on sex and procreation, love and intimacy were not necessarily integral parts of the marriage contract and institution. Romantic ideals of love and intimacy slowly became incorporated into institutional norms for marriage so that the norm for modern marriages is to include all three of the other components—love, intimacy, and sex.

The Romans conceived marriage as a privilege for the upper class. This notion of privilege carried over to Europe in the Middle Ages. To get married, one had to wait until there was a house or cottage available, or until there was permission to build one. In the sixteenth century, the acquisition of the resources necessary to marry might take years, and in bad times, might never be obtained. This marriage pattern resulted in a large proportion of the adult population being unmarried and presumably sexually abstinent at any point in time. This pattern lasted in many European countries until the last 100 years. Even by 1870, two-fifths of the women in Lucerne, Switzerland had not been married by the age of 50 (Wrigley 1969).

While this conception of a means test for marriage was brought to the United States by the original colonists, the constraints on marriage were quite different. Generally, anyone could find land and build a cottage or house. Community pressure developed for people to get married and populate, rather than the reverse. In colonial United States, young people married at an early age, as a result of fewer resource constraints.

Many modern societal pressures encourage people to marry today. The first pressure is that most people are reared in a family setting and feel comfortable with that lifestyle. During childhood, children frequently view adulthood as consisting of roles relating to marriage and parenting. Some stigma is still attached to being single. Single people are sometimes treated as less adult. The term typically used to describe an unmarried woman—old maid—is pejorative. The equivalent term for men—bachelor—conveys a sense of temporariness and the idea that marriage will eventually follow, since bachelor is distinguished from "confirmed bachelor." Most forms of entertainment and socializing traditionally revolved around heterosexual couples. To not be a part of a couple is to not fit in socially. Additionally, economic incentives also encourage marriage. Married people may find it easier to get credit to buy an automobile or to obtain a mortgage. Grandparents, parents, and other family members may place further pressure upon young people to get married.

Marriage requires adjustment by each partner. Most people come into a marriage with differences in daily routines, eating habits, personal tastes, and ways of thinking and behaving. Many differences in daily eating and sleeping behavior pass unnoticed until the couple is married, at which point they must adjust to each other. Prior to marriage, partners spend most of their spare time together and are primarily concerned with developing the relationship, rather than exercising individuality or pursuing activities one partner enjoys but not the other. After marriage, adjustment must include development of private time and accommodation of activities that one but not the other enjoys. For young and newly married couples, the additional accommodation of learning household and personal financial tasks must also be made. Individuals who have been on their own or who have been married previously may have a specific approach to handling household and other chores which may require modification if conflict is to be avoided.

Adjustment to marriage involves many facets. Seven major areas of adjustment for newly married couples are sexual relations, financial matters, children, recreation, in-law relationships, religion, and friendships (Wells 1984). Sexual adjustment is made more difficult by high expectations of satisfaction in an area where most people have had the least preparation. Financial matters—how income is obtained and dispersed—have a major influence on the success and happiness of a family. Debates about the amount of time spent at work and the amount of emphasis placed on a job, and whether both partners should work are part of financial adjustment. The other side of financial matters is how to spend money, whether to go into debt to finance consumption, and who makes financial decisions.

Adjustments about children include whether, when, and how many to have, as well as achieving agreement on how they will be reared. One aspect of this is deciding if one partner—typically the wife—should devote full time to child and household care. When a couple decides to have children, further adjustments in many areas are required, given the presence of another person in the household. Recreation would include all of the family's activities other than those involved in running the household and earning a living. Adjustment in this area is often related to financial matters and children. One special area in recreation is whether or not couples spend most of their recreational time, including vacations, together, or whether they spend their time in separate activities.

Friendship adjustment is strongly related to adjustment surrounding recreation, since frequently recreational activities include other people. One traditional pattern employed in many ethnic groups was to separate friendships into separate activities, so that men engaged in recreational activities with other men, while women socialized with women. In modern suburban middle-class United States, increased mobility often means that couples leave old friendships acquired prior to or separately from marriage behind. New friendships are developed either through work or through the neighborhood, where roles and behavior of each spouse are more clearly specified.

In-laws have always complicated marital adjustment, sometimes by espousing views about how the couple should handle finances and children. In-laws can exacerbate existing tensions about differences in living and spending patterns. Usually fights over in-laws reflect deeper problems in the marriage which surface around this issue. Conflicts over religion may occur when partners are of different religions, or hold different values about the relative importance of religion. Couples more easily accommodate differences in beliefs than differences in outward religious practices and behavior. Conflict over religion based on different socialization experiences may worsen relationships with in-laws. Children may require more adjustment to religious differences, since couples may not feel strongly religious themselves, but may feel that their children should grow up in a religious tradition.

To what extent do modern marriages meet the ideal merging of love, intimacy, and sex within a marital relationship? Survey data indicate modern marriages fall short of the ideal merger, especially for women. In a 1976 survey, more wives than husbands wished their spouse talked more about thoughts and feelings. Similarly, more wives felt resentment and irritation with husbands than was conversely true.

Nor is the same marriage experienced similarly by the male and female partner. Despite the traditionally held belief that marriage is more beneficial for women, "his" marriage is often more advantageous to the man than "her" marriage is for the woman, producing greater happiness and better health for the man (Bernard 1972). More recent survey data confirm that husbands are generally happier with marriage than wives. Of husbands, 88 percent versus 80 percent of wives said they would marry the same person again if they had it to do over again. Slightly more husbands than wives said they could imagine spending the rest of their lives with their current spouse. Similarly, 17 percent of wives versus 11 percent of husbands said the likelihood of divorce was high (Rubinstein 1983). Fewer wives reported positive companionship in marriage. Only half as many wives as husbands say there is nothing about their marriage that is not as nice as they would like (Bernard 1972).

The number of suicides for men and women indicate mental illness, stress, and extreme unhappiness. While marriage is somewhat protective for both marriage partners, it protects men more. Only half as many white married men as white single men commit suicide, while three-fourths as many married women as single women do. Similarly, the difference in overall death rates between married and unmarried women is not as great as between married and unmarried men (Bernard 1972).

One concept useful in understanding marriages is the marriage life cycle, as altered by crises (Nye and Berardo 1966). This cycle involves a set of stages that most marriages go through, beginning with the wedding and ending with the death of the spouses or divorce. The stages are defined, based on the presence of children in the home, the ages and school placement of the children, and the occupational or retirement status of the major breadwinner. Each stage represents a basic shift in the structure of the family. The nine stages are newly married couple, child-bearing years, families with young children, children in school, adolescent children, launching stage, empty nest, retirement years, and postmarital years.

In contrast to the romantic view that marriage results in constant or increasing happiness with the passage of time, several studies of marital satisfaction have found a U-shaped curve across the various stages in the marriage life cycle. With the U-shaped curve, satisfaction is high in the early stages, decreases in the middle stages, and rises again in the later stages (Rollins and Feldman 1970; Miller 1975; Duvall 1977). This U-shaped curve is especially true for families with children, since couples without children tend to maintain a relatively steady level of satisfaction throughout the duration of the marriage (Le Masters 1974). The existence of children in the family creates more strain in the family group. The most difficult stages are generally when children are in their preteen and teenage years. During this time, many families have problems, both with the demands of the children for autonomy, and finances. These problems account for the drop in marital satisfaction during this period. As children reach adulthood, leave home, and attain independence, conflict over parenting diminishes and financial difficulties may lessen.

The early years or newly married couple stage are sometimes called the honeymoon stage. This period is one that married couples remember as the happiest. For couples who are compatible, this period of high satisfaction builds a foundation for later more stressful stages. For some young couples, however, this period of high satisfaction does not last long. Most divorces occur during the third and fourth year of marriage. Half of all divorces have occurred by the end of the seventh year (Schoen 1975).

The early years phase traditionally ended with the decision to have children. While the interval between marriage and birth of the first child is quite variable, the majority of couples have a child somewhere between two to five years after marriage. The birth of the first child usually requires major adjustments in household roles and financial matters. Adjustments continue as the baby grows into a preschooler and enters school.

The middle years of marriage generally begin when children become teenagers, and include the stages of having adolescent children, the launching stage, and the empty nest. These are often difficult years for a marriage, when marital satisfaction decreases. The financial demands of having children are great at this stage. In traditional families, career pressures may be great on the male breadwinner, and may be compounded by tensions from wives who were previously homemakers reentering the labor force. Even though this period is relatively low in satisfaction, marriages that survive to this point usually last longer still.

The last two stages of retirement and postmarital years require major role transitions. In traditional families, retirement is a major transition for the husband, and has implications for the total marriage. More time is available for companionship and togetherness. The couple must learn to deal with a frequently lessened financial condition. Health problems may also occur. When one partner dies—more typically the male—widowhood brings major adjustments, including the creation of new friendship patterns. Financial worries may also increase. Children and parents may reverse roles, with children assuming a strong advising role to now aged parents.

There are several critiques of the exposition of the traditional marriage life cycle. The original development of the concept assumed that men were the providers and women the homemakers. It also assumed that families had children and that divorce was infrequent. Divorce is more frequent today. The proportion of childless couples has increased. Also, fewer couples retain a traditional lifestyle of the male as a provider with a nonworking wife. Most women work at various points during their life cycle, and increasing numbers of women work throughout the child-bearing years with only a short leave of absence for birth. The marriages described in the traditional life cycle are now a minority. While the life cycle remains useful, revisions are needed to make it more applicable to modern circumstances.

In addition to the presence of children, a major factor affecting satisfaction with marriage is the quality and frequency of sex. The rate of sex tends to decrease over the course of a marriage. For young couples, the average rate is three times a week. By the middle 30s and early 40s, the average is one and a half to two times a week. For couples 50 and over, the figures drop to once a week or less (Gagnon 1977).

If marital satisfaction becomes too low, divorce may occur. Marriages are most likely to end in divorce when both partners become unhappy with the marriage at the same time. One partner may become unhappy, but if the other partner does not have equivalently low satisfaction, the more satisfied partner may work hard enough to hold the marriage together. If both partners experience a substantial drop in satisfaction at the same time, no one is working to hold the marriage together and divorce may result. Discovered extramarital affairs commonly place great stress upon a marriage because both partners become unhappy simultaneously. The person engaging in the affair was most likely dissatisfied originally, at least with some aspects of the marriage, and turned outside the marriage to find increased satisfaction. The newly discovered knowledge of a partner's affair decreases the satisfaction of the nonparticipating spouse, and lessens willingness or interest in working to keep the marriage together.

INEQUALITY IN COUPLE RELATIONSHIPS

The degree of inequality in couple relationships, whether or not the couple are legally married or living together, influences the satisfaction of each partner, and the stability of the relationship. The money each individual partner brings to a relationship affects equality within the relationship. Money establishes the balance of power on an interpersonal level. The partner with greater income tends to exercise a disproportionate influence in purchasing decisions concerning large items, and in deciding expenditures on recreational and leisure activities (Blumstein and Schwartz 1983). Women on average earn less money than men and more typically enter a male-female relationship with the lower income of the two. Currently, many married couples still accept the validity of the male provider role, reinforcing the power of men in intimate relationships independently of how much each partner earns.

Inequality may persist in the performance of household tasks, despite legal changes promoting equality in the external work environment. In modern U.S. society, housework is generally a private service provided by women for men and children. Household tasks are distributed on the basis of gender. Men and male children most frequently perform household tasks external to the home, such as mowing the lawn, taking out the garbage, and raking leaves. Women and female children engage in housecleaning, laundry, meal preparation, and washing and drying dishes (Andersen 1983; Roper Organization 1980).

In a 1975 study, only 26 percent of husbands sampled spent time cleaning, versus 86 percent of wives. Of the wives, 93 percent contributed on average 8.5 hours per week to cooking, versus only 27 percent of husbands who contributed 2.5 hours per week (Meissner et al. 1975). If women do not work outside the home, perhaps greater hours of work within the home do not represent inequality. For those couples in which both husbands and wives work, unequal contributions to household tasks are likely to signify inequality for women. Wives who work do spend less time on housework than nonemployed wives, but husbands of working wives do not spend a substantially greater proportion of their time on housework than do husbands of nonworking wives (Hartmann 1981; Pleck 1979).

Inequality may also exist in what each partner expects to get from a couple relationship. While women often bear a disproportionate burden of household chores, they also expect more from a couple relationship and therefore are more likely to be disappointed. In a 1976 survey, more wives than husbands wished their spouse talked more about thoughts and feelings. Similarly, more wives felt resentment and irritation with husbands than was conversely true. A recent survey found husbands generally happier with marriage than wives. Despite some changes in the status of women, inequality still persists in couple relationships, leading to the continuation of "his" and "her" marriages.

5 The Impact of Birth Control on Personal Relationships

Reproduction, more than production, has driven the relationship between the sexes throughout history. Women have been defined largely by their reproductive roles as nurturing, less geographically mobile, and risk averters. Before modern birth control, sex was integrally tied to procreation. Society only condoned sex in the context of marriage, especially for women, since the family was the societal institution which assumed the financial and emotional responsibility of rearing children. After reliable and effective birth control was widely available, sex outside the context of marriage became more common, affecting all components of male-female interaction. Once sex is no longer linked to marriage, the possibilities for different sequences in male-female relationships increase dramatically.

This chapter will employ the probability theory of permutations to explore the increased number of available sequences for male-female interaction. Under pre-birth control conditions, the number of choices for interaction were limited and norms governing behavior were explicit and widely recognized. Under post-birth control conditions, changes in behavioral norms have not kept pace with the increase in potential choices for interaction, producing a period of flux and confusion.

THE IMPACT OF BIRTH CONTROL ON COMPONENTS OF MALE-FEMALE RELATIONSHIPS

Love

The impact of modern birth control technology on male-female romantic love has been considerable and multi-faceted. In the pre-birth control era, men and women often became romantically infatuated with potential partners for whom a strong sexual attraction was evolving. Romantic love and sexual attraction were often blurred and difficult to separate. Social norms discouraged sexual experimentation, especially for women, so that the only safe and societally accepted interpretation of sexual arousal was as romantic love.

After birth control techniques were more reliable and more widely disseminated, the strong prohibitions against sexual experimentation began to diminish. The likelihood of choosing love partners on sexual attraction alone also diminished. While male-female love continues to include an element of sexual attraction, and while that element remains an important component of relationships between men and women, the probability of confusing sexual attraction alone with image-reinforcing love has declined. The impact of birth control on love has been particularly great for adolescents. Being less experienced in male-female relationships, adolescents in the past were particularly likely to confuse sexual attraction with love. Adolescents still mistake sexual attraction for love, but the availability of birth control diminishes this probability.

Love and romance remain important concepts, particularly for women. In a recent survey, women report falling in love for the first time earlier than men do. More women than men view romance as important and describe themselves as romantic. Men view romance as more characteristic of women, and rate their partners as being more romantic than themselves (Rubinstein 1983).

Intimacy

Birth control technology has also altered intimacy in male-female relationships. Before birth control, intimate relationships were predominantly between members of the same sex or within the context of marriage. In same-sex intimate relationships, the issue of unwanted pregnancies and procreation was moot. Male-female relationships before marriage were presumed to be preludes to marriage. After marriage, male-female friendships (except with spouses) were discouraged by a variety of norms. Men were encouraged to associate with each other in their leisure activities through men's clubs, team sports, and neighborhood bars. Married women were discouraged from friendships with men except as part of a couple. The informal norms against male-female friendships impeded the advancement of career women. Most powerful positions in organizations were occupied by men. Women were less likely to experience a mentor relationship, a form of intimacy, and were often excluded from informal information dissemination and decision-making sessions.

Traditional sex stereotypes were often maintained, even in platonic relationships with no romantic attraction. Typically, the male was the initiator of male-female friendships. The male may have approached the female for a date, but subsequently, the two may have discovered that while there was no romantic attraction, they liked each other. In a female friend, the male could confide emotions such as fear, anxiety, and insecurity. Revealing these emotions to male friends could create discomfort, since the stereotypical image of masculinity prevented the revelation of weakness, especially to men. In a female friend, the male found a non-threatening confidante who boosted his ego. Yet rarely did the intimacy run both ways. Should the female try to reveal similarly intimate and emotional details, the male may have become uninterested, bored, or sought a change of subject (Chafetz 1974).

The marital status of individuals also affected the development of cross-sex friendships and intimacy. Married women often had little opportunity to interact with men outside of couple relationships or well-defined work or service roles. The absence of any extended interaction precluded the development of intimacy and friendship. Married men had more opportunity for extended interaction but were often reluctant to become friends with women at work, usually single women, since the interaction might be interpreted as sexual.

After increased birth control usage, the danger of intimate relationships between men and women culminating in sexual intercourse and unwanted pregnancy declined, increasing the acceptability of strong friendships between men and women. Platonic opposite sex roommates and behavior in sexually integrated dorms indicate that opposite sex friendships frequently evolve into intimacy without sex. Intimate cross-sex relationships, even after birth control, are still more likely to occur among single people, since many people still experience emotions developed from a more traditional pre-birth control morality. Intimacy between men and women may still result in sex, but the possibility for a wide variety of male-female friendships outside of romantic love and marriage has dramatically expanded. Among men and women who are both married, women are more likely to initiate cross-sex friendships. The continued reluctance of many married men to engage in intimate friendships with women especially holds for men married to traditional women.

Sex

Birth control dissemination has reduced fear of pregnancy, increasing sexual behaviors previously regarded as taboo. Traditional social norms only condoned sexual intercourse among persons legally married to each other. Marriage and sex manuals illustrate norms of legitimate sexual behavior. Nineteenth century sex manuals often portrayed sex as an unfortunate procreative necessity, arguing that modest women seldom desired sexual gratification for themselves (Gordon and Shankweiler 1971). During the last quarter of the nineteenth century, manuals began to portray sex as intrinsically fulfilling and not just for procreation (Gordon and Bernstein 1970).

By the first half of the twentieth century, many marriage manuals portrayed sex within marriage as potentially enjoyable for the wife as well as the husband. However, many nineteenth century ideas about women's sexuality were retained. The manuals were aimed at middle-class women, who were still assumed to have little overt interest in sex. Men were expected to be more experienced and knowledgeable with stronger and more overt sex drives. Women's sexual experiences were assumed to occur only within marriage, making women dependent upon men to awaken their sexual potential (Weinberg and Hammersmith 1983).

Analysis of 49 major sex and marriage manuals between 1950 and 1980 reflects three different models of female sexuality: the different and unequal, humanistic sexuality, and sexual autonomy models. While the different and unequal model rejected the notion of the early twentieth century that sex was a woman's distasteful duty, it still retained the concept of a fundamental difference between male and female sexuality. Female sexuality was viewed as naturally emotional, and male sexuality as more animalistic or physical. It therefore continued the notion of earlier sex manuals that female sexuality remained dormant until awakened by a more experienced male. These manuals also romanticized marriage, assumed sex occurred within a marital context, and encouraged wives to be sexually responsive in order to please their husbands.

The humanistic sexuality model dominated sex and marriage manuals published in the early 1970s, and appears in some manuals published subsequently. Sexuality is taken out of the context of marriage and marital roles, and is portrayed as a basic human quality, although there is still the assumption of a loving relationship between the partners. Sexual inhibitions within traditional roles are discouraged. These manuals reject the view of women as sexually passive and dormant.

Sexual autonomy was the most popular model in manuals published between 1975 and 1980. This model, for the first time, portrays women as independent agents who are in control of their own sexuality, and focuses more on sex as a private individual experience than as part of a couple relationship. Orgasm is viewed as every woman's right. The woman is responsible for achieving her own sexual satisfaction. Especially in the manuals written by women, this model politicizes female sexuality, making linkages between behavior in bed and in the general society. This model is also devoid of the moral and romantic connotations traditionally associated with female sexuality (Weinberg and Hammersmith 1983).

The development of these three models of female sexuality parallels birth control developments. The different and unequal model is still limited in its view of women's sexuality, but is less restrictive than earlier views. The latter two models were possible only with freedom from inhibitions caused by fear of unwanted pregnancy. These models developed only after the dissemination of the pill and the IUD.

Increasingly, with the improvement in birth control technology, behavior has deviated from this traditional norm. Studies of sexual practices on college campuses between 1960 and 1970 confirm that the proportion of women having intercourse at each age has increased (Cannon and Long 1971). Similarly, a nation-wide survey in 1971 of unmarried teenagers from 15 to 19 found 28 percent had experienced sexual intercourse. This figure increased substantially in a second nation-wide survey (Kantner and Zelnick 1972; Zelnick and Kantner 1977).

To clearly compare rates of premarital sexual intercourse before the introduction of the pill and the IUD with afterward, the Kinsey data from the late 1940s and early 1950s are useful. Kinsey, Pomeroy, and Martin (1948) found that 71.5 percent of all males had engaged in intercourse prior to marriage, but among those who attended college, only 38 percent had done so by age 19. Zelnick and Kantner (1980) interviewed men and women aged 17 through 21 who lived in large metropolitan areas. The overall rate of premarital intercourse was 70.3 percent, a figure very similar to the Kinsey findings. One important factor in comparing these figures, however, is that in the Kinsey data, most of the respondents were married. Much of the premarital sexual experience with both men and women is with the person they later married. In the more recent sample, most of the respondents were unmarried. For the men who had never married, the rate of premarital intercourse was 83 percent, leading to the conclusion that rates of premarital intercourse have increased slightly among men.

For women, there has been a much greater increase in premarital intercourse over the last 25 years. Kinsey et al. (1953) found that 50 percent of the women in his sample had engaged in premarital intercourse, although half had done so only with their future husband. By age 20, only 20 percent had engaged in premarital intercourse. In the Zelnick and Kantner data (1980), the rate for never married women was 87 percent versus 46 percent among the never married 15- through 18-year-olds. For never married 19-year-olds, the rate was 69 percent.

The advent of new and highly effective methods of birth control appears to be the major explanation for the increased incidence of premarital sexual experiences among young women (Heer and Grossbard-Shechtman 1981). Among college students, the traditional double standard which permitted premarital and extramarital sex for men but prohibited it for women is disappearing. The new standard permits premarital sex for both men and women. The students' rationale for this value shift was that later first marriages increased the opportunity for premarital sex for both men and women (Marzano 1983).

Underlying the shift in values toward premarital sex is the reality that premarital sex no longer carries the same potential danger for women of undesired pregnancies, due to improved birth control technology and dissemination. Ironically, rates of teenage pregnancies are increasing. Norms against premarital sex for teenagers have declined without offsetting effective use of modern birth control techniques.

Birth control has affected extramarital sexuality as well as premarital sexuality. Based on the Kinsey data, a quarter to a third of married men in the late 1940s had extramarital intercourse at least once in a five-year period. Mean frequency ranged widely from 5 to 50 times per year. For college men, the amount of extramarital intercourse increased gradually with age, peaking in the late 30s and early 40s. For working-class men, extramarital sex was begun earlier and decreased with age. By contrast, in one recent survey, 72 percent of men married two years or more had engaged in extramarital sex. The overwhelming majority did not tell their wives, at least at that time. Most men felt extramarital sex was more acceptable if love was not involved, since love for a third party would compete with affection for their wives (Hite 1981). The norm of monogamy remains, since only 3 percent of the Hite sample had open marriages where sex with persons other than the marriage partner was overtly acknowledged and viewed as acceptable for both partners.

Kinsey data from the late 1940s are also available on rates of extramarital intercourse for women. Women showed a pattern of increasing extramarital activity with age, from about 10 percent in early marriage to about 20 percent later in life. The mean number of times per year for women was somewhat less, ranging from about 5 to 30. A recent survey conducted by *Redbook* magazine found that slightly less than half of working women ages 35 to 39 had experienced extramarital sex, compared to 27 percent of nonworking wives. The Kinsey figure for the equivalent age group was 26 percent. For the age group 20 to 25, 25 percent reported extramarital sex versus 9 percent in the Kinsey data (Gagnon 1977).

The liberalization of sexual behavior applies to nontraditional as well as married couples. In another sample comparing married couples, cohabitating heterosexual couples, gay male couples, and lesbian couples, married couples were the most monogamous. Of husbands, 26 percent and 21 percent of wives reported at least one instance on nonmonogamy. Equivalent figures for male and female cohabitants were 33 and 30 percent, while 82 percent of gay men and 28 percent of lesbians reported sex outside of their couple relationship. In all categories, men reported a greater number of outside sex partners (Blumstein and Schwartz 1983).

Marriage

Modern birth control has been a major factor altering the institution of marriage. Couples are both more willing to wait until older ages before engaging in first marriage and more willing to divorce. Beginning at the turn of the century through the 1950s, the age of first marriage was declining for both men and women. In 1956, the lowest median age was recorded for both sexes. The median age of first marriage has been increasing since then. In 1959, the age of women at first marriage was 20.2 while for men it was 22.5. By 1980, the median age had increased for both women (22.1) and men (24.6) (Bureau of the Census 1981a; U.S. Department of Commerce 1980). The proportion of women from 20 to 24 who were unmarried increased from 28 percent in 1960 to 40 percent in 1970 (Lipman-Blumen 1976). By 1980, 50.2 percent of women in that age group were unmarried, as were 68.6 percent of men (Bureau of the Census 1981a; Richardson 1981).

Marriage rates have declined as birth control has allowed more varied relationships including intimacy and sex outside of marriage. Men are more likely to be married (63.4 percent) than women (59 percent), although a greater proportion of men are more likely to have never married (29.3 percent) than women (22.4 percent) (Bureau of the Census 1981b).

Divorce and remarriage rates began to rise around 1960, reaching unprecedented highs around 1980. While in 1960, the divorce rate was 35 per 1,000 persons in the population, by 1980, the divorce rate was 100 per 1,000 (Bureau of the Census 1981a). Traditionally, the remarriage rate has tended to equal the divorce rate. More recently, divorce rates have continued to rise while remarriage rates have leveled off, especially among women with high educational, occupational, and economic levels (Lipman-Blumen 1976; Skolnick 1978). Men tend to remarry sooner and more often than women (Glick and Norton 1977).

THE IMPACT OF BIRTH CONTROL ON THE SEQUENCING OF MALE-FEMALE RELATIONSHIP COMPONENTS

Traditional Sequences

Two moralities and value systems have emerged historically concerning sex and appropriate sex roles. The old morality preceded effective birth control and existed for much of human history. Many norms from this older value system still have wide appeal. The new morality began with the introduction and dissemination of birth control. It is less restrictive than the old morality, and its norms are still emerging.

Under the old morality, sex implied love and intimacy, relationships were considered to be predominantly permanent, sex was sanctioned only after and within marriage, and the love partner was expeceted to fulfill all sexual needs, expecially for women. Under the new morality, sex may or may not imply love and intimacy, relationships may be temporary as well as permanent, premarital and sometimes extramarital sex are increasingly acceptable, and some sexual needs may be fulfilled outside the partner relationship. (See Table 5-1).

TABLE 5-1.   Changes in Morality After Modern Birth Control

Old morality	New morality
Sex implies love and intimacy	Sex may or may not imply love and intimacy
Predominantly permanent relationships	Both temporary and permanent relationships
Sex only after marriage	Premarital sex acceptable
Sex only within marriage	Sex within and sometimes outside of marriage
Partner fulfills all sexual needs, especially for women	Some sexual needs may be fulfilled outside partner relationship

Implicit in the old morality surrounding pre-birth control male-female relationships was the unstated but ubiquitous assumption that all male-female interaction would ultimately result in sex. Before safe and predictable birth control technology, sex resulted in children who required care, a function traditionally provided through marriage and families. Consequently, in the old morality, marriage necessarily had to precede sex.

The ordering of marriage before sex has always been a stronger norm for women than for men. Part of the traditional double standard was the sanctioning of premarital sex for men but not for women. Men were expected to "sow their wild oats" before settling down into marriage. This looser standard both allowed men to gain sexual experience, which they brought to a marriage, and increased their willingness to settle into the responsibilities of marriage. Men of the middle and upper classes did not engage in premarital sex with women who were regarded as suitable marriage partners, but rather selected prostitutes and other socially unsuitable women for their premarital experimentation. Women, by contrast, were not allowed the same freedom. Society divided women into "madonnas" who were acceptable marriage partners for middle- and upper-class men, and "whores," who were not. A woman who experimented with sex before marriage ran the danger of crossing over from the former category into the latter.

Several sequences of the four components of love, intimacy, sex, and marriage are possible, but under the old morality, sequences in which marriage did not precede sex were not socially sanctioned, especially in the middle classes. Limiting the sequencing of the four components significantly restricts the number of possible permutations of the four relationship components. Before birth control, the number of sequences for ordering the four components of male-female relationships was small, since marriage had to precede sex. In essence, marriage and sex were treated as one item, since the probability of marriage without sex immediately following was low. The reason for marriage under tratitional norms was to have intercourse, control the sexuality of women, produce heirs, and link families economically.

The function of sex has changed across the reproductive eras, as birth control and reproductive technologies have been introduced, disseminated, and used. In the first reproductive era with limited birth control, the primary function of sex was reproduction. The old morality was based upon this function of sex as reproduction. Sex was limited to a marriage relationship since marriage was the social institution designed to handle the care and rearing of children. Sex before marriage in an era of limited birth control made probable the birth of children outside of marriage, making uncertain their future care. Limiting sex to the institution of marriage also allowed clear determination of paternity, and therefore economic responsibility for children.

In the era of widespread birth control, sex began to assume a function of communication as well as reproduction, serving as an important means for the expression of emotional warmth and commitment. While the absence of heirs in the era of limited birth control served as grounds for divorce in many societies, lack of adequate sexual communication is more typically a reason for divorce in the era of widespread birth control. In the upcoming era of artificial procreation, reproduction will continue to recede as a function of sex and communication will assume even greater importance. (See Table 5-2.)

The introduction of birth control increased the number of probable sequences of components in male-female relationships. The number of permutations is the number of ways a set of items can be arranged when the sequence or order matters. The formula for the number of permutations of N things is N factorial (N!) where $N! = N \times (N - 1) \times (N - 2). \ldots . \times 2 \times 1$.

TABLE 5-2. The Changing Function of Sex Across Reproduction Eras

Reproduction era	Function of sex
Limited birth control	Predominantly reproduction
Widespread birth control	Reproduction and communication
Artificial procreation	Predominantly communication

Without any restrictions, the number of four-way permutations for ordering four components would be $4! = 4 \times 3 \times 2 \times 1 = 24$. These represent all possible sequences of four components.

Additional permutations of four components include three-way, two-way, and one-way permutations. Three-way permutations are all possible sequences of all possible three-component subsets of the original four components. For four components, this equals 24. The general formula for permutations of N items taken R at a time $= N!/(N\text{-}R)!$ (See Tables 5.1 and 5.2). Similarly, for four items, there are 12 two-way and 4 one-way permutations. The total number of permutations for four components is the sum of four-way, three-way, two-way, and one-way permutations, or 64 possible sequences.

Before birth control, the number of sequences available was mathematically equivalent to ordering three things not four, since marriage and sex were treated as one item. For three components, the number of permutations for ordering three items is the sum of all three-way, two-way, and one-way permutations. The number of three-way permutations is $3! = 3 \times 2 \times 1 = 6$. The number of two-way permutations is $3!/(3-2)! = 6$. The number of one-way permutations is $3!/(3-1)! = 3$. The total number of three-way, two-way, and one-way permutations is 15, quite a reduced number from the 64 that would have been available without the restriction that marriage precede sex.

There are six three-way sequences of relationship components under the old morality, assuming marriage preceded sex and were together treated as one component. (See Table 5-3.) Sequence 3—intimacy, love, marriage-sex—might be a scenario equivalent to marrying the girl or boy next door whom one had known for a long time before falling in love. Sequence 1—love, intimacy, marriage-sex—is the romantic love ideal of meeting a romantic stranger, falling in love, and becoming intimate before marriage and sex. Sequence 2—love, marriage-sex, intimacy—is an infatuation that progresses to marriage quickly and possibly prematurely. Sequence 4—intimacy, marriage-sex, love—was more likely to occur when either partner married for family prestige and status or financial security. Women

TABLE 5-3. Possible Permutations Under
Pre-Birth Control Morality

Societies without arranged marriages

(1) L I M-S
(2) L M-S I
(3) I L M-S
(4) I M-S L

Societies with arranged marriages

(5) M-S L I
(6) M-S I L

N! = 3! = 3 × 2 × 1 = 6.
L, Love; I, Intimacy; M, Marriage; S, Sex.
Marriage and sex have been linked together as one component under pre-birth control morality.

marrying older men may have fit this sequence of marrying a decent husband with little regard for romance—which they hoped would eventually develop. Sequences 5 and 6 occurred in many traditional societies with arranged marriages where frequently the partners had never met or had met only briefly prior to marriage. In these cultures, ideal romantic love, particularly within marriage, was not emphasized. In Sequence 5, romantic love emerged soon after marriage, whereas in Sequence 6, romantic love evolved slowly across time.

Of the six 2-way permutations in the traditional pre-birth control morality where marriage preceded sex, four occurred in societies without arranged marriages and two in societies with arranged marriages. In Sequence 12, romantic love never evolves within the arranged marriage, as contrasted with Sequence 6 where romantic love evolves slowly across time. In Sequence 11, love emerges in an arranged marriage but not intimacy. This scenario was most likely to occur in a sex-segregated society where interactions between the sexes were ritualized, role bound, and limited.

Societies without arranged marriages have four possible two-way permutations under the pre-birth control morality. Sequences 7 and 8 include the linked component, marriage-sex, plus one other component. In Sequence 7, love precedes marriage-sex. This sequence occurs when individuals fall in love, get married, but intimacy does not subsequently evolve. This permutation was particularly likely to occur among couples who married young and later evolved different interests which did not overlap or encourage mutual friends and experiences. In Sequence 8, intimacy precedes marriage-sex. This sequence was most likely to occur between individuals who married for children or convenience or money, but who never experienced love.

The remaining two-way permutations preclude marriage-sex. In Sequence 9, intimacy precedes love but never culminates in marriage-sex. This situation may evolve among coworkers or friends who grow to love each other but never act on the feelings by pursuing marriage and sex. Other situations where Sequence 9 may occur would include circumstances where one partner in an intimate and loving relationship is judged to be socially unsuitable for marriage, a judgment that may be encouraged by either parents or peers. Another possibility for Sequence 9 is when one or both partners are already married to other people and are not willing to get divorced. Sequence 10 where love precedes intimacy may arise in similar situations as Sequence 9. The difference is that the romantic attraction occurs before intimacy.

With three components, there are three one-way permutations. Intimacy alone may occur in male-female friendships. Such friendships with nonrelatives were not encouraged in pre-birth control morality. Love alone reflected an unrequited romantic passion. This type of relationship was also not encouraged. it was most socially approved in an aberrant distant form where individuals may have developed an attraction for movie stars and other celebrities with little potential for reciprocation. The last one-way permutation, marriage-sex alone, portrays an emotionally barren marriage. While the exact frequency of this permutation is unknown, literature and psychological evidence indicate that such marriages existed, despite public images of happy communicative unions.

Social class variants on socially sanctioned sequences of male-female relationship components have always existed. Illegitimacy rates are historical proof of sex outside of marriage. The existence of a double standard implied that norms for sex outside of marriage were not as strong for men as women. The norms against sex outside of marriage were also not as strongly observed among lower classes as among middle and upper classes. If pregnancy resulted, however, marriage was expected to follow, thus upholding the appearance of the norm to a higher degree than actually occurred.

Among upper classes in some pre-birth control societies, romantic love and intimacy often did not follow marriage and sex, as in the ideal. Sequences of the four components in a conjugal relationship were sometimes abbreviated before all four components materialized. Marriage, as a major economic unit for the care of children and the production of heirs, however, was regarded as permanent. To accommodate the discrepancy between the ideal and the reality, norms allowed extramarital affairs for men, and eventually for women as well. Those affairs could imply intimacy, romantic love, and sex, or could be just sexual liaisons. Probably the class least likely to deviate from the ideal of finding love, intimacy, and sex strictly within marriage was the middle class.

Post-Birth Control Sequences

After the introduction and dessemination of modern birth control, marriage is no longer necessarily a prerequisite for and precursor of sex. Breaking the linkage between sex and marriage increases the number of theoretical sequences of the four components of male-female relationships to 64: 24 four-way, 24 three-way, 12 two-way, and 4 one-way permutations. (See Table 5-4.)

TABLE 5-4.   Possible Permutations Including Marriage Under Post-Birth Control Morality

Likely sequences

(1) I L M S	(6) L I S M
(2) I L S M	(7) L I M S
(3) I M S L	(8) L M S I
(4) I S L M	(9) L S M I
(5) I S M L	(10) L S I M

(11) S L I M
(12) S L M I
(13) S I L M
(14) S I M L
(15) S M I L
(16) S M L I

Unlikely sequences

(17) I M L S
(18) L M I S

(19) M L I S
(20) M L S I
(21) M I L S
(22) M I S L
(23) M S I L
(24) M S L I

$N! = 4! = 4 \times 3 \times 2 \times 1 = 24$.

L, Love; I, Intimacy; M, Marriage; S, Sex.

Of these 24 four-way permutations, the six sequences where marriage precedes all other components are highly unlikely in modern society. Given the decline in industrial society of arranged marriages, the likelihood marriage would be the initial phase of a relationship is small. Two other four-way sequences which impose a third component between marriage and sex are possible but uncommon (Sequence 17—intimacy, marriage, love, sex; and Sequence 18—love, marriage, intimacy, sex) since marriage is a license for sex.

Removing the unlikely sequences leaves 16 of the 24 possible four-way permutations as likely. These are Sequences 1–16 in Table 5–4. In Sequences 1–5, intimacy is the initial component in the relationship, while in Sequences 6–10, love and romantic attraction form the beginning of the relationship. Sex precedes marriage in 6 of these 10 sequences. These six sequences placing sex before marriage were not likely nor socially sanctioned under pre-birth control morality. In Sequences 11–16, the relationship begins with sex. Relationshps where the initial component is sex were particularly taboo under traditional mores. Of the 16 likely four-way sequences under post-birth control morality, 12 were not permitted under pre-birth control morality, since they order sex before marriage.

Birth control also expands the possibility that marriage will not be a part of a male-female relationship. Prior to birth control, the fear that any type of male-female interaction could result in sex and unwanted offspring often restricted relationships to sequences including marriage. This restriction, while particularly true for sequences containing sex, even carried over to cross-sex intimacy and love.

Under post-birth control morality, there are 24 three-way permutations. Ten of these, Sequences 39–48, are unlikely. Sequences 39–44 are unlikely since marriage is the first component, an improbable occurrence in a modern society. Where these sequences would occur would be within groups with arranged marriages. While such traditional groups do still exist in the modern world, for example, in traditional restrictive Arab countries, they are not typical of western society.

Sequences 44–48 include marriage but omit sex. It is particularly unlikely that a marriage would begin without sex, especially if the partners are young. In addition to money, dissatisfaction with sex is one of the two most common causes of marital difficulties and divorce. In some marriages of long duration, sex may have been present initially, but across time may atrophy into nonexistence, at least with the marriage partner. Other forces, such as custom, money, convention, and children may hold the sexless marriage together. In these marriages, however, while sex may be absent at a particular point in time, it was present at certain stages, so that a relationship including marriage in which sex was never present is highly unlikely.

Fourteen three-way permutations of the four components under post-birth control morality are likely. Sequences 25–30 all include sex but exclude marriage—an order unlikely and not socially sanctioned under pre-birth control morality. Many male-female relationships now resemble one of these sequences. This includes the increasing numbers of cohabiting couples who live together, maintain a household, but do not marry. In 1981, the Census Bureau estimated there were 1.8 million of these couples, 4 percent of all couples. The number of such couples has increased threefold since 1970. In other countries, the cohabitation rate is even higher. In Sweden, 12 percent of all couples live together without marriage. Generally, cohabiting couples live in a household without children. When children are present, they are most likely the result of a previous marriage or relationship (Blumstein and Schwartz 1983).

The remaining eight likely three-way permutations include marriage which is preceded by love, sex, intimacy, or some two-way combination of these. Sequence 31 to Sequence 34 are loveless marriages where romantic passion was never strong and where the marriage partner does not reinforce a desired self-image. However, in these marriages, intimacy emerges at some point, often before marriage. Sequence 31, intimacy-marriage-sex, could easily have occurred under the pre-birth control morality as well as the post-birth control morality. Sex-marriage-intimacy, Sequence 34, while not sanctioned under the old morality, may have occurred in some shotgun marriages stimulated by pregnancy. The likelihood of Sequences 32 and 33, mixtures of intimacy and sex ending in marriage, has increased with birth control.

Sequences 35 through 38 omit intimacy. These sequences generally emerge more quickly than sequences including intimacy, since intimacy requires the slow development of trust and detailed knowledge of the other person. Of the three-way permutations, relationships that include marriage but exclude intimacy are more likely to end in divorce than marriages that include intimacy but exclude love. Across time with the problems of daily living, the romantic aspect of love may decline. Another component of love is reinforcing a positive self-image of the partner. Unless this reinforcement is based on detailed knowledge of the other person's character, then across time, such reinforcement may also become less valued.

Only in Sequence 35 does sex follow marriage, a socially sanctioned sequence under the old morality. Sequence 38 (sex-marriage-love), like Sequence 34, may have also been a shotgun marriage, where marriage was stimulated by pregnancy, under the old morality. Sequences 36 and 37 where some mixture of love and sex precedes marriage are more likely under the new morality.

Two-way permutations of four components total twelve in number, seven likely and five unlikely. Of the five unlikely sequences, three order marriages first, and unlikely occurrence except in societies with arranged marriages, and two include marriage but no sex, a situation even more improbable.

Of the seven likely permutations, Sequences 49 and 50 include just intimacy and love. While these two sequences could imply romantic relationships, which are never actualized sexually, owing to social norms, these sequences also could include deeply based but not romantic or sexual male-female friendships. Intimate male-female friendships are more likely after birth control, since the fears of both sexual involvement and the accusation of sexual involvement have diminished. Sequences 51–54 include sex and either intimacy or love. These sequences were made possible by the newer post-birth control morality and represent sexual relationships which do not end in marriage. Sequence 55, the emotionally barren marriage is still possible. The growth in divorces and remarriage may be indicators of less tolerance for emotionally barren marriages under the post-birth control morality.

There are four one-way permutations, representing each of the four relationship components experienced alone. Sex alone often becomes the one-night stand found in singles bars, conventions, and other locations that facilitate casual encounters. The frequency of one-night stands and other casual sexual relationships has increased in the post-birth control era. While men have always enjoyed casual sexual encounters through the institution of prostitution, the increase in participation in sex alone has been especially dramatic for the majority of women. For women, under the old morality, casual sex often precluded other types of relationships with other components of male-female relationships, especially love and marriage, a limitation not applicable to men. In the new morality, casual sex may not as readily preclude other types of relationships as the double standard for sexual behavior erodes.

Intimacy alone represents another one-way permutation. Intimacy alone, as with intimacy combined with nonromantic love, typifies male-female friendships which were discouraged in pre-birth control morality. Romantic love that never advances to include sex or intimacy still may occur, especially during youth or in aberrant form, as part of unreciprocated hero or celebrity infatuation. Marriage alone is unlikely.

SOCIETAL IMPACT OF THE NEW MORALITY

Under the new morality made possible by improved birth control, tremendous confusion and uncertainty in how men and women relate to each other has occurred over the past two decades. There are two sources of confusion, both partially attributable to the development and dissemination of effective birth control techniques:

TABLE 5-5. Possible Permutations Excluding Marriage Under Post-Birth Control Morality

Likely sequences

(1) S
(2) I

(3) S I
(4) S L
(5) I L
(6) I S
(7) L S
(8) L I

(9) S I L
(10) S L I
(11) S I L
(12) I S L
(13) L I S
(14) L S I

Unlikely sequences

(15) L

$P = N!/(N\text{-}R)! = 3!/(3\text{-}1)! = (3 \times 2!)/2! = 3.$
$P = N!/(N\text{-}R)! = 3!/(3\text{-}2)! = (3 \times 2 \times 1!)/1! = 6.$
$N! = 3! = 3 \times 2 \times 1 = 6.$
Total $= 3 + 6 + 6 = 15.$
L, Love; I, Intimacy; M, Marriage; S, Sex.

(1) Each of the four components of male-female relationships—love, intimacy, sex, and marriage—has been changing in the post-birth control era. Many taboos on sex before and outside of marriage have been lifted, causing changes in the contexts in which love, intimacy, and marriage occur.

(2) The number of sequences of these four components has increased dramatically. Before birth control, the only socially acceptable permutations sequenced marriage before sex, especially for women. This occurred because sex could not be reliably separated from procreation. Sequencing marriage before sex assured that children would be born in the context of a family, the basic unit for raising children. After birth control, the linkage sequencing marriage before sex was severed. New possibilities for both combining and ordering the components of male-female relationships became possible. The number of sequences possible has increased

from 15 under pre-birth control morality to 64 under post-birth control morality, a dramatic 327 percent increase.

Birth control and its new yet emerging morality have freed men and women from the constraints of marriage before exploring sexuality. Marriage and child rearing may be delayed while careers or other objectives are pursued. Women now can control both the number and the timing of offspring, a type of control not enjoyed previously. Prior to reliable birth control, one way for society to limit unwanted pregnancies and illegitimate births was to restrict the type and nature of male-female interactions. Part of this restriction involved the acceptance by both men and women of the notion that sex and overt sexuality were unappealing and unattractive for women. In the absence of reliable birth control, sexual activity did become distasteful for many women since it led to greater numbers of children, limiting the freedom of women to engage in any activities other than mothering and household duties. Now, both the need for repression of sexuality and its actual suppression have diminished. Subsequent to the widespread use of birth control, women can more readily enjoy sex, since the fear of an unwanted pregnancy has been removed.

These dramatic changes in a relatively short historical period have increased the uncertainty in how men and women relate. Prescribed guidelines before were restrictive, but clarified and simplified choices. Now expectations are being altered. The old morality which was adapted to a pre-birth control culture is crumbling, but the new post-birth control morality is still emerging. The choices available to individuals and couples have increased dramatically, while new guidelines about appropriate behavior have not matched the growth in choices.

In the old morality, premarital and extramarital sex was clearly undesirable, especially for women, since the consequences of intercourse might be pregnancy outside of marriage. Under the new morality, the reduction in the fear of pregnancy has led to changing norms toward premarital sex, extramarital sex, and births outside of marriage. New guidelines for appropriate behavior are less uniform and less explicit, creating confusion. More couples are living together and establishing joint households without marriage. More adults are having extramarital sex since the consequences of doing so are less severe after birth control than before. Teenagers face greater pressures for premarital sex and uncertainty about how to respond appropriately. Under the old morality, cues in male-female relationships were clearer and the number of potential sequences was restricted. Under the new morality, each individual has a greater number of choices in developing male-female relationships. The increased number of choices enhances both freedom and uncertainty simultaneously.

6 Home Technologies and Sex Role Changes

The two basic activities in which the human species must successfully engage to survive are production and reproduction. This book argues that innovations in reproductive technologies, rather than productive technologies, are the source of fundamental shifts in sex roles. Reproduction technologies have been the major determinant of sex roles throughout history. Throughout most of history, the reproductive era of limited birth control has existed. In this era, the roles of women differed fundamentally from the roles of men, due to differences in childbearing and the care and feeding of young children. Women were less geographically mobile, more risk averse, and emphasized nurturing over production. Men were more geographically mobile, risk seeking, and emphasized production over nurturing.

Throughout the era of limited birth control, changes in production technologies have modified but did not fundamentally alter these basic stereotypical sex roles. Only with the advent and dissemination of birth control did the sex-based stereotyping begin to crumble. In the reproductive era of widespread birth control, changes in productive technologies have further accelerated changes in sex roles initiated by reproductive innovations. Productive technologies have magnified sex role shifts, but were insufficient alone to precipitate these shifts.

Two types of productive technologies, those for household tasks and those for work outside the home, have affected the role of women in society and have given impetus to the women's liberation movement. Historians and political theorists have paid much greater attention to changes in productive technologies outside the home, particularly those originating with the Industrial Revolution, than to changes in technologies inside the home. Historians were not accustomed to thinking of housework, typically done by women, as valuable contributions to the economy. The full impact of technological change on women is still not completely explored (Bernard 1981; Cowan 1974; 1976b; 1977). This chapter examines the impact of household technologies on the role of women, while the next chapter explores the impact of workplace technologies.

TIME- VERSUS LABOR-SAVING HOUSEHOLD TECHNOLOGIES

Improvements in home technologies may be labor saving, conserving human muscle power, or time saving, or both. Among the most important improvements in home technologies were leaps from oil lamps to electric lamps, coal stoves to gas or electric stoves, kitchen heating to central heating, and outdoor plumbing to indoor plumbing. Other examples include the shift from homemade to store bought clothing and from homemade to store bought baked goods and bread. These major shifts were both time and labor saving, as well as raising the overall standard of living. Other more minor improvements were primarily time saving: paring and coring devices introduced in 1838 and egg beaters in 1857. Some devices such as chopping machines and churns were labor saving if not necessarily time saving (Andrews and Andrews 1974).

Major home technological changes were largely dependent on electrification and the introduction of indoor plumbing. In 1900 most U.S. homes had neither electricity nor running water. By the 1930s, around 60 percent of U.S. homes had electricity, making possible mechanical refrigerators, gas and electric ranges, and washing machines. By the beginning of World War II, 70 percent of homes had indoor plumbing (Cowan 1976a and 1976b; Vanek 1978b).

Neither labor-saving nor time-saving improvements in household technologies alone caused changes in the roles of women. While initially, many newer home technologies appeared to be time saving, their long run impact is less clear. Standards of home care and cleanliness rose with new technologies, often resulting in as much time being spent in housework in order to meet the newer higher standards. Change of clothing, for example, moved from occurring weekly to daily. Before irons, families slept on unpressed sheets; after irons, only pressed sheets were appropriate. In one study, shifting standards resulted in urban women spending more time on housework in order to meet elevated norms than did rural women who had fewer amenities (Folsom 1943).

Also confounding evaluations of the impact of time- and labor-saving home technologies were parallel reductions in the number of domestic workers. Domestic workers were more likely to be employed before the introduction of time- and labor-saving technologies than afterward. Part of the advantage of new home technologies was offset by the decrease in the domestic labor supply. Between 1890 and 1920, the ratio between general population and the number of servants decreased by 50 percent. Illustrating this trend, the number of persons throughout the country engaged in domestic service decreased from 1,851,000 in 1910 to 1,411,000 in 1920. During the same time period, the number of households rose from 20.3 million to 24.4 million. The number of paid domestic servants decreased from 98.9 per 1,000 population in 1900 to only 58 in 1920 (Filene 1974; Cowan 1976a).

Between 1920 and 1980, the amount of time spent on specific tasks, such as food preparation, sewing, mending, and cleaning, decreased, but total time spent on housework actually increased. The introduction of cheaper clothing and linens produced a greater amount of clothing and linen per household, raising the total time per household spent doing laundry. The invention of the automobile saved transportation time across a given distance. However, coupled with suburbanization, the automobile increased time spent transporting family members, especially children, and shopping (Vanek 1978a).

FOOD PRODUCTION

Food preparation in the home is greatly affected by methods for preserving food. If safe and effective methods had been available for storing food, especially before refrigeration, time and energy devoted to food production could occur in a more cyclical manner. Improvements in food preservation also allowed more food production and preparation to occur outside of the home, reducing the amount of time and energy required within the home.

One of the first major changes in food storage was the development of preservation of foods by enclosing them in glass vessels, and hermetically sealing the vessels. This technique supplemented and partially replaced the older techniques of cold storage, pickling in brine, and use of spices. Tin plate cannisters were quickly substituted for glass jars in the 1810s. Fish was being canned in New York in 1818. In 1819, Underwood began canning meat in Boston (Oliver 1956; Williams 1978). During the 1850s, a machine press was invented to cut can tops and bottoms. Soon a machine die was developed to produce a can bottom in one operation. By the early 1900s, the presence of automatic continuous assembly lines for cans had reduced their cost to a small amount, facilitating the spread of canning as a food preparation technique.

These innovations in the production of cans were followed by the application of automated techniques to the development of the filling, causing commercially sold canned goods to shift from being luxury items to being widely disseminated products. Although canned foods were available in

U.S. markets as early as the mid-nineteenth century, they did not become a standard part of the middle-class diet until the 1920s, based on women's magazines and cookbooks (Cowan 1976b).

In addition to canning, advances were made in the production of dairy products and breads which reduced food preparation time in the household. Some early factory produced butter was available in the United States in the 1860s and 1870s. First disseminated in cities, the use of factory produced butter spread to rural areas so that by 1900, many farmers were buying butter instead of making their own. The first factory produced cheese in the United States was available in 1850. Cheese making was taken over by factories by the 1880s (Oliver 1956).

Innovations in milling techniques and preservatives to extend the shelf life of flour facilitated the dissemination of "store bought" bread. Across time, bread from small local bakeries became available in urban areas eventually to be supplemented by mass-produced factorymade bread. By the early 1920s, some convenience foods became available in the United States. These included cold breakfast cereals, pancake mixes, bouillon cubes, and packaged desserts.

Refrigeration has also had a profound impact on household food preparation. Refrigeration was first used on specially designed box cars on trains to facilitate both the distribution of food and ice for home iceboxes. Before electricity was used to produce ice, household iceboxes were filled with bought ice. This natural ice was harvested from cold areas in the midwest and was transported to towns throughout the country by means of refrigeration cars. There was never enough natural ice to equal the demand for it. If the winter was warm, as in 1889, severe ice shortages occurred in northern and southern areas by July.

Refrigerators for homes became available in the late 1910s, but most U.S. homes at that time did not have the requisite electricity. Only later when electrification spread did the use of home refrigeration spread also. High costs of home refrigeration further impeded its spread. In 1919, the price of a refrigerator measured in 1963 dollars was $1,660 (Vanek 1978 a and b). By 1930, only 13 percent of the nation's families owned a refrigerator.

Starting in the nineteenth century, gas cookers became available. The cookers were usually of heavy black cast iron with burners at the sides and an oven ventilated at the top. Separate gas-heated hot plates with a griller-toaster beneath it were also manufactured and sold to the public. Gas cookers replaced cooking by coal or wood. Early electric stoves were first demonstrated in the Columbian Exhibition of 1893 in Chicago. The wide dissemination of electric stoves, however, did not occur rapidly, partially due to the slow dissemination of electricity. After World War I, advertisements for wood and coal stoves disappeared from major women's magazines (Cowan 1976b). In Muncie, Indiana, in 1924, gas cooking was available in two out of three homes. By 1935, only 5 percent of homes valued over $2,000 were still using coal or wood stoves (Lynd and Lynd 1929; 1937). Electrical ranges were disseminated more slowly. In 1930, only 5 percent of homes owned an electrical range (Vanek 1978 a and b).

Gas or electric stoves, compared to wood and coal stoves, did eliminate a number of household chores, such as loading the fuel or removing the ashes. In addition, gas and electric stoves were easier to light, maintain, and to regulate, making cooking less burdensome. The newer stoves made keeping the kitchen clean much easier, especially compared to the large amount of dust produced from coal stoves. Gas and electric stoves also did not heat the kitchen to insufferable temperatures during the summer, as did their predecessors.

Many innovations in food production, preservation, and preparation served to reduce the time and effort expended by homemakers to feed their families. Canning and convenience foods reduced food preparation time. Refrigeration and food preservatives reduced the frequency of food shopping trips and made a wider variety of foods available. Gas and electric stoves made cooking food easier and more pleasant. Despite these advances, gender-based roles still predominantly determined food preparation in the home. Women remained the primary cooks.

Additionally, standards about appropriate levels of nutrition and quality of food rose, requiring additional time and effort and partially offsetting labor- and time-saving advances. In the 1920s, middle-class mothers learned to compulsively weigh infants and children on the advice of women's magazines and some pediatricians. Adequate weight gain was viewed as a measure of adequate nutrition and good food preparation. In more recent times, gourmet cooking has become a new standard for middle-class families, despite the necessity for elaborate shopping and preparation requiring great expenditures of time. Women, more than men, continue to be judged by their abilities to cook.

CLOTHING PRODUCTION

The making of fabrics for clothes and for other goods has always been a necessity. In earlier eras, this activity was often performed in the home, and was labor and time consuming. In early United States, most of the material used in clothing was homespun, unless it was imported fabric from England. The homespun clothing was made by women and girls in the family with hand labor. Even in these prerevolutionary times, commercial weavers were available to weave cloth from homespun threads, although family manufacture of cloth was more common. In most of the colonies, except for the poorest of families, shoe production was performed by craftsmen cobblers. Their products were known for durability and long wear rather than style (Oliver 1956).

Starting in the 1820s and later in frontier areas, spinning began to move outside the home. While women still made their own clothes and the clothes of their family members, they typically bought already produced cloth. There were always tailors and dressmakers available for wealthy families, and eventually, even the clothes of average citizens were completely made outside the home. As early as 1831, in New York, a small tailoring establishment advertised their excess custom order suits for sale as ready-to-wear clothing.

With the invention of the sewing machine in 1846, the time required to produce finished clothing from prepared cloth was reduced greatly, whether done inside or outside the home. The wide use of the sewing machine was made possible by Singer's 1851 invention of the foot-operated treadle method of operation, leaving both hands free to guide the cloth. After the invention of the sewing machine, the manufacture of ready-made clothing increased dramatically. In Boston, New York, Philadelphia, and Cincinnati, the manufacture of ready-made clothing doubled in three years. The value of ready-made clothing increased from $40 million in 1850 to over $70 million a decade later. While clothing production became increasingly commercial, women in the home were still responsible for the care and maintenance of clothes (Oliver 1956).

One major technological advance in the manufacture of clothes which also affected their care and maintenance was the development of manmade fibers. Before the development of these manmade fibers, the only four fabrics available for clothing were wool, cotton, linen and silk. Each required substantial care. Cotton required the least care, since it could be washed, although cotton required ironing. Everyday clothes were typically made of cotton. Wool could not be washed and had to be professionally cleaned. Linen could be washed but wrinkled even more than cotton and was expensive. Silk was a luxury item, afforded only by the rich. Nor could silk, which required special care, be washed.

Early chemically produced fabrics included rayon and nylon. Rayon-type fabrics were first marketed as celanese in the early 1920s. The name rayon was applied in 1924. Nylon products were first introduced in the 1930s, but were not perfected until World War II. These fabrics were silk like in texture, but were cheaper, more durable, and required less maintenance than silk. Before these products, most women could not afford silk stockings and used cotton instead. Nylon soon replaced cotton as the basic fabric for stockings and undergarments. Orlon, the first manmade substitute for wool, was developed much later. Orlon was first produced in the laboratory in 1941, but commercial production did not occur until ten years later (Oliver 1956).

These newer manmade fibers required less care than the older natural fibers. However, rising standards of cleanliness for clothes partially offset the reduction in labor manmade fibers made possible. With rising affluence, the average citizen also began to have more clothes. Standards shifted from wearing the same clothes for an extended period of time to wearing different clothes on different successive days. Infrequent washings and cleanings were replaced by frequent washings, sometimes after every use. Traditionally, men's shirts were made with removable collars and cuffs so that the same shirt could be worn all week without cleaning. This style was replaced by shirts without removable collars and cuffs which required more frequent laundering. Undergarments, previously washed weekly, were changed daily.

In earlier eras, the most time-consuming aspect of clothing was its production. As production gradually moved outside the home with the passage of the homespun age and the development of new technologies, the predominant home activities involving clothing increasingly were concerned with cleaning and maintenance. In more recent and more affluent times, shopping for clothing has also become a time-consuming activity. In most households, care, maintenance, and often shopping for clothing remains the role of the woman.

LIGHTING, HEATING, AND COOLING

The first advancement beyond candles for lighting in the home was whale oil. While whale oil, compared to the candle, was a superior illuminant, the supply was greatly limited. In the early 1850s in England, paraffin oil was produced from coal. Around the same time in the United States, kerosene was produced from coal. Kerosene rapidly replaced candles and whale oil as a source of lighting. By the 1890s, gas was available to middle-class houses and was used for home illumination. However, many major advances in home lighting awaited the dissemination and use of electricity.

Inventors from the 1840s forward were intrigued with the idea of developing a usable electric light for home usage. The first commercially successful electric light was developed by Thomas Edison in 1880. Prior to Edison, the few early users of electricity purchased small electrical plants which were individually installed in the home. Edison revolutionized the concept of home electrification by demonstrating how centralized electrical plants could be used to supply many users. Centralized electrical plants laid the groundwork for other electrical appliances as well as the widespread dissemination of electrified illumination. Electric lights were not only eventually superior in illumination, but also were safer and required less maintenance, since oil lamps needed periodic cleaning. The eventual availability of other electrical appliances, including irons, washing machines, and clothes dryers held the promise of freeing women from drudgery and altering the tasks that homemakers performed.

Much domestic effort in earlier eras focused upon maintaining coal or wood stoves for heating. Two advances eventually changed home heating systems, reducing required maintenance—a shift from wood and coal as fuels to oil, gas, and later electricity, and a change from space heaters to central home-heating systems. While coal and wood furnaces required continual stoking, oil and gas furnaces did not. Even in 1950, coal was still the dominant fuel used in heating, but its use was dropping, from 55 percent in 1940 to 35 percent in 1950. The use of gas heating tripled between 1940 and 1950. By 1950, oil and electricity were the other major sources of fuel.

Centralized systems were a substantial advance from space heaters and stoves which often roasted home residents on the front side while freezing them on the back side. In Minnesota in 1928, furnaces and central heating were common only among families with cash income over $6,000. In urban areas, the dissemination of central heating had begun earlier. In Muncie, Indiana, in 1924, most of the homes of the business class had basement or central heating. A survey in 1935 indicated that only 22 percent of dwellings valued over $2,000 were heated by a kitchen stove (Vanek 1978 a and b; Lynd and Lynd; 1937). By1950, half of the nation's homes were equipped with central heating plants, a 50 percent increase from 1940. With the exception of the poorest homes, most houses are now heated centrally.

The shift to central heating required the development of both more efficient furnaces and a means to distribute the heat throughout a building. Warm air and hot water systems were tried experimentally, but steam heating systems were the first centralized systems to be used in many buildings. The development of the steel radiator in 1874 allowed steam heating systems to be installed in major public buildings, industrial settings, and homes of the wealthy. The process of manufacturing cast iron radiators was developed in the 1890s. This shift to less expensive cast iron made possible the spread of central heating into middle-class homes.

Early experiments in air conditioning began in textile plants in the 1830s, but were not particularly successful. In the 1890s, systems of forcing air over ice racks were tried in places such as Carnegie Hall and the New York Stock Exchange, but this technique also proved unsatisfactory. Carrier developed the modern idea of air conditioning—combining humidification of the air with heating or cooling features. This technique was patented in 1904. In the 1920s, air conditioning began to be used in commercial movie theaters.

Room air conditioners which cooled a limited space were the first to be used in the home. As with heating, these space coolers were later replaced by centralized systems. While initially a luxury, air conditioning units and systems were first disseminated among the homes of the wealthy, eventually filtering down to the homes of the middle class. Many poor still do not have access to air conditioning.

Both heating and air conditioning advances increased the overall comfort of the home and made houses more habitable for homemakers. While heating advances clearly reduced the amount of work at home to be done as well as increasing comfort, air conditioning advances primarily affected comfort. Neither affected male-female roles in any dramatic fashion, although increased comfort may have facilitated physical interaction and intercourse.

CLEANING AND SANITATION

Many technological advances which facilitated domestic cleaning and sanitation depended upon electricity. The vacuum cleaner, patented in 1901, was the second device to use an electric motor, following the development of the electric rotary fan in 1889 by Westinghouse. The earliest vacuum cleaners were large pieces of machinery mounted on a horse-drawn cart. Suction tubes were passed through the windows of the house to clean rooms. In 1909 the first handpowered vacuum tubes were developed, but required two people to operate them, one to work the wheel or handle and a second to pass the nozzle over the carpet, under the assumption that homes wealthy enough to afford vacuum cleaners could also afford servants to operate them. In 1908, the Hoover Company assumed the patent for an upright model operated by one person. By 1930, 44 percent of urban families owned a vacuum cleaner.

The vacuum cleaner replaced the carpet beater and represented a substantial improvement in the initial physical labor that had to be expended with the earlier technology. The carpet beater required hauling the carpet outside and beating it with a special implement. The vacuum cleaner removed the necessity of taking the carpet outside, lessening the amount of physical effort, as well as leaving the carpets cleaner. However, the vacuum cleaner did not reduce the amount of time devoted to housework, since standards in cleanliness rose.

In addition to housecleaning, ironing represented a household drudgery. Early sad-irons in the United States were heavy iron boxes with wooden handles, into which a red hot slug of iron heated in the kitchen fire was dropped. Later irons evolved to their now familiar shape and were heated on the top of stoves or in front of open fires. Late in the nineteenth century, irons were heated on the hot plate of a gas cooker. Electrical irons were first produced in 1894, and were gradually improved, first with enameling in the 1930s and then with thermostats. After World War II, steam irons represented an additional advance.

Ironing was traditionally one of the most arduous household chores, especialy before the development of electric irons. This was particularly true in warm climates in the summer, since the stove had to be kept hot most of the day, making the kitchen almost unbearable. Advertisements for electric irons first began to appear in ladies' magazines after World War I. Since they were relatively inexpensive, the innovation spread quickly. A survey of 100 Ford employees in 1929 found that 98 had electric irons in their home (Cowan 1976a).

Sanitation and disposal of human wastes is another area where techonogical advances greatly affected the quality of life. The water closet began to come into general use in the early nineteenth century, but existing cesspools were not able to cope with the increased flow of water-borne sewage. The nineteenth century was an era of severe river pollution from human wastes. Cast iron pipes made possible the separation of water supply from sewage, a particularly essential protection when cities became larger making traditional water systems of aqueducts, small pipes, or individual wells inadequate. By the 1820s, wealthier homes were often equipped with baths and running water. One famous illustration was the home of Longfellow which contained both water closets and a kitchen sink.

Not until the 1880s did many U.S. communities establish water works and sewer systems, making modern home plumbing and sanitation possible. The installation of plumbing in homes was slow, however, due to both costs and debates about the desirability of this technological innovation. For example, one popular magazine in 1904 contained an article entitled, "Is Bathing Good for Us?" (Oliver 1956).

The availability of both indoor plumbing and running hot water considerably lessened the frequent and arduous house chore, typically performed by women and children, of transporting and heating water. In middle-class homes during the late 1800s, hot water had to be heated in kettles over a kitchen range and carried to the bathroom. A predecessor to modern plumbing was a mini-pipe system linking the kitchen range to receptacles in the bathroom. By the early 1900s, large wealthy households had installed this forerunner system to modern plumbing.

The 1920s in the United States was an era of bathroom mania. At least one and sometimes multiple bathrooms were placed in older homes, and newly constructed homes contained bathrooms. Before World War I, bathrooms were custom-made for each house, and most bathroom fixtures were handmade from porcelain, making bathrooms very expensive. Industrialization and mass production after World War I reduced the cost of bathrooms. Fittings became standardized, and cast iron enamelware reduced the cost of bathroom fixtures. The first recessed double-shell cast-iron enamel bathtub was available for purchase in the United States in the early 1920s. By 1930, the U.S. bathroom attained its standard form of a recessed tub, tiled floors and walls, a single unit toilet, enameled sink, and medicine chest. This form has persisted to the modern era in middle-class homes. Along with the dissemination of bathrooms came the growth of modernized systems for heating water.

Running water became widely available to many families in the early decades of the twentieth century, although the modernization of plumbing facilities progressed more slowly than general electrification. In Zanesville, Ohio in 1926, 61 percent of the homes had indoor plumbing and centrally heated water (Cowan 1976a). In Muncie, Indiana, 83 percent of the homes had hot and cold running water by 1935 (Lynd and Lynd 1937). Not until 1940 did 70 percent of the nation's homes have indoor running water. Sharp differences emerged between urban and rural residences. By 1940, only 17 percent of farm homes had indoor running water, versus 93 percent of urban homes.

Washing clothes, a major household chore typically performed by women, is heavily dependent on the mechanical effort required to churn clothes in soapy water. In the nineteenth century, most clothes were washed in a wooden tub with a hand-operated dolly. Water was heated on a fire and poured into the tub. In the 1920s, gas-fired wash boilers became available. These were light copper cauldrons on legs with a gas burner under it to heat the water. Clothes still had to be swirled by hand, although heated water was available.

Also in the early 1920s, a slight improvement occurred. This was wooden tub washers with electric motors bolted to the underside to oscillate the dolly. These had frequent problems of electric shocks and short circuits, caused by water trickling onto the motor. In this apparatus, while the motor performed the oscillation, the water was heated externally and poured into the tub. By the late 1920s, a true electric washing machine was designed, formed of metal with a waterproof motor. In early versions, however, water still had to be heated externally and poured into the tub. A survey of 100 Ford workers in 1929 found that 49 had electrical washing machines in their homes.

Soap production also constituted a major household chore in earlier times. Laundry soap powders were not available until the 1920s. Prior to that time, bars of laundry soap had to be boiled and scraped.

The washing machine initially did not dramatically reduce the time spent on household laundry. These machines did not go through cycles automatically and did not spin dry. A homemaker had to watch to stop and start the machine at appropriate times, add soap, and on some models attach drain pipes. Clothes had to be run through a wringer manually. Spin dry features on washing machine did not become available until the 1920s. By the 1950s, fully automatic washers did reduce the amount of time required to clean a single load of clothes. However, rising standards of cleanliness and esthetics raised the number of loads washed per week. In most households, women still did the wash. Also with the dissemination of automatic washers, much laundry in middle-class and affluent families that was previously sent out to commercial cleaners was now washed in the home.

IMPACT OF HOME TECHNOLOGIES ON THE ROLE OF WOMEN

Many of the time- and labor-saving advantages of home improvements have been offset by rising standards. During the 1920s, middle- and upper-class homemakers were especially urged to raise standards of cleanliness and nutrition. This was an era of concern about household germs, vitamins, and roughage. Also, greater emphasis was placed on women as purchasers of an increased array of consumer goods, and on the role of the homemaker in child care.

In earlier eras, women were made to feel guilty for such "egregious" acts as abandoning their children and families, or being promiscuous with their affections. Beginning in the 1920s, guilt was extended to such transgressions as sending children to school in scuffed shoes or dirty or unironed clothes, having an odor behind the bathroom sink, or not fixing a hot breakfast for the family. Home technology innovations did not significantly alter gender-based roles or the total amount of time spent by women in housework.

For middle-class women, the time spent in housework frequently increased during the 1920s, and the nature of the task of house management changed. Before World War I, middle- and upper-class households generally included a paid or unpaid servant. While paid workers were often hired from members of lower social classes, unpaid workers included maiden aunts or unmarried daughters. By the 1930s, the number of paid household workers declined greatly. In Indiana, the ratio of households to servants increased from 13.5 to 1 in 1890, to 30.5 to 1 in 1920. In the United States, the number of paid domestic servants per thousand population decreased from 99 in 1900 to 58 in 1920. In the Muncie, Indiana study, housewives from business families reported they employed only half as many womanhours of domestic servants as had their mothers (Cowan 1976a).

Home technologies have in many ways leveled class differences. Technological home inventions have reduced the differential in time spent in housework by upper- and lower-class women. In 1930, highly educated urban women spent less time than rural homemakers in the routine household chores of food preparation, care of the home, and care of clothing and linens. They spent more time on tasks such as family care, purchasing, and general household management. Today, household patterns that were found among high status women in the past are more common among women in every class stratum. The remaining minor difference is that upper-class women still spend more time on consumption and purchasing than do lower-class women.

Home technologies have made life more pleasant and less arduous for all family members, and especially for women. These technologies—improvements in heating, cleaning, clothing production and maintenance, cooking and food preparation, and sanitation—have changed the type of work performed in the household, but have not altered the basic social role of women as more nurturing, less geographically mobile, and more risk averse than men. Women still disproportionately perform household chores. Rising standards have significantly undercut time-saving gains from household technologies.

7 *Work Technologies and Sex Role Changes*

As with home technology improvements, advances in work place technologies have altered perceptions of women and their role in the labor force. Some technological innovations, particularly those in the industrial sector, have more sharply differentiated the productive roles of men and women. Other technological innovations, including many dealing with offices and communications, have accelerated the growth of women in the labor force. The alterations caused by work place technologies in both the perceptions and actual roles of women have not changed the basis for gender-based stereotypes. Despite work place technological advances, women remained in roles that were less geographically mobile, more nurturing, and more risk averse. Men dominated the roles that called for greater geographic mobility, emphasis on production rather than consumption and nurturing, and greater risk taking. Only changes in reproductive technologies make possible a fundamental alteration of these basic gender-based roles.

AGRICULTURAL TECHNOLOGIES

In the past, a prevalent assumption was that the role of women steadily improved with improvements in production technologies. More recent studies question that assumption of steady improvement, and indicate that not only have the changes in sex roles emanating from production technologies been at best minimally progressive, but sometimes have actually worsened the status of women, especially within the family. Tilly and Scott (1978) have studied the productive activity of married women across historical eras. They have found a U-shaped pattern, with the productive activity of married women being relatively high in preindustrial household economies, lower in industrial economies, and becoming higher again with the development of a modern service sector. In eighteenth century France and England, data indicate that wives had an important role in the household economy, and, from this status, were important in deciding on the allocation of family resources. Even during the 1800s on U.S. farms, farm wives often produced both the basic necessities for subsistence, and developed separate cash crops. Some women retained personal control over the revenues from their cash crop, increasing their autonomy (Vanek 1980).

With industrialization came a growth in the idealized image of woman as a woman of leisure. The model of the ideal upper-class woman depicted women of leisure who spent time on refined arts and culture rather than productive activities directly related to economic survival. Middle-class families began to aspire to the same model. The ideal wife and mother did not participate in the labor force, or make major family decisions. Women who were aggressive or decisive, especially in economic affairs, were guilty of "henpecking" their husbands. In middle-class homes, wives were expected to devote substantial time and effort to enhancing the well-being of their husbands and children, rather than in engaging in productive activity and earning money outside of the home. This image of the ideal woman contrasts sharply with the earlier image of farm wives, where men and women both were expected to work long hours in productive tasks of economic consequence. In 1920, one-third of the nation's families still lived on farms where productive roles, while different, were equal in their recognized economic contribution.

Many of the agricultural technological innovations have reduced the recognized role of women in that sector. With improvements in technology, agricultural production has shifted from predominantly small family-based farms to large agri-businesses. As the family farm diminished in inportance, replaced by larger corporate farms, the role of women declined. First, the development of the Farm-All Tractor in the 1920s, along with the combine and improved tractors with rubber tires in the 1930s, greatly increased the mechanization of the typical farm. Mechanization of farm labor greatly improved efficiency. In 1955, the average U.S. farmer was 110 percent more productive than in 1935. By 1955, there were 36 percent fewer farmers, each working fewer hours, yet they produced 43 percent more than farmers 20 years earlier (Oliver 1956).

As farm efficiency rose at an unprecedented rate, farming increasingly became mechanized. Men assumed responsibility for buying, maintaining, and running expensive farm machinery. The farm activities from which women had traditionally earned money and gained independence also became increasingly specialized and mechanized. Throughout the twentieth century, the proportion of the labor force in farming has declined, as the industrial sector grew.

INDUSTRIAL TECHNOLOGIES

The Industrial Revolution created centralized work places with new technologies distinct from their predecessor cottage industries. With the Industrial Revolution, production shifted from the home to centralized, standardized, and more mechanized factories. With a few exceptions, such as selected textile plants, men were the major labor supply for factories and industrial occupations. Firms that did hire females often used younger unmarried women. Women served as a reserve labor force whose prevailing low wages drove down male wages. In mid-nineteenth century United States, women's wages were about half of men's (Woody 1929).

As soon as possible, men organized to prevent factories from hiring cheaper labor which would drive down industrial wages. Women were effectively precluded from high-paying industrial jobs, both through labor unions and through protective legislation. Industrial work technologies did not dramatically expand employment opportunities for women. Women employed in the industrial labor force have continued to be concentrated in low-wage industries such as textiles, garment-making, jewelry, and toys (Cowan 1979).

The number of areas of production affected by the Industrial Revolution are both numerous and diverse. They may be divided into those where women constituted a substantial portion of the labor force, and those where women were rarely employed. The textile industry is an example of the former, while the steel industry is an example of the latter.

The Textile Industry

The New England cotton industry was the first in the United States to incorporate the factory system of production and the use of labor-saving machinery. Some early factory production relied on machinery, such as the Arkwright Water-Twist Frame in 1769. The introduction of the power loom in 1813 and 1814 was a major impetus to high volume factory production. This technology was applied first in Waltham, Massachusetts in a plant that integrated all processes involved in cotton manufacture. In 1824, Lowell, Massachusetts was incorporated as a center for cotton textile production in the United States. By 1827 there were 25 factories in the town. The Lowell mills developed a system of using women for employees. These female employees were usually young unmarried women from middle-class farm families who lived in special boarding houses run by the companies. Further improvements in technology occurred in Rhode Island in 1828 with the transition from water to steam power. Those mills located close to railroads which could easily transport coal were among the first to switch to the new steam technology (Oliver 1956).

Early production of wool remained in the home longer than did cotton. Both early fulling machines and carding machines were set up as community shops rather than factories, with the wool returned to the household for spinning. In the 1820s, a new carding machine, the Goulding Condenser, was introduced and stimulated the development of wool factories. Fringing machines in the 1830s accelerated this process, as did the development of Crompton's loom, which allowed fancy weaving in pattern. By the 1850 census, 24 of the 31 U.S. states had factories engaged in some part of wool manufacturing. While there were more male employees (22,000) than female (16,000), as with cotton weaving, the textile industry was a major source of employment for women (Oliver 1956).

By the mid-1870s, cloth production was the leading industry in the United States. Before the Civil War, the industry was located almost exclusively in New England. In the 1870s, some wool manufacture was established in midwestern cities, such as Cincinnati, Milwaukee, and Chicago. In the 1880s, the textile industry also expanded to the South. Three major inventions after the Civil War contributed to more rapid bulk production of cloth. More effective carding devices made of steel were developed. An improved ring spindle was developed; by the mid-1890s it had doubled the speed of that process. The automatic loom in the 1890s led to the replacement of most hand operations, and greatly increased the number of looms that an individual employee could attend. The period between 1880 to 1900 saw major advances in cutting and sewing material for garments, including mechanical cutters, buttonhole machines, mechanical pressers, and power-driven sewing machines (Pyke 1967).

Changes in the wool and cloth industry in the early part of the twentieth century were less related to technological development than to changing volume and patterns of world trade. Two new areas of textile manufacture—artificial fibers and the manufacture of dye—were the result of improved technology. By the 1920s and 1930s, rayon production was booming. Artificial fibers spurred the development of textile plants in the south, partially at the expense of the northern industry. After World War II, the United States became the major world producer of synthetic fibers. In recent decades, the U.S. textile industry has increasingly moved its factories abroad to developing countries where labor is cheaper (Williams 1978).

Early textile employment provided comparatively good wages for women, compared to other employment opportunities. This is no longer true. The lack of unionization has helped to diminish the ability of the industry to compete in the wages it offers. In 1820, when textile mills were new, they were viewed as attractive employment opportunities for middle-class women. By 1920, a comparative drop in wages, coupled with a status change from a new and innovative industry to an older more mature one, caused textile employment to be much less attractive to middle-class women who moved into clerical and office jobs.

The Steel Industry

Steel was a major industry in which few women were employed. Its predecessor, the iron industry, was also initially developed in New England. One of the earliest products made with iron were engines to transport water for fire fighting. While wrought iron was produced in New England, a different process was developed in Pennsylvania using a blast furnace. By 1771 there were more than 50 iron furnaces and forges operating in Pennsylvania. The furnace operation used considerable human muscle power, requiring the services of 10 to 12 large and muscular men, inhibiting the employment of women.

The industry was stimulated by a new process which used iron recovered from the banks of discarded cinders and led to the development of stamping mills. By the time of the American Revolution, the colonies were the third largest producer of iron in the world, ranking only behind Russia and Sweden. The United States produced one-seventh of the world's output. Throughout this time period, most iron production remained in blacksmiths' shops, and local forges and foundries.

By 1805, the iron industry began an important westward expansion into Pittsburgh. The first major technological improvements in U.S. manufacture, including a rolling mill for sheet metal in 1818 and the rolling and puddling machine in 1819, were developed in western Pennsylvania. Casting developed as a separate industry with special foundries. Subsequent improvements resulted from improvements in fuels used in iron furnaces, from charcoal to anthracite, to bituminous coal and coke. In 1846 in Kentucky, the pneumatic or air-blown process—heating iron by blasts of air—was discovered. With this process, improved iron, sometimes called "mild steel," was produced.

The Bessemer converter was an improvement upon previous processes, allowing the speedier conversion of iron into steel. The first commercial use of the process occurred in the 1860s in Pennsylvania. Andrew Carnegie was instrumental in improving both the organization of steel production and the methods used. Carnegie brought together the mineral resources of the Lake Superior region, coal fields, lake steamers, and the railroads to Pittsburgh. He also funded the construction of plants incorporating technological advances. Carnegie also employed expert chemists and metallurgists who improved the quality of the steel produced, and made it possible to produce large quantities more cheaply.

One of the greatest technological improvements was in the organization of the plant itself. These organizational improvements included expanded use of machinery, the creation of work stations, use of belts and pulleys, and many of the structures now identified with the modern factory. Subsequent improvements included the electrification of the plants, and the adoption of the open-hearth process. Electric lights in the 1890s made work faster and plants safer. Detailed hand labor, such as operation of hooks and tongs, was replaced by electric-driven feed tables. The open-hearth furnace allowed the production of a tougher steel more easily tailor-made to particular uses. By 1910, 66 percent of U.S. steel production was from open hearths. Oxygen steel making was introduced in the late 1940s and eventually replaced the open-hearth process.

Iron and steel production never employed many women. In the early years of the industry, workers often needed physical strength and brawn, characteristics attributed to men but not women. Men traditionally worked stripped to the waist because of the intense heat and wore goggles to protect their eyes from molten metal and flying sparks. These steel workers perceived themselves as the aristocrats of the labor world who combined strength, mechanical abilities, and a capacity to work under sometimes dangerous conditions. Steel workers were among the best paid of all industrial workers, in contrast with the more heavily female textile workers who were among the worst paid.

Although electrification displaced and mechanized many of the more arduous tasks, some, such as the puddling of steel were not mechanized until after World War I. Despite much modernization in the 1900s, the employment of women in the steel industry continued to be inhibited by several factors, including the reduction of the number of workers required from mechanization and the strength and heavy physical labor still required. By World War II, when men in the civilian labor force where in short supply relative to the war generated demand, women moved into many traditionally male industries, including some steel production. After the war, however, traditional employment patterns prevailed, so that few women, even today, work in the industry.

Industrialization generally has improved the number of goods and the material lives of U.S. citizens. It did not, however, significantly alter the dominant sex role stereotyping that men were more production oriented, geographically mobile, and willing to take risks, while women were more nurturing, less geographically mobile, and risk averse. While in agricultural society, women were often more heavily involved in food production which occurred in or close to the home, the centralization of production into factories through the technological innovations of industrialism further segregated women from production and accentuated traditional sex role stereotypes. Even when women did participate in industrial production, as in the textile industry, little occurred to change the image of women as the weaker and more nurturing sex.

TRANSPORTATION TECHNOLOGIES

Improvements in transportation facilitated the process of industrialization but did not directly alter the role of women in society. Early transportation consisted of stage coaches, horses both on land and with canals, and steamboats on rivers. It was railroads, however, that marked the greatest advance in pre-Civil War transportation technology.

Railroads

Beyond the advantages of speed and power, railroads were dependable and, unlike canals, operated year round. Early wood-burning engines were replaced by coal-burning engines. In addition to the development of the locomotive, railroads required many engineering advances in the design of bridges and track construction. Railroads reached their peak in the 30-year period after the Civil War, with steel replacing iron tracks, more powerful locomotives, and safer and more comfortable coaches.

A major improvement in railroad transportation, especially for long distances, was the establishment of a uniform track gauge (the width between the rails). In 1860, there were 11 different gauges on northern railroads. Travel from Maine to New Orleans required 13 train changes, due to gauge differences. The building of the Union Pacific line solidified the recognition of the need for national gauge standards.

Trains improved the lives of women but did not affect their fundamental role in society. Trains made long distance travel for both women and men easier, safer, and more feasible, marginally decreasing the isolation of women. Trains, especially when Pullman sleepers and dining cars were added, were considered a more appropriate means of travel for middle-class women than were stage coaches, horseback, and other earlier methods. Trains also facilitated the distribution of commercially produced home products, appliances, and clothing that altered the tasks women performed in the home, but women were not employed in the industry or in the manufacture of locomotives, rails, and railroad cars.

The Bicycle and Automobile

An often overlooked transportation innovation is the now humble bicycle. The era between the early 1880s until the advent of the automobile was the age of the bicycle. Everyone who could afford a bicycle purchased one. Bicycles sometimes allowed women to escape from restricted home life, but did not change the primary role women played in the home. While women continued to be viewed as the less geographically mobile, more nurturing, and more risk averse of the sexes, the bicycle did stimulate minor dress reforms, especially the development of bloomers—a type of pants—to replace cumbersome long skirts.

The automobile revolutionized twentieth century transportation, leaving a fundamental impact on the U.S. landscape, industry, and social patterns. In the 1890s, U.S. mechanics and bicycle builders experimented with horseless buggies powered by steam, electricity, and gasoline. Gradually, the internal combustion engine powered by gasoline won as the most practical of the possible types of engines.

Henry Ford began experimentation with building a simple, cheap car in the early 1900s. By 1908, he had developed the famous Model T, which remained available in an almost unchanged form for about 20 years. It was sufficiently simple that most customers could operate it and make repairs. Ford emphasized the standardization of parts, and developed the conveyor assembly line of production.

A major technological improvement in cars was the development of the electric self-starter, first introduced in 1911. The prior method of starting cars with a hand crank could be an arduous ordeal. Women began to drive cars in much larger numbers after the introduction of the self-starter.

Improved roads were a necessity for cars to become useful and reliable, especially outside of urban areas. Interest mounted in the development of good roads, resulting in federal aid incorporated in a national defense act to build good highways. Cars also became more comfortable in the 1920s, with improved low pressure balloon tires, closed passenger compartments, and the installation of heaters.

The numbers of commercial automobiles produced and sold declined during the Depression in the 1930s, and even more sharply, due to rationing, in World War II. At the end of World War II, a huge pent-up demand for new cars was unleashed. By the 1950s, the availability of many new improved cars and improved roads with greater federal money facilitated a movement by U.S. middle-class families to the growing suburbs.

The movement of families to the suburbs in the 1950s, along with the increased birth rate, reinforced the traditional roles of women as more nurturing, less geographically mobile, and less willing to take risks than men. Women were often isolated in suburban homes in bedroom communities all day while their husbands commuted to jobs in distant cities. The differences in male and female roles were even more sharply defined in suburbia than they had been in urban environments. Women continued to assume the responsibility for child care, managing the home, and often taking care of exhausted husbands in the evening.

The automobile increased the mobility of women and the opportunity to shop and visit at greater distances from the home, but it also added the new task of chauffering children. While in urban areas many children could walk or take public transportation to school, public libraries, movies, and after-school lessons, in suburban areas the wife frequently had to transport the children in the family car. Rather than freeing women from domestic tasks and allowing them greater freedom to pursue careers, automobiles and the suburbanization that automobiles facilitated tied women's schedules more closely to activities of their children.

Airplanes

The last major technological innovation in transportation was the development of the airplane. The first successful flight of an airplane was in 1903 by the Wright brothers at Kitty Hawk, North Carolina. By 1910, the Wright brothers had established an aerial express between Dayton and Columbus, Ohio, but overall, there was little commercial use of airlines until after World War I. World War I demonstrated the possibilities of aviation, and provided the country with thousands of trained pilots. Commercial use of airlines began to increase, first with the development of air mail service in the 1920s, and with growth of airlines of passenger service in the 1930s. After World War II, jet engines were perfected and greatly increased the speed and reliability of commercial aircraft, making the airplane the dominant method of travel for long distances.

Airplanes made the entire society more geographically mobile, especially initially the middle and upper class. It ultimately changed the concept of distance, increasing the willingness of people to move for educational and job opportunities. The plane did not, however, significantly alter the role of women visa-à-vis that of men.

OFFICE AND COMMUNICATIONS TECHNOLOGIES

Beginning in the late 1800s, new office-related technologies changed the nature of white-collar work and expanded the number of office jobs. Among these were the typewriter and the telephone. Generally, office and communication technologies offered new employment opportunities for women and facilitated their movement into the labor force. However, women remained in stereotypical "female" jobs which were routine and nonmanagerial. Their employment was often viewed as temporary.

The Typewriter

The typewriter gradually transformed office work (Oliver 1956). Although early typewriters were available in the 1860s and 1870s, sales efforts for typewriters were not initially directed toward commercial use. Typewriters were viewed as too impersonal for business use, but appropriate for writers, clergymen, and court reporters. Office letters at first remained the job of predominantly male clerks and private male secretaries who were usually training for higher management positions in business.

By 1878, typewriters with both upper- and lower-case letters and standardized keyboards were available. With the standardization of the keyboard and better quality type, typewriters became acceptable for business. To use the machines efficiently required special training. Typing and the training it required were increasingly viewed as female activities. The job of private secretary switched from being a male job that was an apprenticeship for management to being a lower-level female job. Female private secretaries not only typed but also performed domestic service tasks in the office, such as preparing coffee and keeping the office orderly. The linkage between being a private secretary and becoming a manager was severed as women began to dominate the secretarial ranks. As typing was increasingly viewed as mundane, typists in a general typing pool were regarded as among the lowest ranking of white-collar workers. Secretarial jobs were appropriate for middle-class women whose families were in depressed circumstances, or for young unmarried girls.

The Telephone

The telephone, developed in 1876, changed both the office and commercial work. It accelerated the speed of business and commercial life, making the geographic concentration of similar businesses less necessary. It was preceded by the development of the telegraph in 1837. The telegraph did increase the speed of communication. However, in many ways, it was only an extension of the mails, where messages were written and delivered to the appropriate office, with written replies. By contrast, the telephone extended the sense of hearing across greater distances by allowing private simultaneous communication between two people in different geographic locations (Pyke 1967).

Alexander Graham Bell began work on the early telephone in 1874. By 1875 a rough version was produced that was publicly demonstrated in 1876. A year later, a successful conversation over a distance of two miles between Boston and Cambridge occurred. In that same year, five Boston banks installed telephones. Within three years, over 50,000 phones were in service and telephone conversations were possible across distances of 40 to 50 miles. By 1900, over half of the people of the United States were within talking distance of each other.

Entering businesses at about the same time as the typewriter, the telephone required a new type of employee to be present to answer the phone and take messages. Combined with the typewriter, the effect of these technologies was to expand the number of clerical jobs. In many small offices, the woman hired to type also answered the phones. In larger offices, separate receptionists were hired to greet visitors and direct them to appropriate personnel, both in person and over the phone. The job of receptionist did not alter the sex-linked roles of women in business or society, but rather represented an extension of the traditional role of the wife as hostess into the world of commerce. As with secretarial jobs, receptionists were not on a management career track. The job of receptionist was viewed as appropriate for young unmarried women or widows, and later for married women who needed to supplement the family income.

The Computer

A mid-twentieth century invention which has radically altered both the office and the industrial work place is the computer. Computers were first developed during World War II. The first commercial electronic computer—the UNIVAC I— was installed at the U.S. Bureau of Census in 1951. Computer technology rapidly expanded, passing from first generation vacuum tube technology to solid state circuitry and miniaturization in a period of three decades.

The first generation of computers was based on electronic valves, or vacuum tubes, as the switching elements. These required the first generation machines to be very large, use large quantities of electric power, and produce heat that had to be removed by forced air cooling systems. From about 1958 to 1964, second generation machines were developed using the switching transistor. Machines were somewhat smaller, more powerful, and more reliable.

Third generation machines were introduced in 1964. Incorporated on a single chip of silicon were all of the necessary components—transistors, and capacitors—for logical operations. These integrated circuits made better and cheaper manufacturing processes for computers possible, further lowering the costs and increasing the power of computers. Fourth generation machines developed in 1970 used large scale integration (LSI) where a single chip included virtually all the electronics of a complete processor. The 1980s have been the decade of the personal computer revolution which provided further impetus for the computerization of society. The fifth generation of ever more powerful super computers capable of handling huge data banks for weather forecasting and resource management, among other tasks, looms on the horizon.

Computers have altered all facets of modern living. Introduced in many industrial processes, computers have made routine programmed decisions without human error, leaving humans to make quality checks and judgment calls. They have altered the industrial work place through robotics, further alleviating the need for human muscle power to engage in hot, heavy, and repetitive tasks.

In the office, computers have changed word processing, data analysis, information storage, and electronic communications dramatically. Some studies indicate that the introduction of computer technology into the office initially accelerated male-female stratification. The new upper level technical jobs were heavily dominated by males. The level of skill in traditional female clerical jobs as well as, in some instances, the number of those jobs, decreased (Feldberg and Glenn 1983; Helfgott 1966; Rothberg 1969). However, the long-term impact of computerization is still unfolding.

LABOR FORCE PARTICIPATION

The labor force participation of women has changed across the last century, particularly in the decades of the 1960s and 1970s. However, many aspects of women as workers in the market economy have remained stable. Women workers in general are paid less than male workers, a fact that often remains true even when men and women are in similar types of jobs. Most of the time, sex stereotyping has resulted in gender segregation in types of jobs held by men and women. Technological improvements did not significantly alter the types of jobs women held in the labor force, relative to the types of jobs men held. Contributing to the differences in pay and job status is that women, until recently, have been considered both by themselves and others to be transient participants in the labor force.

The Participation of Women Until the 1920s

The foundations of inequality in the labor force were laid early. In the communal economy of the early Jamestown settlement, unmarried or poor women worked as laundresses in return for a portion from the communal store. Most men received grants of land, and men excluded from land grants were bakers and cooks. When unmarried people came into the Salem and Plymouth colonies, only the men were given allotments of land. Also in the colonial period, when girl children were put out for an apprenticeship, there was no requirement to teach them a trade (Cowan 1979).

The proportion of women working outside the home in the United States has been increasing since the Civil War, but until World War II, the rate of increase in female labor participation was relatively slow. Domestic service was the major employment sector for U.S. women 100 years ago. In 1870, half of all women wage earners in the United States were domestic workers. In 1890, the Census reported 1.2 million women working as housekeepers, chambermaids, cooks, and servants. While some of these women worked in offices or commercial establishments, the majority worked as live-in servants in private homes. Certain types of women were more likely to become domestic workers. Half of the women in domestic service were the children of immigrants. Another quarter were black. Of the few who were married, most were black. Some were widows, but most were unmarried girls who worked until they married (Smuts 1959).

Labor force participation rates of women experienced a moderate increase in the first two decades of the twentieth century, an era of the introduction of barrier methods of birth control. In 1890, 16 percent of the total labor force in the United States was female. By 1910, the proportion had increased to 21 percent. The female labor force as a percent of the total female population in that time period increased from 18 to 24 percent. In both periods, a very small proportion of the female labor force was married. In 1890, only 5 percent of married women were working, a figure, although still small, almost doubled to 11 percent by 1910 (Filene 1974).

Outside of domestic service, in 1890, women were employed in factories in unskilled and semiskilled jobs. Women outnumbered men in clothing factories, and were about half of the labor force in textile and tobacco factories. Women were also an important minority in shoe and food processing industries. Some few women were even employed in foundries and tin-plate mills, but in all industrial settings, women were clearly hired for different jobs than were men. In general, their jobs required less skill, lower pay, and few chances for advancement. The industrial female labor force continued to be composed predominantly of young unmarried girls, particularly from immigrant families (Smuts 1959).

One other large group of women employed outside the home were women school teachers. Women began to replace men in elementary classrooms as early as the 1830s. By 1890, women teachers outnumbered men by two to one. Like domestic and factory workers, most teachers were young and single. Their social class origins were typically different from those of female factory workers. Most teachers were of native stock and from middle-class families. Teaching was the predominant professional occupation available to middle-class women. Female teachers were unmarried because many communities had laws requiring the replacement of women teachers who married. In many communities, these laws remained in effect until the teacher shortage during World War II. Since there was an abundant supply of young unmarried women seeking employment relative to the number of teaching jobs available, women teachers were typically paid a third to a half as much as men teachers (Smuts 1959).

Nursing, while a professional job for modern women, was not a professional occupation in 1890. Then, as now, it was predominantly a woman's field. There were few trained nurses available in 1890. Of the 40,000 nurses and midwives listed in the 1890 census, most had no training. The few with training had at most one to two years of supervised hospital experience before entering private practice. Until more formal education based on the Florence Nightingale model of hospital experience was required for nursing, the field was considered inappropriate for middle-class native born women. One indication of the low status of the field was that during the Spanish-American War, even though the professional nursing association volunteered the services of its members, the War Department instead selected the Daughters of the American Revolution, an untrained volunteer group, to provide nursing services (Smuts 1959).

At the turn of the century, office work and sales clerking in commercial stores opened as employment opportunities for women. By 1890, women were already likely to be the typists and stenographers in office jobs. Some women were also bookkeepers and clerks. Female office workers were most likely of native parentage, and like most women workers, were young and single. Selling in stores, working as stock clerks, package wrappers, and mail order clerks became open to women by 1890. The sales jobs women held were different from those held by men. They were more likely to be found in the bargain basement, in departments with low-priced items, or in departments that sold women's clothing and accessories. Department store sales jobs often represented a step toward upward mobility for the daughters of immigrants, since these jobs had higher status than semiskilled factory work or domestic work.

The Participation of Women from the 1920s

In the 1920s, women entered the labor force at an accelerated rate, with the female labor force growing 26 percent during this decade. By the 1920s, almost one out of every four persons in the labor force was female. The pattern of women workers being young and unmarried continued, as did discrimination against female employment, especially at higher levels. In 1919, within the federal government, women were excluded from 60 percent of all civil service examinations, and 64 percent of all scientific and professional positions. Exemplary of this discrimination is that 14 female lawyers who passed the civil service exam for law clerks instead were appointed to general clerical positions at half the salary. When the Women's Bureau was established as a permanent agency, the salaries of its professional experts were limited to $1,800, whereas in the Bureau of Labor Statistics, similar experts received $3,000 (Chafe 1972).

One reproductive technological innovation that greatly affected the labor force participation rates of women was the development of small, safe, and disposable sanitary napkins to absorb monthly menstrual flows. Prior to this innovation, women used cloths and rags which were bulky and had to be laboriously laundered. Garments for women were often long, cumbersome, and bulky, in order to hide the presence of these rags during the monthly period. Between 1854 and 1914, over 20 different patents for types of napkins, sanitary supports, and menstrual receivers were granted. None received wide public acceptance.

In 1920, the Kimberly Clark Company had a surplus of cellulose from wood fibers which had been used for bandages in World War I. Company executives knew that the wood cellulose was more absorbent than any competing fiber, but did not consider using it for menstrual pads until they discovered that army nurses had been using the material for that purpose. The company began marketing the first disposable sanitary napkin. Despite the high initial costs and difficulties in advertising, the innovation was well received, and contributed to a revolution in dress for women. Menstrual pads were later followed by even less bulky and constrictive tampons which were inserted and worn internally (Bullough 1979).

In the 1930s, the effect of the Depression on female labor force participation overrode the impact of technological innovations. During that period, more married women, often with unemployed or underemployed husbands, entered the labor force to help support their families. The first half of the 1940s was dominated by World War II. Due to the wartime shortage of able bodied men, women entered the labor force in massive numbers. Factories and the federal government facilitated this entry in order to maintain wartime production by establishing day-care facilities for children of working women.

The most significant change in female labor participation during World War II was an increase in the age and change in the marital status of women workers. Before the war, a majority of women workers were age 32 or under. Over the next four years, 60 percent of all the women added to the labor force were over age 35. The proportion of women employed during the war jumped from 25 percent to 36 percent, a 57 percent increase. The proportion of married women employed increased from 15 percent in 1940 to over 24 percent by the end of 1945 (Chafe 1972).

Most of the women employed during the war wanted to keep working afterward. A Women's Bureau survey found that three out of four women working at the end of the war wished to keep their jobs. By 1950, however, the female proportion of the labor force had shrunk from 36 percent at the end of the war to 29 percent. Various methods were used to fire wartime female workers. The concept of "last hired first fired" worked against newly hired women who had less seniority. Under the Selective Service Act, veterans took priority over wartime workers in civilian jobs. The aircraft industry laid off 800,000 workers, most of whom were women, in the two months after V-J Day. In the auto industry, the percentage of women fell from 25 percent of all auto workers in 1944 to 7 percent in 1946, only 1 percent higher than the 6 percent employed in 1939.

The termination of support for child care made staying in the labor force more difficult for married women with small children. All federal support for child-care facilities ended in 1946. Many states had also installed child-care programs which were terminated after the war. A number of companies reimposed both age and marital status restrictions on women employees, as well as nepotism bans against hiring wives.

During the post-World War II period, labor force participation of women has increased, particularly in the 1960s and 1970s. By 1981, 52 percent of all women worked in the labor force. This contrasts with 77 percent of all men. While the percent of male labor force participants was still 48 percent higher than the percent of females, male labor force participation has been modestly declining while female participation has been increasing. In 1950, only 34 percent of women were in the labor force versus 86 percent of men. During the next 30 years, female participation increased 53 percent, while male participation declined 11 percent.

The Modern Working Woman

Not only are more women working, but the composition of the female labor force has changed. In 1900 when labor force participation rates for women were low, the median age of working women was 26. The median age rose to 40 in 1960, with a sizable jump in the participation of "empty nest" women, ages 45 to 59. The subsequent increase in the participation of women ages 20 to 34, an age group in earlier eras predominantly engaging in childbearing rather than labor force participation, caused the median age to drop to 34 in 1980. By 1981, almost 70 percent of women ages 20 to 24, and 67 percent of women ages 25 to 44 were working outside the home.

The marital and family status of the female work force has also changed. While early female workers at the turn of the century were predominantly young unmarried women, modern participants are more likely to be or have been married. Of the never married women, 62% were in the labor force in 1981. For married women with a husband present, 51 percent worked outside the home. Even more likely to work outside the home are married women with a husband absent (61 percent) or divorced women (75 percent).

Mothers with children are more likely to work now than before. Between 1950 and 1981, the labor force participation rate of mothers tripled. Particularly striking in the decade of the 1970s was the increase in labor force participation of married mothers with preschool children. While in 1970, only 30 percent of these mothers worked, by 1981, 48 percent worked (Women's Bureau 1983).

Despite the increased rates of working women, there are still important differences between male and female workers. On the average, women earn about 60 percent of the earnings of male workers. One explanation for this is the large amount of occupational segregation by sex. In the 1980s, as in the 1900s, men and women still work at different types of jobs. Women largely work in clerical, service, or lower-paid traditional female professional jobs such as teaching and nursing. Although two-thirds of the women are in white-collar jobs, most are in clerical positions. Another large segment of the female labor force is in "pink-collar" ghettos, working in service positions such as waitresses, maids, and hairdressers (Howe 1977). In 1981, two out of every five women workers were employed in one of ten occupations: secretary, bookkeeper, sales clerk, cashier, waitress, registered nurse, elementary school teacher, private household worker, typist, and nursing aid.

Despite this concentration in traditionally female and poorly paid jobs, women have made some inroads into male professions. The percent of lawyers who are women tripled from 1972 to 1981, from 4 to 14 percent. Gains were not quite as large during the same time period in the medical field. The number of women physicians doubled so that 14 percent of all physicians were women in 1981. In the field of dentistry, almost previously exclusively male, similar gains occurred. In 1970, only 2 percent of dentists were women. By 1981, 5 percent of dentists were female.

Although women dominated teaching at the elementary and secondary levels, college teaching has traditionally been a male bastion. The number of women college teachers increased 60 percent between 1972 and 1981. In 1981, women constituted 35 percent of all college teachers. Despite the inroads, women are still far more likely to be concentrated at lower academic ranks. Recently, of all instructors, 50 percent were women, versus 9 percent of full processors, the top academic rank. Women with Ph.D.s still earn less than men, although the difference is not quite as great as the gap in male and female earnings for the general labor force. Women Ph.D.s earn 23 percent less than men, regardless of field, experience, quality of training, and nature of jobs (Andersen 1983).

Education does not translate into high earnings for women as easily as it does for men. Over half of all women who had completed college had incomes in 1981 about equal to the median income for men with only eight years of education. Women with a high school education had a lower median income than men who had not completed elementary school. In all educational groups, women earn substantially less than men at the same educational level. The gap was least for women with the lowest and highest amounts of education. Women in these categories earned about two-thirds the amount received by men. The worst categories were women with some high school education or high school graduates, who earned 59 percent of their male counterparts.

While the rates of labor force participation by women have increased, the greatest change in this century has occurred in the type and family status of women who participate. Early female labor force participants were young and unmarried or never married. Modern female workers are far more diverse, and include married women and mothers with small children. The change in the composition of the female labor force was largely made possible by the introduction and dissemination of modern birth control, which allowed women to control both the numbers and timing of children. This ability to control the number and timing of children is particularly important for the small but growing number of women entering traditionally male professions which require long periods of education, training, and apprenticeship. Despite the dramatic shift in both the number and type of women workers and some improvement in the number of women in professional jobs, the majority of women continue to work in sex segregated, poorly paid, and low prestige positions.

8   *Women's Movements*

The struggle for equality by women includes legal and political changes, as well as interpersonal changes. For the overall role of women in society to change, improvements along many dimensions are necessary. Technological changes, especially in birth control, begin the change process. Changes in the family structure and interpersonal relationships both precede and follow political responses and legal changes. Improvements in the status of women in society have depended greatly upon these political responses. Two women's movements have dramatically shaped public policy affecting equality for women. The first movement began in the 1800s and culminated in women achieving the right to vote after World War I. The second movement began in the 1960s. It failed in the objective of passing the Equal Rights Amendment for women, but succeeded in changing discriminatory laws in several policy areas.

CONDITIONS PROMPTING THE WOMEN'S MOVEMENTS

Severe inequality in the social, political, and economic status of women in the United States existed through the 1800s and into the 1900s. Before 1850, women could not vote in most elections in the United States, including presidential elections. They suffered discrimination in various jobs, particularly if they were married. In a field eventually dominated by women—education—women teachers were often required to quit if they married, leading to the stereotype of the "spinster school teacher." Women were not expected to receive a high school education. It was even rarer for women to attend college. Most male colleges would not accept women.

With the creation of women's colleges after the Civil War, some college education became available to affluent women, but employment discrimination by marital status remained, even in women's colleges. Women who married were usually required to resign. Although Barnard College by exception allowed a woman president to retain her position after marriage in the early twentieth century, when she had a child she was forced to resign.

After the Civil War, more states, especially midwestern states, began to allow women to attend the state university. Oberlin and Antioch, both private schools, had begun admitting women by the early 1850s. Iowa in 1858 was the first state university to accept women. Wisconsin admitted women to the normal school courses designed to train public school teachers in 1863. The first woman student was allowed to enroll at the University of Michigan in 1870.

Although a few eastern schools also began admitting women—Boston University in 1869 and Cornell in 1874—the more prevalent pattern in the east and later, also in the south, was to establish separate women's colleges. Women's colleges established in the east in the 1800s included Vassar College, founded in 1861, followed by Wellesley and Smith in 1875.

Women continued to be prohibited from attending professional schools until recently. Particularly discriminatory practices were prevalent in medicine and law. In 1849, Elizabeth Blackwell, later to become a famous female physician, had to apply to 29 medical schools before finding one that would enroll her. In response, she established a medical school for women which served as the major source of training for women until the modern era. During this same period in the 1800s, many states prohibited women from being admitted to the bar (Flexner 1959).

In most states, married women legally were unable to control their own earnings, manage property, or sign legal papers. This common law doctrine was called *femme couverte,* and assumed that wives were chattel of their husbands with no independent standing or legal rights. The one exception to this doctrine was a negotiated premarital agreement to put property in trust for the wife. The husband still retained control of the income from the property, although the property remained in the woman's name. These prohibitions on property ownership and retention of income did not apply to single women, called *femme sole.* Between 1839 and 1850, many states passed some reforms recognizing the rights of married women to hold legal property. By 1890, most states had given wives control over their inherited property and their earnings, and women had a reasonable chance in the case of divorce of getting at least joint custody of the children (Banner 1974).

Discriminatory laws about the family and business, however, remained. Many states had laws that women could not enter into business partnerships without the consent of their husbands. Husbands frequently had the legal right to decide where the family would live. In most states, a wife was required to take her husband's name upon marriage, and lost her separate credit rating.

The unequal status of women was especially evident in laws regulating sexual conduct. Often, adultery by the husband was not sufficient grounds for divorce, although adultery by the wife was. The double standard of sexual behavior was applied in issues surrounding prostitution. Traditionally, men were not prosecuted for patronizing prostitutes, although women were prosecuted for offering sexual services for pay.

Rape laws also manifested a double standard designed to protect women who were viewed as more helpless. Rape was essentially a crime by men against women, where the possibilities of female assault on men or homosexual rape of men were not addressed. The origin of rape laws, however, was not to protect women and their right to control their own bodies, but to protect the property of one man from violation by another. Some critics argued that rape laws, in fact, protected the accused more than the victim. Traditionally a man could not be convicted solely on the testimony of the victim. Corroborative evidence was required, including proof of penetration, and proof that the act occurred without consent. Women's prior sexual habits and moral character were frequently issues in rape cases.

Married women lost legal protection against assault within the home. Although state rules varied, two different interpretations of English common law were used. In some states, the first beating was legal. Police could be called in for repeat beatings, although generally prosecution as a criminal assault did not result. In many other states, the ancient "rule of thumb" was applied. A husband could strike his wife with a stick no thicker than a thumb (Walum 1977). Since domestic violence was rarely regarded as a criminal assault, women who wished to use the courts to prevent physical violence had to get a warrant against the husband from civil court, a far more cumbersome procedure often making the wife the antagonist of her husband and frequently further provoking his rage.

Despite marginal improvements, many laws continued to discriminate against women. The most important were voting laws. Only in four states in 1890 could women vote in general, federal, state, and local elections. Some states allowed women to vote in special elections, such as municipal or school board elections. Generally, because women could not vote, they could not sit on juries or hold public office.

THE FIRST FEMINIST MOVEMENT

Each of the major feminist movements in twentieth century United States may be linked to and was driven by technological change. The origins of the first feminist movement in the United States coincide with the abolition movement of the Civil War. In 1848, the first "Declaration of

Rights" was issued by women in upstate New York. It argued that men had established an absolute tyranny over women, depriving them of legal rights, profitable employment, educational opportunities, and the right to vote (Dubois 1978). Every year from 1850 to 1860, national women's rights conferences were held. These early conferences focused less on obtaining the right to vote than on achieving rights for women to control property and earnings, have better opportunities for education and employment, and acquire legal status to sue and bear witness.

All organized suffrage activity promoting the rights of women ground to a halt during the Civil War. Much of the reform effort during and after that focused on freedom and the vote for blacks. Quickly apparent after the war was the need for a constitutional amendment to protect the voting rights of blacks. The fourteenth and fifteenth amendments were approved to meet this need. Leaders of the women's movement had hoped that the voting franchise would be extended to women at the same time that it was extended to blacks—an event which did not materialize. Although reconciled to this not being likely, feminist leaders were upset with the development of the fourteenth amendment in particular. Nowhere in the original Constitution and Bill of Rights was the word "male" explicitly used. In the fourteenth amendment, however, "male" was used three times, always in conjunction with the word "citizen." This raised the question of whether women were actually citizens of the United States (Flexner 1959).

At the time of the American Revolution, the question of whether women could vote, as well as questions of property and family law, were considered state matters. In fact, in New Jersey, women had voted in some parts of the state, prior to the adoption of a state constitution which limited the right to vote. In many states, the right to vote was originally limited to white male property owners. It was eventually broadened to include all white males over the age of 21. In a few northern and western states, the race limitation was removed before the Civil War. The fourteenth and fifteenth amendments further extended the right to vote to all males, regardless of race, in remaining states. The insertion of the word "male" into the fourteenth amendment made clear to feminists that achieving the right to vote for women would require a separate constitutional amendment.

The political failure after 1865 in which blacks but not women achieved the right to vote led feminists to split into two different suffrage organizations in 1869 and remained separate until merging in 1889. Societal interest in women's rights remained low over the next 20 years (Coolidge 1966). By the late 1800s, more organizations promoting women's rights were being created. Not all women reformers agreed on the importance of obtaining voting rights.

The late 1800s was a period of growth of a number of women's organizations such as the Association of Collegiate Alumnae, the Young Women's Christian Association, and various women's clubs, which were part of social feminism. These groups supported improved education opportunities for women, enacting child laws, improving conditions for women workers, and reforming property and family laws, as well as laws for all of society. Many women in these organizations participated in the subsequent revitalization of the first feminist movement. These women were of upper middle and middle-class origins. Their class standing exposed them to the new barrier methods of birth control being developed in Europe.

The first women's movement did not gain great momentum until the early 1900s when women rallied behind the suffrage issue. The main thrust of the first movement from that point forward was to obtain the vote for women. Two arguments were used to persuade men to given women this right: the justice argument and the expediency argument. The justice argument extended the rationalization that colonists had made when settling the New World—that men were created equal and had the inalienable right to consent to the laws by which they were governed. Feminists contended that women were also equal and deserved the right of consent (Kraditor 1965; Buhle and Buhle 1978; Gluck 1976).

The expediency argument took several forms. Under one version, women were to bolster the shrinking power of the white majority to offset gains made by blacks and immigrants. Women should be extended the vote to allow the dominant white Protestant group to retain power. Others argued women needed the ballot for self-protection since women faced hazards to morals and health in factories and elsewhere. Underlying this version was the notion that women represented a better and higher system of values. Given the right to vote, women would use this right to reform and elevate society. This second version emphasized the potential of women to support child labor laws, laws regulating food and drug purity, cleaning up corrupt city governments, and most controversially, the temperance movement (Kraditor 1965).

A federal suffrage amendment extending voting rights to women came only after a long series of state political battles focusing on the female franchise. In 1890, Wyoming entered the United States as the first state with full suffrage for women, followed by Colorado in 1893, and Utah and Idaho in 1896. Despite many state level campaigns, no new states passed suffrage amendments between 1896 and 1910. By the beginning of 1914, five states plus the territory of Alaska gave women the right to vote, raising the total to nine states. Two more states followed suit in 1914. Almost all of the early states enfranchising women were western, with the least western being Kansas. Illinois was the first state east of the Mississippi to give women voting rights. In 1913, the state of Illinois gave women the right to vote for president, but excluded them from voting for other offices. This raised questions about how to extend voting rights to women, as well as the earlier question of whether to extend them (Kraditor 1965; Buhle and Buhle 1978; Coolidge 1966; Catt and Schuler 1926).

The political movement for women's suffrage was confounded by related but separate political movements. In the very beginning, many women were drawn to the abolition movement. Male supporters of the abolitionist movement often supported rights for women. Among the signers of the call to the first national woman's rights convention in 1850 were the major abolition leaders of the day, including Wendell Phillips, William Lloyd Garrison, and Bronson Alcott. When blacks obtained the right to vote through constitutional amendment, the coalition and overlap between supporters of blacks and women was greatly strained.

The feminist movement also had some overlap with the temperance movement. The temperance movement was also begun in the 1840s. Although at first it excluded women, by the 1850s, there was a linkage with feminist leaders. Temperance concerns faded during the Civil War, but were revived in the 1870s with a stronger feminist orientation (Buhle and Buhle 1978).

Temperance legislation, its movement leaders argued, was needed to protect women and children from irresponsible husbands who would squander family resources on drinking. Many women were drawn into the suffrage movement through their prior interest in temperance. There was a great deal of overlap between membership in suffrage organizations and membership in the Women's Christian Temperance Union (WCTU). While most temperance men were in favor of women's suffrage, in wet areas, especially in the east, opponents of prohibition became opponents of suffrage because of the belief that women voters would vote for prohibition in greater numbers.

Another movement which confounded feminist suffrage politics was the Nativist movement which sought to prevent the dilution of political power of native-born Americans. As part of the expediency argument, some suffrage leaders contended that giving the vote to white women would help to ensure the supremacy of white Anglo-Saxon U.S. citizens over the foreign born. These leaders advocated suffrage with an educational qualification, generating controversy and schism in the women's movement. In the south, women's suffrage coupled with an education requirement was sometimes presented as a "solution" to the race problem by increasing the white vote (Kraditor 1965).

Though the first feminist movement had some success through state campaigns, the major thrust was to pass a federal amendment guaranteeing women the right to vote. The Women's Party created in 1914 under Alice Paul especially espoused this goal, and employed more militant tactics. Their members engaged in such radical actions as chaining themselves to the White House fence and heckling speakers of the party in power. Their philosophy was to hold the political party in power (then the Democrats) responsible for the achievement of suffrage (Buhle and Buhle 1978;

Coolidge 1966; Irwin 1971). The National American Woman Suffrage Association (NAWSA), the older and more established suffrage organization, disavowed such militant tactics, and instead urged quiet pressure and lobbying in the legislature.

With President Wilson's belated support, the nineteenth amendment was eventually passed through the House in 1918 as a wartime measure. It passed the following year in May of 1919 and was ratified by the necessary number of states (three-quarters of the state legislatures) in August of 1920. This victory, occurring after a lengthy and arduous battle, was the political culmination of the first feminist movement.

Birth control played a major role in precipitating the first woman's movement. Most critical was the development and dissemination of barrier methods of birth control at the turn of the century to upper-middle-class women, giving the leaders of women's suffrage more effective control over their bodies and the timing and birth of children. The more socially minded feminists were supporters of the extension of the freedom birth control granted to working and lower-class women. They were supportive of birth control dissemination efforts, including those of Margaret Sanger.

Middle-class women had less access to new birth control technologies, though private discussions of how to limit births were linked with the growth of the women's club movement (Banner 1974; Chafe 1972). During this era, middle-class women were not entering the labor force, but rather were gradually augmenting their social roles by engaging in volunteer civic and cultural clubs, many of which were oriented toward charity and reform. In these clubs, formerly housebound women, especially those in middle and working classes, were introduced to the concerns of the broader world. They acquired political and organizational skills which they later applied to politics in both the first and second feminist movement (Smuts 1959; Filene 1974; Bernard 1981).

THE SECOND FEMINIST MOVEMENT

During the interstitial period between the two women's movements, supporters of women's rights maintained a low profile, but limited feminist activity continued to occur. The NAWSA transformed into the National League of Women Voters, with the goals of dissemination of political information and general government reform. The Women's Party, after the passage of suffrage, reorganized and opened a new fight for legal equality, proposing an Equal Rights Amendment to the Constitution in 1921. While the Women's Party actively pursued the passage of an ERA and was joined in this pursuit by other organizations, little headway was made toward this goal until the beginning of the second feminist movement (Lemons 1973).

Other social feminist organizations, such as the General Federation of Women's Clubs and the Consumer League, pushed some social legislation, especially in the early 1920s. These groups were able to garner some political clout in the early 1920s as representatives of the newly enfranchised "American woman's" views. By the late 1920s, a separate and identifiable woman's vote had failed to materialize. Women essentially voted no differently from men. The credibility of social feminist groups as spokespersons for women declined. The Great Depression further eroded the power of women's groups as both politicians and citizens focused attention upon economic survival.

The crisis of the Depression and the all consuming national effort involved in World War II produced a national passion for patterns of the past and a return to traditional family roles for women in the 1950s. Women married earlier and had more children than in the 1920s. During this decade, the birth rate soared as the Baby Boom emerged. Middle-class Americans began a trek to newly developing suburbs, adopting a life-style that emphasized sex stereotyped roles and further segregated women from labor force participation into bedroom communities. The percentage of women employed as professionals declined. Although more women attended college, they became a smaller percentage of the total college enrollment. Broadly based support for feminist issues was not reawakened until a decade later with the beginning of the second feminist movement (O'Neill 1969).

While several social factors including popular books and the civil rights movement contributed to the growth of the second feminist movement, technological change was also a major precipitating factor. The second feminist movement began in the 1960s and extended into the 1970s and 1980s. At the beginning of the 1960s, women were moving into the labor force in greater numbers but had not yet developed a sense of collective consciousness. President Kennedy alerted the nation to women's concerns in 1961 by appointing a Commission on the Status of Women. Many states followed this example and also began a formal inquiry into the role and status of women.

In the early 1960s, young women displayed a concern for social issues which led into a second feminist movement. They joined in sit-ins at lunch counters, other activities of the black civil rights movements, and joined the Peace Corps, venturing overseas. In 1963, Betty Friedan produced a consciousness-raising book, *The Feminine Mystique,* which publicized for middle-class women their unequal lot. Friedan identified "the problem which has not name"—the isolation of women in the family—as a major source of the problems of women. The reproductive role of women, along with social norms that mothers should stay home with their children, were why women were isolated and atomized in their homes. Women in this era were often limited to a social world no broader than their neighborhoods. Friedan's book was one factor laying the seeds for the second feminist movement.

As with the first feminist movement, the second movement frequently overlapped with the struggle for black equality. The second feminist movement was linked to the 1960s civil rights movement. Between 1963 and 1965, white college students from the north began to go south to assist in the struggle for civil liberties and voting rights for disenfranchised blacks. The women who participated in the civil rights struggle for blacks noticed that they were often relegated to demeaning clerical tasks and were denied an equal role in policy decisions. The actual treatment of women, combined with the civil rights movement's emphasis on the examination of the roots of oppression, caused young women in the civil rights movement to question their overall role in U.S. society (Chafe 1972; Rothschild 1979).

In 1966 the National Organization for Women (NOW) was founded, marking the real beginning of the second feminist movement as an organized political force. This organization viewed the goals of feminism to be an extension of equal rights to women. The technique for accomplishing these goals was to be traditional interest group politics within the existing political system. Although NOW was the largest of the women's groups in the second movement, and the group most clearly focused upon achieving objectives through the political system, other types of women's groups also grew (Freeman 1973).

Many smaller more locally based groups engaged in consciousness raising and mutual support for female group members. Some women focused on community goals such as the formation of rape crisis centers and shelters for battered women. Women's caucuses within political parties and professional organizations formed and frequently argued for greater female representation within their organizational hierarchies.

In the 1970s, a number of other organizations also developed political goals at the national level. These included the National Women's Political Caucus (NWPC) and the Women's Equity Action League (WEAL). NWPC focused on elections and campaign work, especially support for women candidates. WEAL lobbied for a variety of national legislative goals, and provided financial support for women involved in precedent-setting discrimination cases (Costain 1981). Later in the 1970s, other traditional women's groups such as the National Federation of Business and Professional Women (BPW) and the American Association of University Women (AAUW) joined in lobbying with feminist groups.

Within feminist organizations in the 1970s, dissension and internal strife occurred over both the goals and tactics. The NWPC was torn by whether to establish a program of strong lobbying and whether to fund a national office at a high level. NOW also experienced internal debates over several issues. Was NOW becoming too reformist and elitist, serving only the needs of upper middle-class professional women? What should the organization do—continue to focus on achieving legislative and legal reform, or become involved in the establishment of community service centers for women? As the deadline for ERA passage approached, other goals became subordinated to winning approval of the amendment.

The ERA was a U.S. Constitutional amendment providing that "equality of rights under the law shall not be denied or abridged by the United States or any state on account of sex." Across time, consensus emerged that passing the ERA was the primary goal of the second feminist movement. Subsidiary goals were to pass legislation or otherwise obtain favorable judicial and regulatory outcomes. Policies addressed included the labor force issues of equal pay for equal work, and later equal pay for comparable worth. Other social issues addressed were equality for women in sports, education, commercial credit, retirement pay and pensions, job protection for pregnant women, prosecution of rapists and counseling for victims, and increasing the number of women in executive and political offices (Freeman 1975).

In the second feminist movement, the issue of the right to abortion coincided with feminist goals, although the two remained separate political movements with partially overlapping membership. The National Abortion Rights Action League (NARAL) was the major political movement aimed at revising state abortion laws. In 1973, the Supreme Court established the right of women to abortion. Since that time, a number of right-wing and antifeminist groups have focused on challenging that Supreme Court decision, either through further court cases, or through a proposed constitutional amendment to ban abortion.

In 1972, almost 50 years after its initial introduction as a continuation of the first feminist movement, the Equal Rights Amendment (ERA) to the Constitution was passed by both houses of Congress and sent to the states for ratification. In that same year, 22 state legislatures approved the amendment. After that, momentum for passage began to decrease. Opponents of the ERA organized in force. By November of 1978, only 13 additional states had ratified the ERA (Boles 1979). Part of the controversy over the ERA included the abortion debate, as well as other fears such as drafting women for combat military service. Tactics used by proponents of the ERA included calling economic boycotts of conventions in nonratifying states. Opposition to ERA was predominantly clustered in the same group of southern states that had also opposed ratification of the suffrage amendment granting women the right to vote.

By June of 1980, only 35 states had ratified ERA, three short of the required number. Four states that had passed the ERA later rescinded their approval in an unprecedented legislative change of heart, raising unresolved questions about the constitutionality of state rescissions. Although proponents were not able to pass ERA within the original time limit set by Congress, they were able to secure an extension of the time allowed for state legislative ratification of the ERA. Despite this minor victory, proponents failed in securing the major victory of successful ratification within the time extension.

Even though ratification of the ERA was not obtained, many other political and legislative victories were gained through the second feminist movement. These included Title IX assuring women greater access to athletic training and other educational opportunities, some lower court decisions on equal pay for equal work and more recently for comparable worth, job protection for pregnant women, fair credit treatment for women, and equal opportunity in hiring and promotion. The ERA has now been reintroduced into Congress, although its political fate in the 1980s and beyond is unclear.

With the election of Ronald Reagan as President, conservative forces gained power in all aspects of U.S. life. Reagan was supported by conservative groups that opposed passage of the ERA, other social legislation for women, and abortion. Although organizations such as NOW and WEAL continue to maintain and pursue a political agenda, public support for feminist reforms lessened in the 1980s. Given the substantial swing in the political climate toward conservative values and policies in this decade, the likelihood of congressional initiation and state adoption of the ERA in the 1980s, along with other legal reforms promoting women's rights, is unlikely.

Social and economic factors played some role in the growth of the second feminist movement. The rise in greater affluence of middle-class families and the concomitant move to suburbs created an isolation problem for some women. At least some suburban mothers raised their daughters to expect more from life than traditionally raised females expected. The daughters expected institutional treatment similar to that of males. The glaring discrepancy between expectations and reality, even in the civil rights and radical movements, fueled feminism (Rothschild 1983).

A "marriage squeeze" for women in the 1960s further accelerated the second feminist movement (Guttentag and Secord 1983). Marriage squeezes occur because men and women typically marry at different ages. Older men marry younger women, and the number of births in age cohorts fluctuate. Men in the 1950s experienced a marriage squeeze. More men were born in the decade of 1920 to 1930 than were women born in the 1930s during the Depression who were of a suitable marriage age for men born before 1930. By the 1960s, the ratios had reversed and a marriage squeeze developed for women. Women in the 1960s Baby Boom were in a large size cohort, preceded by a particularly small size cohort. The Depression and the war reduced the number of births in that era, reducing the number of suitably aged men for first wave Baby Boom women (Heer and Grossbard-Shectman 1981). Many of these women were less likely to marry early or to marry at all, heightening their concerns about opportunities for women.

As with the first feminist movement, birth control technology played a major role in the second women's movement. The introduction and dissemination of the pill and the IUD preceded the second feminist movement by half a decade. The early dissemination of the pill to young women, especially on college campuses, gave them unprecedented control over procreation. This began a change in how women perceived their bodies, sexuality, and roles in society which fueled the second feminist movement. While older barrier methods constituted reliable but often inconvenient methods to control the timing and number of births, the pill and the IUD represented substantial improvements in birth control in that they were both reliable and convenient. The greater freedom from fears of unwanted births made possible by these innovations, especially for unmarried women, was one major factor in the development of the second feminist movement.

Birth control technology has played a critical role in both directly and indirectly precipitating and fueling both women's movements. With the first women's movement, barrier methods of birth control helped to change the role and expectations of women and culminated with the passage of suffrage for women. The second women's movement was preceded by the introduction and dissemination of even more effective and convenient birth control, the pill and the IUD, which further increased the ability of women to control procreation and altered their self-perceptions. The increased availability of abortion also greatly augmented women's sense of control over their own bodies. These birth control innovations, more than technological changes in either the home or work environments, led to greatly increased rates of labor force participation by women, feeding the initiation and continuation of the second feminist political movement.

9 Legal Changes and Policy Outputs: Pay Equity and The Work Environment

Both the first and second feminist movements focused on particular legislative and policy goals. The first movement achieved its major policy objective—the passage of the nineteenth amendment giving women the right to vote. The second movement did not achieve its major policy objective—the passage of the Equal Rights Amendment (ERA) assuring women equal treatment under the law. Despite this defeat, the second feminist movement has achieved a number of legal and policy changes. Many of these changes would have been covered by the ERA. In the absence of a constitutional ERA, however, specific legislation in a variety of policy areas was and is required to achieve equal treatment of women.

As a result of the feminist movements, progress toward equality has been made in four major areas. This chapter examines the area of labor force participation. Policy changes have affected the pay of women, retirement benefits and pensions, sexual harassment, pregnancy benefits, day care, and the role of women in the military. Chapter 10 explores policy changes pertaining to the family and sex, including commercial credit, family violence, abortion, and rape. In the area of education, legislation has affected the status of women as workers, women as students, and women as athletes. Chapter 10 also examines these policy areas. Chapter 11 reviews the relatively modest inroads women have made in achieving elected and appointed political office.

PROTECTIVE LEGISLATION

Much early legislation regulating the participation of women in the labor force was oriented toward protecting women, rather than establishing their equality. Examples of such legislation included restrictions on the amount and time of hours worked, and prohibitions against women performing work thought to exceed their physical capacity. Many states had laws requiring women to cease work for a specified time during and after childbirth.

In the past, feminists did not agree about the desirability of special laws protecting women workers, since protective legislation legitimized the prevalent notion that men and women performed different work. One part of the feminist movement collaborated with labor unions to promote protective legislation, while another part of the movement was opposed to it. Susan Anthony was among the latter, arguing that protective laws would set women apart from their male peers. In *Muller v. Oregon* in 1908, labor and women jointly brought the case to the U.S. Supreme Court where the court ruled that special protective legislation was justified in order to protect women's health and safety.

Protective legislation was not directed toward improving the economic status of women, which remained inferior to that of male workers. Often, protective legislation actually hindered the economic status of women workers. Women were prevented from working at night when they would have received differential shift pay. In some states, women were prohibited from working more than a set number of hours, which precluded them from overtime work and pay. Many factors, however, in addition to protective legislation, continued to hurt women economically (Lipman-Blumen 1984).

A consistent earnings gap between men and women has prevailed to the present day. Through the 1970s, women's earnings as a percentage of men's were 57 to 59 percent. In 1980, women's earnings rose very slightly to 60 percent of men's. The average woman earned $11,590, while the average man earned $19,712. Part of the explanation for this differential in earnings is that men and women work in different jobs. For men in 1981, the three highest ranking jobs in terms of median weekly earnings were aerospace and aeronautical engineers ($619), stocks and bonds sales agents ($589), and chemical engineers ($583). There were not enough females in these job categories to report averages for women. In two occupational groups with large numbers of women—registered nurses and school teachers—median weekly earnings were $331 and $321.

Occupational segregation is not the only explanation for male and female earnings differences. Even when men and women work in the same field, women are paid less. The median weekly earnings for male lawyers were $574, 40 percent more than the $407 paid female lawyers. The weekly earnings for female lawyers were comparable to the weekly earnings of male postal carriers—an occupation that ranked fortieth in men's earnings. A similar differential exists for physicians and dentists. Men earn $561 a week versus $401 for women. In the growing field of computer systems analysts, the female wage was $422 versus $546 for men (U.S. Department of Labor 1982).

EQUAL PAY FOR EQUAL WORK

The Equal Pay Act of 1963

The first federal law against sex discrimination in employment was the Equal Pay Act of 1963. Previously, several states had enacted similar laws regulating pay, and selected federal agencies had policies prohibiting discrimination in pay between men and women during World War I and World War II. This federal act was an outgrowth of a commission created by President Kennedy in 1961 on the status of women. The act was an amendment to the Fair Labor Standards Act of 1938, and applied to all employees covered by the minimum wage standards of that law. While the Equal Pay Act covered 30 million workers, 15 million were excluded, including people in executive, administrative, professional, and traveling sales jobs. The act required employers to pay men and women equal compensation for work of equal skill, effort, and responsibility, and performed under similar working conditions. Wage differentials based on seniority, merit, quantity and quality of production, and any other factors unrelated to sex were permitted (Buckley 1975; U.S. Department of Labor 1982).

Originally, the U.S. Department of Labor was charged with enforcement of the Equal Pay Act. Of the first 15 pay discrimination cases tried, the Department of Labor won only four. The reason for the poor showing by the department was a disagreement between labor and the courts over the interpretation of "equal" as it applied to skill, effort, and responsibility. In 1970 in the case of *Shultz v. Wheaton Glass Company*, proponents of strict enforcement won a major victory when the court agreed that equal work standards required only that compared jobs be substantially equal, not identical.

Proponents of strict enforcement lost ground, however, in the 1973 case of *Hodgson v. Robert Hall Clothes, Inc.* The grounds for charges of discrimination in this case were that saleswomen selling women's clothes were paid lower wages than salesmen selling men's clothes. The company argued that women's clothes were less expensive and less profitable than men's clothes, justifying the lower wage for women clerks. The court ruled that salespeople in each department were not interchangeable, owing to potential embarrassment to customers and consequent reduction in sales volume. The court upheld the sex-based wage differential (Buckley 1975).

Litigation surrounding the Equal Pay Act established several principles. Foremost was that to be compared for potential pay discrimination, jobs only had to be substantially equal in effort and skill, not identical. Once the federal government or a plaintiff has established wage differentials, the burden is on the employer to prove that sex is not the basis for this discrimination. If some but not all members of one sex perform significant extra duties on the job, only the employees performing the extra duties are entitled to a higher wage.

Heavy lifting, or other duties women are deemed unable to perform, are not automatically a justifiable reason for higher wage rates for men. Employers must prove the advantage in dollars and cents, and women must be given opportunities to perform the more strenuous activities on the same terms. Men on night shifts cannot be paid higher than women on night shifts. Mental as well as physical effort must be considered in establishing equality of effort. Concurrent employment of the two sexes is not required to make a wage comparison, so that employers cannot arbitrarily pay lower wages to a female employee replacing a male employee (U.S. Department of Labor 1982).

Two major expansions of the Equal Pay Act occurred in 1972 and 1974, as a result of feminist pressure from the second women's movement. In 1972, coverage was extended to executive, administrative, and professional employees, and outside salespeople. In 1974, coverage was extended to most federal, state, and local government employees.

Title VII of the 1964 Civil Rights Act

The most frequently used federal legislation to safeguard equal opportunity for women has been Title VII of the 1964 Civil Rights Act. The original intent of this act was to protect blacks and other racial minorities. In addition to Title VII, which deals with employment, other titles cover voting, public accommodations, and equal access to public schools. Equal opportunity for women was only included in Title VII as an amendment to the original bill. Protection for women was accidental, resulting from a political miscalculation by opponents of the act. Southern congressmen who wished to defeat the bill strongly supported the amendment including women in hopes that the presence of the amendment would strike fellow members of Congress as ludicrous, causing the delay or defeat of the entire act. To the surprise of these opponents, both the amendment and the act were passed.

Since the ERA prohibiting any discrimination on the basis of sex was not passed, this accidental inclusion of women into the 1964 Civil Rights Act remains the strongest legal protection against discrimination women currently have. While passage of the Civil Rights Act was not part of the second feminist movement, the subsequent employment of it to protect women was integrally tied to the movement. Initially, few cases involving sexual discrimination were brought under the act. By 1969, enough cases had arisen to stimulate the development of sex discrimination guidelines.

Title VII of the Civil Rights Act created the Equal Employment Opportunity Commission (EEOC) to establish regulations and carry out the provisions of the title. The five commissioners are appointed by the president, with approval by the Senate. Initially, the powers of the EEOC were limited to investigation and conciliation. Coverage was limited to business establishments in the private sector. In 1972, these powers were extended to include litigation authority and to extend coverage to educational institutions and state and local government employees. Currently, the law covers all private and public employers of 15 or more workers. It also covers public and private employment agencies and labor unions with 15 or more members.

One early question about the protection Title VII offered women was a question of precedence. Many states at that time had protective legislation which prohibited or limited the employment of women under dangerous or less desirable working conditions. Examples included prohibiting women from lifting weights in excess of a specified limit, proscribing employment during certain night hours, or proscribing employment of women for more than a specified number of hours per day or per week. Pushed by feminists, the EEOC issued guidelines in 1969 that found that protective laws discriminated against women rather than protected them, and therefore were not a defense for unlawful practices (Buckley 1975).

What are unlawful employment practices under the 1964 Civil Rights Act? According to Title VII, it is unlawful for an employer to discriminate because of sex in hiring, firing, wages, salaries, promotions, or terms and conditions of employment. It is unlawful for labor unions to discriminate in membership, applications for membership, or referrals for employment. It is also unlawful for employment agencies to discriminate in classifying or referring persons for employment. Exceptions are allowed if sex is a bona fide occupational qualification, such as for an actor or actress. Differentials in compensation based on seniority and merit systems are permitted.

Guidelines developed under Title VII further define discriminatory practices. Refusal to hire an individual may not be based on assumed employment characteristics of women as a category or on the preferences of customers or existing employees. Jobs may not be separately classified as male or female, nor may there be separate lines of progression or seniority systems for men and women. Advertising of jobs in newspapers and employment announcements under male and female headings is illegal.

Discrimination against women in fringe benefits, including pensions and retirement plans, is prohibited. Before the Civil Rights Act, many businesses commonly required female employees to make larger contributions to pension funds than male employees for equivalent benefit structures. The justification of unequal contributions was based on the greater expected life span of female employees. The city of Los Angeles required unequal pension contributions based on sex and was challenged in court for this practice. In the Supreme Court case of *City of Los Angeles v. Manhart,* the court upheld the EEOC guideline that unequal contributions were illegal. Under the same guidelines, unequal retirement payments, given equal contributions, were challenged and declared illegal.

In addition to the lack of coverage for women working for small employers, another limitation on Title VII is that charges of discrimination must be filed within 180 days of the alleged unlawful practice. There are several exceptions to this time limit. EEOC allows a deferral period for states and localities with fair employment practice laws that provide the same protection as Title VII. If a complaint is sent to an appropriate state agency first, the deadline for filing with EEOC is 300 days from the unlawful act, or within 30 days of a notice that the state agency has finished its proceedings. Critics of this time limit argue that the allowed six months is insufficient time to prompt the traumatic decision to pursue legal action against an employer. For institutions, such as universities or large corporations, with elaborate internal grievance procedures, the six months time limit may not be sufficiently long to allow the internal process to be exhausted before filing with the EEOC.

COMPARABLE WORTH

An issue in the 1980s concerning pay equity is the question of equal pay for comparable worth. This principle seeks to raise wages for work performed predominantly by women to the level of wages of comparable although not identical work performed predominantly by men (Gold 1983). Continued job segregation by sex has pushed comparable worth to the forefront of pay equity concerns. In 1970, half of all women workers were concentrated in only 17 occupations, most of which paid lower wages than similar or less skilled work performed by men. By the late 1970s, women still represented 98 percent of all secretaries, 97 percent of all nurses, 95 percent of all household workers, over 75 percent of all clerical workers, and 64 percent of all service workers. For men and women to be fully integrated in the job market and performing the same work—a condition for applying guidelines about equal pay for equal work—two-thirds to three-quarters of all working women would have to change occupations.

Several studies have evaluated jobs on the basis of knowledge, skills, and responsibility requirements. On average, these studies conclude that female jobs are paid 20 percent less than male jobs of comparable worth. In Maryland, in 1979, the starting salary for a public school teacher in Montgomery County, Maryland, was $12,323. This was a predominantly female job requiring a bachelor's degree and two years of experience.Liquor store clerks in the same county were making a similar salary of $12,779. Liquor store clerks were predominantly males with only high school degrees.

In 1978 the state of Washington conducted a detailed evaluation of a large number of state government jobs. The evaluators devised a system to designate comparable requirements and responsibilities. In the low skills category, the predominantly female job of food service worker was paid $637 per month, while the predominantly male job of truck driver was paid $969. In a slightly higher skills category, predominantly female keypunch operators earned $703, while predominantly male stockroom attendants earned $816. A third comparison was made between the predominantly female job of library specialist earning $946, and the predominantly male job of carpenter, earning $1241 (Kahn and Grune 1982).

The first applications of the equal pay for work of comparable value principle occurred during World War I when the War Labor Board applied it to 50 disputed cases. Again, during World War II, the National War Labor Board supported the comparable worth principle. In both cases, when the war ended, the program died. Feminists and personnel experts have maintained an on-going debate about whether Title VII of the 1964 Civil Rights Act covers comparable worth disputes.

Under the Carter administration, several different agencies were interested in developing the comparable worth argument as a way to address sex-based pay inequities. The EEOC under Eleanor Holmes Norton began developing the basis for an enforcement policy, and filed pro comparable worth *amicus curiae* briefs in a number of important court cases. The Woman's Bureau in the Department of Labor acted as a clearinghouse of information on this issue. The Office of Federal Contracts Compliance Programs (OFCCP) normally investigates and monitors discrimination by federal contract holders. This office prepared regulations in December 1980 stating that compensation practices would be scrutinized closely to assure that sex played no role in setting wages. These efforts to advance comparable worth were halted, however, when the Reagan Administration assumed power in 1981. The day before the OFCCP regulations were to be effective, the Reagan administration deferred them.

Prior to 1981, courts issued contradictory rulings on the question of including comparable worth under Title VII of the Civil Rights Act. While several cases supported comparable worth, other cases, such as *Christensen v. Iowa,* did not. In the example, the University of Iowa was found not to discriminate in paying secretaries less than physical plant employees, even though an internal study by the university's personnel department placed the two jobs in the same labor grade. The court accepted the justification of a higher pay scale for physical plant workers owing to prevailing wage rates. In another case where a court ruled against comparable worth, payment of $100 more per month to tree trimmers than to nurses was found to be legal.

In 1981, the U.S. Supreme Court ruled 5-4 in favor of some aspects of comparable worth in the case of *Gunther v. County of Washington, Oregon.* The Gunther decision opens the door for bringing compensation discrimination claims under Title VII without the necessity of showing equal work. The decision provides only weak support for comparable worth. It did not establish what must be proved to show discrimination. Female prison matrons were paid only 70 percent as much as the all male position of corrections officer. The jobs were not identical or equal, because there were fewer female prisoners to guard, resulting in a lower prisoner-guard ratio for the matrons. As a result of the lower ratio, matrons spent part of their work time on clerical duties. Although corrective pay raises were ordered for the matrons, the applicability of the case to other situations is uncertain.

Comparable worth remains an unresolved issue in the 1980s. The lack of support by the Reagan administration has been reflected by Reagan's nominations for positions on the EEOC. Reagan nominees have not been supportive of comparable worth, or of aggressive enforcement of pay equity issues. Courts have been willing to use differential prevailing wage rates for men and women in the local economy as a justification for continued pay inequity for work of comparable worth. Once sex-based wage differentials are present, use of the prevailing wage rate argument to challenge the comparable worth principle assures that sex-based wage differentials will continue unaltered by legal intervention.

SEXUAL HARASSMENT

Title VII of the Civil Rights Act of 1964 not only protects women against pay discrimination, but also covers sexual harassment on the job. Sexual harassment is viewed as a discriminatory and therefore unlawful practice. EEOC clarified the illegality of sexual harassment under Title VII with an amendment to its sex discrimination guidelines in 1980. Sexual harassment is unlawful because it imposes an onerous condition of employment upon an individual based on that individual's sex.

According to the EEOC guidelines, sexual harassment consists of unwelcome sexual advances, requests for sexual favors, and other verbal or physical conduct of a sexual nature which meets one of the following conditions. One criterion is that submission to sexual advances is made explicitly or implicitly a condition of employment. A second criterion is that submission to or rejection of such conduct is used as the basis for employment decisions. A third criterion is that the sexual harassment has the purpose or effect of unreasonably interfering with an individual's work performance, or creating a hostile, intimidating, or offensive working environment (U.S. Department of Labor 1982).

PREGNANCY PROTECTIONS

Early versions of sex discrimination guidelines issued by the EEOC under Title VII did not include pregnancy. In the 1972 revision of the guidelines, pregnancy was added into a disability guideline. Disabilities caused or exacerbated by pregnancy, miscarriage, abortion, childbirth, and recovery were to be treated similarly as other temporary nonjob-related disabilities. Equal treatment extended to insurance, leave, accrual of seniority, and reinstatement.

Several court cases challenged this EEOC interpretation. In 1976 in *General Electric Co. v. Gilbert et al.*, the U.S. Supreme Court ruled that a company's disability benefit plan does not violate Title VII if it fails to cover pregnancy related disabilities. No insurance plan was compelled to provide protection against all risks. The omission of pregnancy from an insurance plan does not constitute discrimination, despite the fact that pregnancy affects only women.

A year later, in *Nashville Gas Co. v. Satty*, the court ruled that Title VII does not require that a company let an employee use accrued sick days for absence owing to pregnancy. The employee was forced to take leave without pay. This ruling did uphold that the employer's policy of denying accumulated seniority to female employees returning from pregnancy leave violated Title VII (Kamerman, Kahn, and Kingston 1983).

A coalition of women's organizations, civil rights groups, and labor organizations were angry at these two court rulings and mobilized to achieve legislative reform. As a result, the Supreme Court decisions were muted by the passage of an amendment to Title VII, the Pregnancy Disability Act of 1978. The amendment extends the definition of sex discrimination to include discrimination based on pregnancy, childbirth, or related medical conditions. It requires employers to treat pregnancy and childbirth similarly to other causes of disability, in terms of employee benefits such as health insurance, disability insurance, or sick leave plans. Payment for abortion by the health insurance plan of the employer was not required, however, unless the life of the mother was endangered or medical complications occur as a result of the abortion.

Mandating that pregnant women take pregnancy leave during gestation at an arbitrarily set time which is not based on inability to work is unlawful. The law protects reinstatement rights of women on leave for pregnancy. This includes credit for previous service, accrued retirement benefits, and accumulated seniority. An employer may not terminate, refuse to hire, or refuse to promote an employee solely because she is pregnant. The act does require an employer to provide a specified number of weeks for pregnancy leave. There have been contradictory appellate court rulings over the EEOC guideline that the Pregnancy Disability Act extended maternity benefits to wives of workers as well as female employees (Kamerman, Kahn, and Kingston 1983).

DAY CARE

Adequate day care is a critical concern for both married and unmarried women who are mothers. Child care is necessary for women to enter into the labor force while children still require the supervision of an adult. The federal government has played a limited role in this area. Generally, federal day-care policy has been related to national emergencies or to poverty issues.

The largest federal day-care programs were during the Great Depression and World War II. Under the Works Projects Administration (WPA) in Roosevelt's first administration, day-care slots for about 40,000 children were financed by a combination of federal and state funds. These were phased out when the emergency had passed. Federally funded day care on a large scale was introduced by the Lanham Act of 1941. Day-care centers were set up to serve the children of workers in defense plants. During the height of World War II, places were available for 1.5 million children. This program was also halted shortly after the end of the war (Adams and Winston 1980).

In 1962, the public welfare amendments included a modest amount of money for day care for the poor. Subsidized day care was considered necessary to get the poor to work. An expanded indigent program was installed in 1967. The Social Security Act was amended to provide funds for 75 percent of the costs of child care for mothers receiving public assistance who were working or in school. One problem with the legislation is that it provided federal subsidies for care without any assurances that adequate centers would be available. A shortage of facilities developed. In 1972, Congress placed a limit on the amount of day-care funds any state could receive. In 1976 federal aid was reduced to only $24 million for all states (Twentieth Century Fund 1975).

No comparable programs for nonindigent citizens are currently available. Responsibility for securing adequate day care is left to the individual working with private sector resources. In recent times, traditional church-sponsored day-care facilities have been supplemented by for-profit day-care chains. By 1970, 60 percent of centers were privately operated for profit. State regulation of day-care facilities is usually a joint responsibility shared by social service agencies and health agencies. In addition to assuring safety and cleanliness, the regulations predominantly focus on worker-child ratios (Feinstein 1979).

One of the largest sources of day care remains individual arrangements in private homes. The United States stands out among western countries in its absence of policies that support maternity and subsidized child care. Provisions of the federal tax code do provide some relief for nonpoor families that use child care. Until 1976, tax deductions were available for child-care expenses, up to a maximum income level. The Tax Reform Act of 1976 replaced the deduction with a credit of 20 to 30 percent of the working parents' total child-care and housekeeping costs, up to a maximum of $400 for one child or $800 for two or more children (Norgren 1982).

A constant problem in the area of day care is the shortage of adequate facilities at costs women can afford. Day-care facilities remain labor intensive, limiting the possible cost savings achievable through personnel reductions. Unmet demand builds up since the low earnings of women limit the amount they can afford to pay for child care. In 1974, there were one million day-care slots available in centers that would have accommodated only one-sixth of the six million children under age six with working mothers. Since that time, the number of children with working mothers has increased dramatically (Adams and Winston 1980). Despite an extension of public schools to include kindergarten, public schools have not expanded their definition of responsibility to include extended care for children beyond normal school hours or younger than normal school age.

Republican administrations have been opposed to federal subsidies for child care and expansion of federal aid for day care since the early 1970s. In 1971, Nixon vetoed the Comprehensive Child-care Act which would have expanded the federal role by establishing a national system of compensatory preschool education and day care for children in low-income families (Norgren 1982). The Reagan administration remains uninterested in child-care policy.

WOMEN IN THE MILITARY

A particularly thorny employment issue has been the role of women in the U.S. military. Before the twentieth century, no woman had regular military status, although women often worked in affiliation with the armed services in jobs such as nursing, cooking, and laundering. The Army established a nurse corps in 1901. The Navy followed suit in 1908. During World War I, some women were enlisted in the Navy and Marine Reserves in nonnursing roles, especially clerical jobs. Between the world wars, the only women in the military were nurses.

When World War II began, all of the services established an auxiliary force for women. Although the original notion was that women would fill medical, administrative, and communication slots, they actually were used in a large number of roles, excepting direct combat. Some women were mechanics and gunnery instructors. Women ferried combat aircraft, and some became prisoners of war. By the end of the war, 260,000 women were serving in the armed services. After the war, these numbers dropped rapidly, so that by 1948, only 14,000 remained. After World War II, the military did propose regular status for women, but with enlistment quotas. Women were not to exceed 2 percent of enlisted personnel, and 10 percent of officers, excepting nurses. Through the 1960s, actual enlistments did not approach these restrictions (Stiehm 1982).

The need for military personnel during the Vietnam War increased pressure on recruiters and along with the growth of the feminist movement, led to new opportunities being opened to women. Under a 1967 law, the 2 percent restriction on enlistment of women was abolished. The previous restriction of only one woman per service being able to hold the rank of colonel or commander was removed, and women were awarded the same retirement rights as men. Two women generals were appointed in 1970.

More changes occurred during the 1970s. In 1971, married women were allowed to enlist or be appointed as officers. Female ROTC programs were begun in 1972. A Supreme Court case in 1973 established that women's dependency benefits should be similar to men's. Previously, women's dependents had to prove their status, while the spouses and children of men were assumed to be dependent. In 1975, involuntary discharge for pregnancy and parenthood was discontinued, and women were allowed to attend service academies. The warrant officer program for women was also expanded. Women ROTC candidates were also allowed to participate in flight programs (Joint Economic Committee 1978).

By 1981, 8 percent of the army was female. This large increase in the numbers of women has raised several questions. Although women now have an opportunity for a military career, many important restrictions and inequities remain. In general, the military sets higher recruitment standards for women. On the average, women military personnel are older and better educated than their male peers. More crucially, women are excluded from combat. Because women cannot command or serve in combat, a principal route to promotion is closed to them. Women top out after lieutenant colonel, since most positions above that rank require combat or combat-related experiences.

Legal Changes and Policy Outputs: Personal Freedoms, Education, and Sports

In addition to issues surrounding pay equity and the work environment, women have been treated unequally in many other areas of living. Many aspects of family and domestic life are affected by the legal system, including how violence is handled, the use of surnames, and the availability of abortion. As a result of feminist pressures, the legal system has changed its response to these issues. Women's legal access to education and sports has expanded, also from feminist pressure.

ABORTION

Until the nineteenth century, abortion was widely accepted in the United States, and the legal status of abortion followed traditional British common law. Under English common law, a fetus was not recognized in criminal cases until quickening had taken place. Quickening is the first sense of fetal movement felt by the mother, and usually occurs in the late fourth to early fifth month of pregnancy. In criminal law during this period, destruction of a fetus in the second half of pregnancy was punished less harshly than destruction of other human life. Abortion was not considered criminal before quickening (Gelb and Palley 1982).

Beginning in the nineteenth century, laws proscribing and punishing abortion began to appear in many states. Between 1821 and 1841, ten states and one territory replaced common law practices with laws making certain kinds of abortion illegal. Several factors prompted this trend. Birth rates were falling in the nineteenth century as the total white fertility rate decreased by half between 1800 and 1900. Abortion laws were aimed at preventing further decline. Underlying this movement was the motive of maintaining the white native population relative to blacks and immigrants (Petchesky 1984).

Related to this desire by the ruling elite to maintain the proportion of white natives, was a push by physicians to outlaw abortion. In the 1840s, competition grew between two groups of physicians. The "regulars," graduates of more prestigious medical schools, were losing patients to "irregulars," physicians with assorted types of training and beliefs about medicine. Irregulars began to advertise their willingness to perform abortions, fueling the fear of regulars that they would continue to lose patients.

The American Medical Association (AMA) represented the regulars. In 1859, the AMA took a formal stand favoring the suppression of abortion. The AMA not only opposed the doctrine of quickening, but called for the nonparticipation of physicians in abortion, and asserted a principle that the fetus was a living being at all stages of gestation. During this controversy, the churches did not take a strong public stand on the abortion issue. By 1900, every state except Kentucky had an antiabortion law. In Kentucky, the state courts outlawed abortion (Petchesky 1984; Gelb and Palley 1982).

The first feminist movement did not deal with the issue of abortion. By the late 1960s, some states began to revise abortion laws. In the more liberal states, abortion was permitted in specific but narrow circumstances, such as when the life or health of the mother was threatened, or in instances of rape or incest. Abortion was a major issue of the second feminist movement. Strategies were developed by feminists to further decriminalize abortion. By 1970, four states—Alaska, Hawaii, New York, and Washington—had decriminalized first trimester abortions. The resulting inequities in access fueled the national debate surrounding abortion.

One simple way to resolve the interstate inequities in access to abortion was through a Supreme Court case. In 1973, the court issued landmark rulings in the companion cases of *Roe v. Wade* and *Doe v. Bolton*. In Roe, the court ruled against a Texas law permitting abortion only to save the life of the mother, arguing that the law interfered with the right to privacy. In Doe, the court declared that states may not make abortions unreasonably difficult by erecting unreasonable or burdensome requirements. In Roe, the court divided pregnancy into three trimesters. State restrictions on abortion during the first trimester were prohibited. During the second trimester, states may regulate abortions to safeguard the life and health of the mother, but may not prohibit abortions. Only during the third trimester could states totally prohibit abortions. The allowable ground for state laws prohibiting abortions in the third trimester is to protect the life of the mother (Frohock 1983).

The two court cases of Roe and Doe remain the basis for abortion policy. Reaction to these cases galvanized strong and outspoken critics of the right to abortion, who formed an antiabortion movement to attempt to amend the U.S. Constitution to remove this choice from women. The feminist movement also coalesced to protect freedom of choice. During the 1970s, debates in Congress focused on whether federal funds could be used to fund abortions through the Medicaid program. In 1977, three different cases (*Beal v. Doe, Maher v. Roe, and Poelker v. Doe*) held that states were not required to fund abortions for indigent women. The Hyde Amendment to the appropriations act for the Department of Health, Education, and Welfare prevented the use of any federal funds for abortion. The Hyde Amendment restrictions on any federal funds was upheld in *Harris v. McRae* in 1980 (Frohock 1983).

A second battle over abortion rights surrounded the proposed Human Life Amendment to the U.S. Constitution. This proposal specified that the word "person" covered all stages of human life, including conception. This approach has not been adopted. An earlier attempt to amend the Constitution—the Federalism Amendment—used a somewhat different approach. The federalism approach stated the right to abortion was not secured by the Constitution, and that Congress and the states have concurrent powers to restrict abortion. In the mid-1980s, neither of these constitutional approaches had passed (Gelb and Palley 1982).

RAPE

Rape is the sexual assault and penetration of one person by another. Male rape of females has been defined as a major crime in English common law. The basis for this definition was that women were viewed as the property of their husbands. The rape of a wife represented the violation of one man's property by another man. While this attitude is less common today in western countries, it still prevails in many developing countries. In the Bangladesh fight for independence from Pakistan, husbands refused to remain with wives who had been raped by the invading Pakistanis.

Many feminists now argue that rape is partially a means to keep women dependent and under male control. As Brownmiller (1976) points out, the potential of rape has a restrictive impact upon all women, regardless of whether they personally have been raped. If women accept a special burden of self-protection, they live and move about in fear, and thus do not have the personal freedom, independence, and self-assurance of men.

Rape provides an example of a serious crime by men against women which is publicly deplored. However, the public denouncements mask an underlying societal ambivalence. A number of traditional myths about rape are only gradually being discredited. One is that women are vindictive or even psychopathic, and may turn an innocent sex partner in to the police out of spite and revenge. A second myth is that women want to be raped. Related to this is that women ask for rape by wearing suggestive clothing or by being in strange dark places. A third is that only "pure" women can be raped, implying that rape is less serious if a woman has a history of previous sexual experience.

These myths have prompted special rules to be required for the proof and conviction of rape. Unlike other crimes, rape must often be corroborated by evidence other than the victim's testimony. In many states, a prosecutor must prove by the presence of semen collected shortly after the rape that the woman was penetrated. In some states, the prosecutor must further prove by physical evidence that the accused was the penetrator. The consequence of these stringent rules of evidence was few convictions for rape in the past. In New York City in 1971, when stringent rules of evidence were required, 1,085 arrests for rape resulted in only 18 convictions (Ross and Barcher 1983).

The second major deviation from normal criminal procedure in rape cases was the determination of whether the woman was a willing partner in the sex act. In some states, the woman must have resisted to prove lack of consent. Bruises or other evidence of physical harm were necessary to establish that a rape occurred. In most states, a tactic by the defense to prove consent was to probe into the woman's past. Evidence bearing on previous sexual activity was brought into court, including whether she was a virgin, the number of different men she had slept with, the type of clothing she wore, and whether in the past she had voluntarily slept with the accused.

In response to feminist pressure, since 1973, half of the states and the federal government have reformed rape evidence laws. The most common reform is to restrict the use of evidence concerning the rape victim's past sexual behavior or reputation. Generally, that evidence is now first presented to a judge, sitting alone without a jury who decides whether it may be admitted at trial. Eight states have repealed their special corroboration requirements so that a rape victim's testimony alone is sufficient evidence. Other reforms are to redefine consent, so that proof of violence and physical abuse is not as important. Another reform is to redefine rape to include forced sex, whether or not actual penetration occurs.

In most states, a man cannot be convicted of raping his wife. The traditional rationale for this exclusion derives from the common law view that through marriage, a wife has consented to all future sexual contacts with the husband. Several states, including Oregon, New Jersey, Iowa, Delaware, and Massachusetts, recently have rewritten rape laws to protect wives from being sexually assaulted by husbands.

The question of before-the-fact complicity also arises in date-rapes. An older study of college dating behavior found that overt male violence or the threat of male violence was present in some dating relationships. Over half of the female respondents indicated that they had been offended by attempts at intercourse. Six percent reported incidents that involved threats or inflicted pain. Only 6 percent of these incidents were reported to parents or college authorities (Kirpatrick and Kanin 1957). Newer research has found similar rates of aggressive behavior on college campuses on dates

(Kanin and Parcell 1981). On one campus, 30 percent of female respondents had experienced an incident of sexual assault. Of these incidents, 10 percent occurred on dates (Lott, Riley, and Howard 1982).

In many instances, the rape victim is still blamed for the incident. Guilt, a sense of shame, and the fear of being subjected to intense questioning in court contribute to victims significantly underreporting incidents of rape. Often, rape occurs between family members, relatives, and acquaintances, which also contributes to underreporting. Estimates of underreporting based on sample surveys in which respondents are asked about involvement in rape incidents indicate that at least half of all rape cases are not reported. Even when rape is reported, arrests occur in only 20 to 50 percent of all cases, depending on the state. Conviction rates are also low (Schur 1984).

Treatment of rape victims in both the courts and the community has improved, due to the feminist movements. Many communities have established rape crisis lines where women can talk to someone immediately and be encouraged to report the crime. Frequently a supportive person will be provided to go with the victim to the hospital and police station. Many police departments have set up special units to investigate rapes, staffed partially with female officers. Despite this, long-term follow through and studies on the psychological consequences of rape for victims are rare.

FAMILY VIOLENCE

Women are also often the victims of other kinds of physical abuse, especially in their own homes. Wife beating was not outlawed in much of western society until the late nineteenth century. Even more time passed until domestic violence and battered women became an issue in the late 1960s and 1970s, prompted by both the feminist movement and the discovery of the relationship of violence against women to child abuse. In any year, an estimated 1.8 to 3.3 million women are battered in their own homes. Despite the myth that wife battering is a lower-class phenomenon, current studies indicate that wife beating is found in all class, race, religious, and age groups, despite higher proportions of incidents among lower socioeconomic and minority groups (Wexler 1982; Schur 1984). One prominent example of wife beating among the educated and higher socioeconomic groups was the case of Fedder, head of the Securities and Exchange Commission in the Reagan Administration. Public disclosures of the fact that the six-foot-seven-inch Fedder periodically beat his five-foot-nine-inch wife led to his resignation, despite a reputation as a good financial regulator.

Legal protection against an abusive spouse falls under state laws. In most states, there are three legal strategies to deal with abuse. One is a divorce or legal separation from an abusive husband, coupled with restraining orders to prohibit the estranged husband from the home of the wife. The second remedy is criminal prosecution of the abused. The third option is securing a protection order which requires the husband to stop abusing or threatening the wife. In some states, protection orders are not available to married couples, unless the woman files for divorce.

Each of these legal strategies has problems. Women often hesitate to pursue the divorce strategy, especially if children are involved, since the consequences are so far reaching. For women who have been removed from the job market for an extended period or who have limited job skills, divorce is equivalent to entering poverty. The fastest growing group among the new poor are divorced women with children.

Protection orders, whether connected with divorce proceedings or not, often are ineffective. In some states, an attorney must be present for a woman to obtain a protection order, a large and difficult expense for many women. Enforcing a protection order is also difficult. Although in theory, the abuser is in contempt of court if the order is violated, and could be fined or jailed, unless the state has made it a special crime to violate the order, police generally do not initiate arrest procedures. To secure relief, the woman must initiate contempt of court proceedings, usually through an attorney. Enforcement is most effective if the court orders a jail sentence, but suspends the sentence upon compliance with the order. Subsequent violations then lead to immediate incarceration.

Although spouse abuse is a crime, police are often reluctant to respond to domestic calls. If the abusive husband is arrested, and the wife files criminal charges, the most common result is probation, not a jail sentence. Thus special protection orders are still required.

Given the complications of obtaining legal relief from abusive husbands and the ineffectiveness of this relief, even if it is obtained, the feminist movement has supported the development of a network of shelters for battered women. Typically, these places will provide temporary shelter for battered women and their children, and will help them secure permanent lodgings and jobs. Federal intervention in this area has remained minimal. Many bills dealing with domestic violence have been introduced, but none have been passed. Some Title XX monies from the Social Security Act have been used to fund shelters for battered wives, although some states prohibit the use of those funds for this purpose.

CRIME AND JUSTICE

Although more likely to be victims of crimes, women are charged with criminal actions much less frequently than men. In recent years women accounted for only 10 percent of all arrests. Women in the criminal justice system in the past have been treated differently from men. At various points, laws in Connecticut, New Jersey, and Pennsylvania provided for unequal sentences for men and women. The U.S. Supreme Court has struck down these laws either on the basis that they violate the fourteenth amendment guarantee of equal protection, or because they violate a state equal rights amendment. When this happened, in Connecticut and Pennsylvania, women were released who had already served more time than the maximum allowable sentence for men for the same crime.

Many states have indeterminant sentencing laws for prisoners of both sexes which makes determination of sex-based discrimination in sentencing patterns difficult. Studies of indeterminant sentencing patterns in California revealed that women received milder sentences than male counterparts, and white females received more lenient treatment than non-white females (Moulds 1982).

Juvenile female offenders, however, are treated more harshly than their male counterparts. Young females are arrested at a much higher rate than young males for offenses that would not be considered criminal were the individual an adult. These offenses include running away from home, promiscuity, incorrigibility, and curfew violations. In some states, legal distinctions exist between men and women. Running away from home may apply to girls up to age 18, but only to boys up to age 16. In 1971, 75 percent of juvenile females in detention centers were being held for status offenses, while for boys, only 20 to 30 percent were there for status offenses. Other evidence indicates that once girls are mandated to training schools, they remain there for longer periods than boys (Ross and Barcher 1983; Moulds 1982).

The adult corollary to the pattern of treating juvenile females more harshly than juvenile males occurs in the legal treatment of women's rights to engage in sexual activity. Women are treated differently in this area, both through gender-based statutes and through differential enforcement. The most prevalent laws defining adult sexual activity as criminal deal with prostitution. Early laws were gender specific, and defined prostitution as a female crime where a woman performed sex in exchange for money or its equivalent. In a number of states, these laws have been challenged, based on the equal protection clause of the fourteenth amendment. More typical now are gender-neutral statutes.

The larger discrimination against women occurs in selected enforcement of prostitution laws. Prostitution is the only crime for which women are arrested more often than men. In 1960, 73 percent of the arrests nationally for prostitution were of women. By 1979, this figure had declined only slightly to 68 percent (Moulds 1982). Although some jurisdictions now also arrest men, the more common approach is to arrest only the women.

A lack of consensus over the appropriate solution to differential treatment by sex of female prostitutes and men hiring prostitutes exists in both the general community and among feminists. Some favor more stringent enforcement and arresting both men and women. Others favor legalization of prostitution, arguing that women will be threatened, physically abused, and forced to work for exploitative pimps and criminal elements until legalization occurs. Given the absence of agreement among feminists on this issue and the fact that prostitution is not central to the lives of most women, little change has occurred. Especially in the conservatism of the 1980s, few politicians appear willing to address legalization of "victimless" crimes, including prostitution.

FAMILY LAW AND DIVORCE

Most laws dealing with women are found under the rubric of family law. This derives from the interpretation in English common law that husband and wife were one, with reciprocal, not equal rights. Change in this interpretation of family law has been pushed by the feminist movement. One example of prior inequality in the law dealt with divorce and alimony. Alimony covers household and personal expenses, work-related costs, training and educational expenses, and recreation for the ex-spouse. In many states, divorced husbands were required to pay alimony to ex-wives, but the reverse was not true. In 1979, the U.S. Supreme Court ruled that alimony laws must be written in sex-neutral terms. The spouse with greater income or wage earning capacity may be ordered to pay alimony if the ex-spouse is in need.

Another trend is toward the granting of short-term rehabilitative alimony. In the past, husbands were often ordered to pay alimony until either the ex-wife remarried or the husband died. Increasingly, courts are placing time limits on the number of years a spouse must pay alimony, requiring payments for a period only long enough to allow the ex-spouse to establish him- or herself in a job. Both the trend toward short-term and sex-neutral alimony have improved the status of men.

Division of property in a divorce follows state laws. In the eight community property states (Arizona, California, Idaho, Louisiana, Nevada, New Mexico, Texas, and Washington), husband and wife each own one-half of all property acquired during the marriage, except for inheritances and gifts. Generally, the property is simply divided into two equal shares. While equal division may be fair if substantial property has been accumulated, many of these states do not have alimony. Women involved in divorces where little or no property has been accumulated, but where the husband has been attending professional school and has high-earning potential, are left with few financial resources (Ross and Barcher 1983).

Forty-two states operate under English common law. In these states, the property belongs to the party whose name is on the legal document of ownership, or to the party whose wages paid for it. In traditional families where the wife stayed home to keep the house and rear children, the courts interpreted this common law provision to mean that only the husband's income bought the property. In a divorce, any claim of the wife to property acquired during the marriage was based upon faithful performance of the marriage vows. If a woman was found at fault in the marriage owing to adultery, desertion, or abandoning the home, she lost all interest in jointly acquired property. An adulterous male retained interest in jointly acquired property, since the courts ruled his wages paid for it.

To remedy this situation, many common law states have passed equitable distribution laws. Courts are to divide all of the property acquired during the marriage between husband and wife at the time of the divorce. Unlike community property states, equitable distribution laws in common law states generally do not require a 50-50 split. The court may consider a variety of factors, including length of marriage, age, health, and earning abilities of spouses, contributions to homemaking and child care, and custody of the children.

A major financial asset in many divorcing families is a pension. Community property states and some common law states also provide for equitable distribution of pension benefits. In other states, pensions are considered the separate property of the person who earned them. The Burger Court has been reluctant to give divorced wives partial rights to the pensions of their ex-husbands. In 1979, the Court refused to recognize the supremacy of state laws which made wives coowners of certain federally controlled pensions. In 1981, the Court ruled that a man receiving military retirement was protected against his ex-wife's claims of coownership (Ross and Barcher 1983).

In 1982, Congress passed a law overturning the 1981 Court decision. This act helped women in states that treat pensions as joint property. This act also gave divorced wives rights to medical, commissary, and survivor benefits. An amendment to the Social Security Act in 1977 does provide some protection of Social Security benefits to ex-wives who had been married for at least ten years. Before then, the marriage requirement for protection was 20 years. Equivalent protection was also extended to the ex-wives of Foreign Service officers.

Whichever party in a divorce has custody of the children may be entitled to child support payments. These payments may include money for food, clothing, shelter, education, medicine, medical insurance, and if financially possible, extras such as summer camp, special lessons, and college education.

Enforcement remains a major problem for alimony and child support.

Studies show that most men default on payments, even in the first year after the divorce. If a husband defaults, an ex-wife must go to court. The court could order garnishment of the salary of the ex-husband. Court expenses often prevented many women from seeking legal relief for default. In 1974, Congress passed Title IV-D of the Social Security Act, requiring states to provide aid to women in collecting child support payments by representing the women in court. If the woman is on public assistance, the aid is free. If the woman is not on public assistance, a small initial fee is charged, and extra charges are taken out of the amount collected.

One solution to the difficulty of enforcing alimony and child support payments would be state laws requiring automatic deductions of these monies from the ex-spouse's wages. New York has passed a law requiring automatic deductions, if the husband has been delinquent in the past. This procedure is effective only as long as the ex-spouse remains at the same job in the same state.

A major problem in divorces is who gets the children. In the past, courts followed the tender year doctrine which presumed that mothers were the better custodian for young children under age seven. In most states, custody decisions are now based on the best interest of the child, without presumption as to which parent is best suited. A growing trend is joint custody, where parents are jointly responsible for the child-making decisions and arrangements on a daily basis. Another trend is split custody, where parents alternately have sole custody of the child, with the other parent having visitation rights. These newer child custody arrangements usually preclude child support payments to the woman, even if she earns less. These trends in custody arrangements have generally benefited men by increasing the probability that fathers will secure legal custody.

Choice of a name presents special questions for women, both at the time of marriage and divorce. Traditionally, women assumed their husband's last name at the time of marriage and kept it until death. In the past, many states required that wives adopt their husband's names. As late as 1981, Kentucky required a married woman to apply for a driver's license in her husband's surname, even if she used her maiden name for all other purposes. By the mid-1980s, most states had abandoned this requirement. Married women may keep and divorced women may reassume their maiden names.

COMMERCIAL CREDIT

Until legal reform, women were treated as second-class citizens by commercial credit institutions. Single women had more trouble obtaining credit than single men. In one example, a 40-year-old woman was required to have her father cosign a bank loan. Married women lacked a credit history, since most records were kept in their husbands' names. Creditors generally required a woman upon marriage to reapply for credit, whereas equivalent requirements were not placed on men. Divorced and widowed women had trouble reestablishing credit, because credit records had been kept in their husbands' names. In addition, divorced women had trouble qualifying for loans because alimony and child support were not counted as income. Loan institutions also frequently refused to count a wife's income when a married couple applied for credit. In other cases, the wife's income would only be counted if she disavowed any intention of having children soon (Chapman 1976).

Women's groups were instrumental in pushing through reforms in the early 1970s in commercial credit. Several groups, including the National Organization of Women (NOW), the Women's Equity Action League (WEAL), and the National Women's Political Caucus (NWPC), formed a coalition to provide technical expertise for the drafting of reform legislation, grassroots support in the form of letters and telephone calls, and other kinds of efforts. Later these feminist groups were joined by more traditional women's groups, such as the American Association of University Women (AAUW), the National Council of Jewish Women, and the National Federation of Business and Professional Women's Clubs.

This coalition of women's groups succeeded in securing the passage of the 1974 Equal Credit Opportunity Act, which banned credit discrimination on the basis of sex. Even after the passage of the authorizing legislation, controversy continued to surround the development of the regulations. The final regulations represented a compromise between creditors and women's groups. Particularly at issue was whether creditors had to provide a statement about the reasons for denying or terminating credit. Feminists wanted a required written statement. Creditors opposed any justification for denial or termination of credit. The compromise was that creditors had to explain their justifications of negative decisions, but not necessarily in writing. Amendments to the act passed in 1976 required written justifications and strengthened several other provisions (Gelb and Palley 1982).

The 1974 Equal Credit Opportunity Act had several provisions. Accounts of married couples are to be listed in both names, with both individuals maintaining a credit history. Lenders were prohibited from inquiring about birth control practices or childbearing intentions. If desired, a lender must open a married woman's account under a hyphenated or maiden name. Credit may not be terminated after a change in the applicant's marital status, unless there is evidence of a new inability or unwillingness to pay. Separate credit may be extended to spouses, if each so desires and qualifies.

Overall the act has been effective in obtaining equal credit opportunity for women. After the initial flurry of activity surrounding enforcement of the new act, few law suits have been brought under its jurisdiction. One indication of success of the law is the increase in female home ownership. In 1980, single women were the purchasers of one-third of all condominiums and one-tenth of all houses in the United States.

EDUCATION AND SPORTS

A number of laws have addressed gender-based inequality in education. Women have experienced unequal treatment as students, as employees, and as participants in school-sponsored sports. In the past, educational opportunities for women have been limited by sex role expectations of proper and improper behavior for men and women. At the elementary and high school levels, girls have been rewarded for being docile, while boys have been encouraged to be aggressive and inquisitive. Girls have often been steered away from mathematics and science.

At the college level, young women experienced several types of discrimination. Many of the most prestigious institutions did not admit women. Particularly in southern states, sex-segregated public institutions were common. Often, the only public colleges available to women had a history of being teachers colleges. Female students were often discouraged from considering advanced professional training. Through much of the 1960s, qualified women were frequently denied admission to law, medical, and other advanced programs. Until the 1970s, most prestigious business schools limited the number of women in entering M. B. A. classes. The admission of women into trade, agricultural, and technical programs was also very low.

Traditionally, women were confined to lower level positions in educational institutions. Almost all elementary teachers were women, but few jobs as principals and superintendents were held by women. Except in women's colleges, women were virtually nonexistent in tenure-track faculty jobs and high level administrative posts.

School-sponsored sports remained a bastion of gender-based discrimination. Many schools and universities did not provide any team sports for girls. Where female teams were provided, they were funded at a significantly lower level, had less equipment, and less access to good practice facilities and practice times. Coaches for male sports have been better paid than coaches for female sports at all educational levels, from junior high schools to universities. Scholarship opportunities for women in athletics were extremely limited or nonexistent.

Major Legal Protections

The decade of the 1960s brought a variety of legislation to protect women, some specifically aimed at education and some more general. The more general legislation includes the Equal Pay Act of 1963, Title VII of the Civil Rights Act of 1964, and the Comprehensive Health Manpower Training Amendments to the Public Health Service Act. Four pieces of legislation focused more explicitly on education: Title IX of the Education Amendments of 1972, the Women's Educational Equity Act of 1974, the Vocational Education Act of 1976, and the Career Education Incentive Act of 1977.

In addition to legislation, the equal protection clause of the fourteenth amendment has been used by women to secure access to previously all male schools. This clause can be used to attack discrimination carried out by state and local governments. Courts have ruled ambiguously on cases brought under this rubric. Some cases have supported the abolition of sex-segregated schools. Such cases resulted in the sexual desegregation of the previously all male University of Virginia at Charlottesville, and the admission of men to the previously all female School of Nursing at the University of Mississippi for Women. The equal protection clause has also resulted in the sexual desegregation of secondary schools, including Boston Latin and Stuyvesant High School in New York City. Suits attempting to admit men to the formerly all female Winthrop College in South Carolina, and girls to the all male Central High School in Philadelphia were not successful (Ross and Barcher 1983).

The Women Educational Equity Act of 1974 authorized a program of grants and contracts to promote equality for women in education. A national advisory council evaluates the act yearly. This is the only federal legislation devoted solely to the achievement of educational equity for women and girls. While very modestly funded, it did provide grants for special projects, including the development of women's studies curricula and the examination of the special needs of rural women and girls. In 1982 attempts to fold the act into a block grant were unsuccessful, but funding was reduced further (Lipman-Blumen 1984; National Advisory Council on Women's Educational Programs 1980).

In 1972, only 5 percent of all employees in agricultural, trade, and technical jobs were women. In 1976, the Vocational Education Act required the appointment of full-time personnel to assist the states in implementing equal access for women in vocational education. States had to provide plans with detailed methods to assure equal access for both sexes. Special groups of women, such as displaced homemakers were given special opportunities. Partially as a result of the act, some women shifted from traditional female areas (clerical, beauty culture, and health services) to mixed programs (data processing, accounting, real estate sales, and hotel and motel management). However, only a slight increase of women in nontraditional technical and heavy industrial jobs occurred (National Advisory Council on Women's Educational Programs 1981).

The Career Education Incentive Act of 1977 established a grant program to increase career awareness and planning. Monies were provided for projects to eliminate sex bias and stereotyping in career education (Mastalli 1977). Despite this, considerable stereotyping in career choices still exists.

Title IX of the Education Amendments of 1972 has been one of the major pieces of federal legislation dealing with sex discrimination in education. This statute prohibits discrimination based on sex in education programs or activities receiving federal financial assistance. Programs directly operated by the federal government were not covered, nor were public undergraduate institutions which traditionally and continually have admitted only one sex. Also excluded were institutions training military and merchant marine personnel, or institutions controlled by religious institutions.

Many educationally related social organizations were not covered, such as university based sororities and fraternities, Girl Scouts and Boy Scouts, the YMCA, and the YWCA. Colleges and universities could provide segregated living facilities by sex, but the same housing rules, regulations, fees, and services must be available to both men and women. Scholarships cannot be restricted to one sex unless the restrictions were established by will, trust, or foreign governments. Previously, public schools often required pregnant girls to withdraw. This school policy was prohibited under Title IX. Unlike the past, schools could not prevent the return of unwed mothers after the births of their babies.

Enforcement of Legal Protections

Little efforts to enforce Title IX were made immediately after its passage. A three-year delay occurred before any regulations defining the discrimination forbidden under Title IX were passed. Title IX was generally ignored initially. Between 1972 and 1976, HEW resolved only one of every five complaints filed with the agency. The average delay on cases it did resolve was 14 months, but many took up to three years. A large backlog of unprocessed complaints grew. HEW had the authority to conduct compliance reviews independently of complaints. By 1976, only 12 of the nation's 16,000 school districts were subjected to a compliance review. Feminist groups sued HEW to compel it to enforce the law. In 1977, HEW agreed to a court order laying out time tables and procedures to handle the backlog. Until 1979, the legal basis for law suits brought by women against discriminatory schools remained unclear. In 1982, a Supreme Court case brought under Title IX established that the act also protected teachers and employees who work directly with students from employment discrimination.

The area in which the application of Title IX has been the most controversial has been that of sports and athletics. Since the development of Title IX regulations was postponed, many of the earlier suits which were successful in protecting the opportunities of women to engage in school sports were brought under the equal protection clause of the fourteenth amendment. The regulations issued under Title IX stated that schools may not bar any student from playing in interscholastic or intramural athletics because of sex. However, schools could sponsor separate teams for boys and girls when team selection is based on competitive skills or the activity is a contact sport. In reality, most team sports are covered by one of those two exemptions. If there is only one team, girls must be allowed to try out for it unless it involves a contact sport.

The regulations also mandate equal athletic opportunity, but do not require that equal amounts of money be spent on boys and girls. The impact of the regulations has been to improve the opportunities for women in athletics. The regulations have, in many instances, pushed schools to create more girls' teams. At the college and university level, some athletic scholarships are available for women whereas before Title IX, there were almost none. In nonrevenue raising sports, the treatment of women has more closely approximated that of men. However, equality in athletic opportunity has not been achieved. Football and men's basketball are big revenue sports for many schools and continue to get the lion's share of athletic resources.

A major court case, *Grove City College v. Bell,* has limited the protection offered by Title IX. Grove City College is a private educational institution that refuses federal financial assistance. However, many of its students received federal funding in the form of Basic Educational Opportunity Grants (Pell grants). The college was asked to sign an assurance of compliance with Title IX and refused to do so, since the school declined institutional federal funds. The controversy in the case centered around the wording of Title IX which forbids sex discrimination in "federally assisted education programs or activities." What constituted a program under the act? How broadly or narrowly should "program" be defined?

The U.S. Justice Department in the Reagan administration has been hostile to Title IX, and filed a brief in the Grove City case supporting the college. The brief supported the position that if an institution received federal money only through grants to its students, then only the financial aid program, not the entire institution, is covered by Title IX. The court ruling contained ambiguities. While one portion supported a broad interpretation that would cover the whole institution, the court also ruled that the receipt of student Pell grants did not trigger institution-wide coverage under Title IX. Only the financial aid program could be regulated under Title IX if the institution did not receive other federal funds. Since almost no athletic programs receive institutional federal funds, the Grove City case undercut the application of Title IX to both athletic programs and to general university programs. Following the Grove City case, as yet unsuccessful legislation was introduced to overturn that decision.

Under the Reagan administration, earlier thrusts to promote sexual equality in educational institutions have been thwarted. Many of the protections for equal opportunity in education rest upon regulations and enforcement of those regulations by executive branch agencies. The administration has been passive in pushing equal opportunity regulations, and in many instances, has argued the opposing case. As a result of the Reagan Administration philosophy, progress toward sexual equality in educational institutions has greatly slowed.

11　*The Dilemmas of High Technology for Changes in the Status of Women*

This chapter will examine the dilemmas high technology presents for changes in the status of women. One area in which technological innovations more slowly produce status changes for women is the political arena. This dilemma is first explored, followed by an examination of the paradoxes technological changes have introduced in the home and the work place and in reproduction.

WOMEN AND POLITICS

Women as Voters and Political Activists

Women are increasingly important as voters. In 1920, the first national election in which women could vote, only one-third of eligible women voted versus two-thirds of eligible men. In 1952, the voter turnout rate was 70 percent for women and 80 percent for men (Campbell et al. 1960). Since 1964, more women than men went to the polls to vote for U.S. president. Part of the difference in the numbers of men and women voting is due to growing similarities in the voting turnout of the two sexes and growing dissimilarities in numbers in the population. Before 1945, men outnumbered women in the United States. Currently, women outnumber men, especially in the older age groups. By 1976, there were 6.5 million more women than men over the age of 18. The political participation gap between men and women voting (expressed in actual numbers) more than doubled between 1964 and 1976 (Baxter and Lansing 1983).

More women are working in political parties, campaigning for others, and in interest groups that are seeking changes for public policy. In recent decades, women have become increasingly important as political activists in electoral campaigns. Survey data from the American National Election studies indicate that increasing numbers of women are trying to influence the votes of others. In 1952, 33 percent of men and 22 percent of women tried to influence others' votes. Both groups increased by 1976, with 44 percent of men and 32 percent of women attempting to change the votes of others.

The proportion of people who are more active, attending political rallies, giving money to candidates, and working for a campaign, is much smaller. In these activities, women have approached the participation rates of men in attending rallies (7 percent) and working for a campaign (4 percent), but not in giving money. In 1952, 6 percent of men and 3 percent of women gave money to a political campaign. The rate of giving for women by 1976 doubled to 7 percent, but still lagged behind the 11 percent figure for men.

Women are also less likely than men to write a letter to a public official. In 1976, 31 percent of men and 25 percent of women reported that they had written to public officials. Part of the explanation of the increase in the number of women writing letters is rising education. Only 10 percent of women with a grade school education had written to public officials, versus 26 percent with a high school education and 40 percent with a college education (Baxter and Lansing 1983). In addition to low educational levels, another factor that may depress political activity is the presence of young children, especially for single parents (Sapiro 1983a).

Women as Elected Officials

Much of this increase in the participation of women is linked to the second wave of birth control, introduced in 1960, and the consequent lower birth rates in the 1960s and 1970s. However, in the 1980s, a political paradox remains. Despite the increased participation of women in some political activities, they remain removed from the centers of power. Women are less likely than men to win elections themselves, or to secure appointments to elite decision-making posts (Baxter and Lansing 1983).

One explanation for the paradox is that unlike status changes for women in other areas, such as employment, education, and sports, changes in status and participation of women as candidates cannot be legislated. Rather, an increase in the number of women candidates and actual office holders depends upon changes in overall public attitudes, which may lag significantly behind technological change. In the 1980s, many U.S. citizens remained opposed to women personally assuming political power. The proportion of people willing to vote for a female presidential candidate held constant from 1958 to 1969 at 55 to 58 percent (Ferree 1974). This proportion increased to 80 percent by 1978. While 80 percent potential support for a female presidential candidate represents a dramatic increase in support for women politicians, 20 percent still refused to vote for a woman candidate on the basis of sex alone. Opposition of 20 percent to a female presidential candidate constitutes a formidable obstacle to electoral success.

In presidential systems, public opinion more directly impinges on selection of the chief national executive than in parliamentary systems. In presidential systems, voters express preferences for chief executives directly. In parliamentary systems, chief executives are selected by members of the dominant party in parliament. In the former, the selection is by the masses; in the latter, the selection is by the party elite, who may place greater importance than the overall electorate on organizational skill, negotiating ability, and contribution to the party. While the United States has not yet elected a female president, three parliamentary systems have selected female chief executives—Golda Meir in Israel, Margaret Thatcher in Great Britain, and Indira Gandhi in India.

Differences in social background affected the willingness of respondents to support female candidates. Using National Opinion Research Center General Social Survey data from 1972 to 1978, more support for women in politics was found among the young, the highly educated, and those who attended church less frequently. Sex, race, and party identification had little impact on support for women in politics (Welch and Sigelman 1982). Changing demographics will further affect general support for female candidates. Over time, less educated older cohorts will be replaced by younger more educated cohorts who are more likely to support women politicians.

For years, women have been said to be the power behind their husbands' political careers. Yet, until the recent past, rarely have women held political office themselves. The few exceptions were typically women whose husbands died while in office. These widows were subsequently elected to their deceased husbands' former positions on a sympathy vote. Examples of this "inheritance" of an office by political wives include Margaret Chase Smith, U.S. Senator from Maine, and Lindy Boggs, U.S. Representative from Louisiana. Lurleen Wallace from Alabama, succeeded her husband, George Wallace, to the governorship, but was largely viewed as a puppet of her still living and very active husband who was constitutionally prevented from succeeding himself. Another notable, Muriel Humphrey, briefly held her husband's Senate seat when Hubert Humphrey died.

In the 1970s, women began to acquire political office on their own. Two women governors who had long been active on their own behalf in party politics—Ella Grasso of Connecticut and Dixie Ray of Washington— were elected governors of their respective states. The number of women elected to city and municipal offices in the late 1970s almost doubled. Yet despite this increase in women officeholders, women remain very underrepresented in the halls of power. In an era when women are becoming involved in (with increasing success) previously male government and corporate hierarchies, they have experienced less success in politics.

Why the paradox of increasing success in nonpolitical arenas and as yet limited success in acquiring political office? Part of the answer lies in the different criteria for success in hierarchical organizations versus democratic politics. In hierarchical organizations, equal opportunity can be legislated and regulated by overseeing government authorities. Compliance on the part of organizations does not require agreement with the principle of equal opportunity for women, but merely fear of prosecution for violating the law. In hierarchical organizations, merit, at least in principle, matters more than popularity.

In democratic politics, no legislation can dictate equal opportunity for women or any other group. Informal ties, organizational skills, fund-raising abilities, and linkages to those currently in power rather than merit criteria to assess who will best perform the job once in office all dominate in determining who wins elections. Recruitment of political leaders is related to achievement in other spheres—educational, occupational, social, and athletic arenas. Until the last decade, women did not have the same access to the most elite universities, and professions such as law and business. Yet elite universities and legal and business professions have been the traditional recruitment grounds for national politicians. Participation in civic clubs, such as the Jay Cees, and athletic clubs are another important route to develop the necessary contacts to run for political office and to finance campaigns. Women historically have been precluded from these outlets.

Women have been more successful in achieving local political offices than in acquiring national political office. Overall, the proportion of women office holders increased from 4 percent in 1975 to 12 percent in 1980. In 1975, 8 percent of state legislators were women. This increased to 12 percent in 1980, and 15 percent by 1984. Women also acquired more leadership positions in state legislatures—8 percent by 1980. Two women—Martha Layne Collins in Kentucky and Madeline Kunin in Vermont—served as governors of their states in 1984. In the same year, five women served as lieutenant governors, 11 as secretaries of state, and 11 as state treasurers.

At the local level, in 1984, women were mayors of 90 cities with populations of 30,000 or more. Prominent among these were the mayors of major cities, including Diane Feinstein of San Francisco, and Katherine Whitmire of Houston (Baxter and Lansing 1983; Lipman-Blumen 1984; Doan and Avery 1985). In the recent past, a woman, Jane Byrne of Chicago, had served as mayor of the third largest city in the United States. In 1975, 2 percent of all county commissioners were women. By 1981, that figure had increased to 7 percent. For other local government offices, the percentage of women in the same time frame increased from 4 to 11 percent (Hedblom 1983).

At the national level, there has been no improvement in the number of female representatives in the U.S. House. By 1984, as in 1975, the proportion of women serving in the House was only 4 percent. Only 2 percent of U.S. Senators in 1984 were women. Since women constitute over 50 percent of the population, they remain greatly underrepresented at all levels of politics. The modest gains in representation that have occurred at the state and local levels have not been replicated at the national level.

Why have women experienced modest gains in electoral success at the local and state level, but no gains at the national level? This pattern of initial local success resembles the pattern experienced by other groups previously excluded from political power, such as the Irish, Italians, Jews, and blacks. For groups excluded from power, national success comes slowly, only after significant experience has been acquired at lower levels of politics. The slow acquisition of national power by women has been experienced by other groups.

Yet women experience additional handicaps in winning elections at higher levels of politics. Women are still viewed societally in terms of domestic roles, while men are viewed in terms of occupational roles. Women politicians have to convince the electorate that their home responsibilities are not too demanding to permit the time commitment required by political office holding. A study of men's and women's campaigns found that women were asked more often how they would manage their family responsibilities if elected, and whether their husbands and children approved of their political activity (Mezy 1978). Men were not asked whether their wives and children approved of their political activity. Rather, familial approval of male political participation was assumed. In the mid-1970s, U.S. Representative Martha Keys of Kansas married fellow Representative Andrew Jacobs of Indiana. They had met while serving on the House, Ways and Means Committee. Each sought reelection in their districts. The political marriage became a campaign issue for Keys, but not for Jacobs (Sapiro 1983b).

Because of the liability that people assume women have due to family responsibilities, many women politicians are either single, widowed, or do not become active in politics until their children are adults (Epstein 1981). For example, Katherine Whitmire, mayor of Houston, was a widow when she sought and obtained political office. Barbara Jordan, former U.S. Representative from Texas and sometime spokesperson for the Democratic Party, never married. Nor had Elizabeth Holtzman, a Harvard lawyer and U.S. Representative from New York who played a visible role in the Watergate hearings in the mid 1970s. Geraldine Ferraro, the Democratic vice-presidential nominee in 1984, had older children before acquiring national attention.

Another difficulty women face is that of raising money for campaigns.

Women have more difficulty raising money, partially because they are more typically nonincumbents, and partially because they are women. Lower budgets for campaigns, resulting from fund-raising difficulties, often lead women to not make full use of modern campaign techniques, including television commercials and polling throughout the campaign. This, in turn, lowers the probability of being elected, especially for challengers.

What factors, if any, facilitate the election of women to political office? Diamond (1977) found that the percentage of women in the lower houses of state legislatures was inversely related to the salary of the position. In states where salaries were low, making state legislative office comparatively less attractive, women were more likely to be elected. Women were also more frequently found in lower houses, which were larger, than in smaller upper houses.

In cities, women are more likely to be mayors when mayors are appointed than when they are elected. This indicates that elites have been more responsive than the general electorate to selecting women as political leaders. Women were more likely to be chosen to a city council in at-large elections than in single-member district elections. One interpretation is that in single-member district elections, women candidates are typically in a one-on-one race versus a man, a situation where sex and discrimination are likely factors in electoral outcomes. In at-large elections, a citizen may vote for one or two women among a multi-candidate field, not having to directly choose between a man and a woman, but voting in some proportions for both. Demographic factors also appear to be related to female electability. Larger wealthier communities but with a lower proportion of home owners are most likely to elect female council members. Larger communities are more likely to elect female mayors than very small communities (Welch and Karnig 1979).

Women as Appointed Officials and Staff

Women have also made modest inroads in acquiring appointive office, but still remain underrepresented relative to their proportion of the overall population. By 1981, 12 percent of appointed positions in governors' cabinets were held by women. Only four states—Arizona, South Carolina, Texas, and Utah—had no women appointed to state cabinet posts. Women, however, appear to be concentrated in traditionally feminine areas. Of the women in state cabinets, 20 percent are in health and human service areas, followed by 10 percent in labor and industrial relations, 8 percent in finance, budget, and fiscal management, and only 4 percent in commerce (Lipman-Blumen 1984).

At the federal level, women are half of all employees, but in 1979 only held 6 percent of all high-ranking positions from GS-13 and above. As at the state level, the success of women at the federal level in achieving a high rank varies greatly by area. In 1979 in the Department of Housing and Urban Development, which had a female secretary, the percentage of women GS-13 through GS-15 was 17 percent, and the percentage of women in the Senior Executive Service and GS-16 through GS-18 was 13 percent. DHEW also had comparatively high proportions of women—20 percent in GS-13 through GS-15, and 12 percent in the Senior Executive Service and GS-16 through GS-18.

By contrast, the Departments of Interior, Agriculture, Transportation, and Defense all had comparatively small proportions of women in high-ranking positions. Defense, typically regarded as a man's world, had only 5 percent women at the GS-13 through GS-15 level, and 2 percent in the highest ranks. Agriculture, also long regarded as a male domain, was only slightly better with 4 percent in each category.

Schedule C jobs are political appointees in noncivil service positions. These jobs rank higher than the highest civil service job. The Carter administration made a concerted effort to include women in these appointments, and appointed women to 31 percent of all Schedule C jobs. This was an increase of 17 percent over the appointments made by the Ford administration. This improvement in female representation in federal political appointments, however, did not last. As of 1983, the Reagan administration appointments of women were under 10 percent (Hedblom 1983).

Do women perform politically sensitive jobs differently from men? One study of male and female congressional staffers answered "maybe"—yes in style, but no in outcome. Johannes (1984) looked specifically at staffers who engaged in casework—active intervention with the federal bureaucracy on behalf of constituents. Casework is a field occupied predominantly by women. In congressional offices, women are more likely to be assigned to conduct casework than to engage in legislative analysis. Women seem more committed to casework than their male counterparts, less skeptical of constituents' problems, more forthright and concerned with norms of equity, and more apt to link casework to other legislative functions. However, men and women were both equally successful in obtaining desired outcomes and dispositions from the bureaucracy.

Women as Party Activists

What role have women played in party politics, often a precursor to electoral activity and political appointments? Women have been less active in party politics than have men. A study of Michigan delegates to national party conventions found rising visibility for women in the Michigan party elites. Part of the increase in visibility for women, however, was due to mandated changes in the Democratic Party rules for selecting convention delegates and officers, which specified quotas for the numbers of women and minorities.

Women active in party politics are becoming more similar to men active in party politics. Between 1964 and 1976, differences between male and female elites in terms of social background, political status, political careers, and perceptions of the political process were decreasing. Issue orientations were predominantly a matter of party rather than gender, except for issues dealing directly with gender roles (Jennings and Farah 1981). In a study of presidential campaign contributors, higher education, childhood family social status, and political interest of parents reduced male-female differences in joining the elite. Parental transmission of party identification is less dominated by fathers and husbands for elite female activists, than for other women in their age groups. Elite female party activists were more likely to come from families where the mother's political beliefs were relevant to the family (Powell, Brown, and Hedges 1981).

The Political Paradox

Women are increasing in participation in all phases of the political process, but are still underrepresented in many areas, especially in elective offices. Women still experience handicaps not encountered by men. To be elected to political office in most cases requires the overt approval of over 50 percent of the electorate, or at least of that portion of it that turns out to vote. There is still a portion of that electorate that will not vote for female candidates simply because they are women. In highly competitive races, and in races where an incumbent is being challenged—the typical type of race women candidates face—a successful candidate cannot afford to automatically lose 15 to 20 percent of the electorate. This proportion of voters who oppose women candidates merely because they are women is diminishing over time, but this diminution is a slow process. Since equality cannot be regulated or mandated in politics but rather depends upon shifts in mass public opinion, change in opportunities and success for women is slower in politics than in other spheres.

Birth control has played a crucial role in the increasing participation of women in all phases both as party activists and candidates for political office. Since the public is quite concerned about whether women candidates can meet their familial obligations in addition to their political obligations—a concern not applied to male candidates—controlling the number and timing of births is crucial for women who contemplate a political career. This public concern, rather than an inability to meet both obligations simultaneously, still makes it difficult for women with small children to enter high level politics.

WOMEN AND PRODUCTION TECHNOLOGIES

High technology is modifying the traditional structure in the U.S. labor force. Foremost among these new technologies is the expansion of the role of the computer and processes for collecting, handling, and manipulating information. Some argue that the economy has shifted from one where materials and physical products are both the means and the ends of production to an economy where information is the predominant material and result of production processes. The wide dissemination of automated processes is a trend characterized by accelerated use of computers for control of production and the increased use of robotics.

These trends have both positive and negative implications for the role of women in society. Among the positive aspects of the introduction and dissemination of high technologies is a reduction in the proportion of heavy labor blue-collar jobs, relatively high-paying jobs from which women have traditionally been excluded. The shop manager and middle management jobs of the future will depend more on overseeing automated processes and less on physical strength, potentially opening up more of these jobs to women. In contrast to earlier industrial processes, high technology also makes possible greater decentralization of work schedules and location. Women may find both flexible work schedules and paid work at home increasingly possible.

High technology in the work place also has potential negative impacts on the status of women. Although high-paying blue-collar jobs are disappearing, many of the new jobs are poorly paid jobs in the growing service sector, which includes such areas as sanitation and cleaning, fast-food chains, and narrowly defined technician jobs and nursing aides in the health-care area. The sophisticated well-paying jobs resulting from new computerized processes may be limited in number. High technology in the office, especially the wide dissemination of word processing, may reduce the number of secretarial jobs. Traditionally, secretarial work has been one of the most secure though not highly paid predominantly female jobs. Increasing requirements for technical skills in secretarial work also set those jobs apart from general administration and further reduce their potential as a route for upward mobility.

New work place technologies are increasingly oriented toward collection, storage, retrieval, and manipulation of data. These technologies often require familiarity with mathematical concepts, science, engineering, and electronics. The elite of this brave new work world are those who develop and expand these new technologies. Yet engineering, electronics, and other scientifically based occupations have typically been male domains. If women are labeled, either by others or by themselves, as inferior in math and science, they will be unable to compete for many positions among the work force elite. The process of labeling and reaction is a long one, beginning in teenage years or earlier. Changing this socialization of women into areas of study that will lead only to low-paying jobs is difficult, requiring changes in many institutions and socializing agents, ranging from parents and teachers to counselors. It also includes changing the expectations and self-images of women themselves.

WOMEN AND REPRODUCTION TECHNOLOGIES

Reproduction technologies will also greatly affect the role and status of women. Improved and more reliable birth control technologies have increased the control women have over their own bodies, allowing women to reliably separate sexual intercourse from procreation for the first time in human history. Women can now control both the total numbers and the timing of children they bear. Improved control has contributed to advancement within the labor force. Birth control is a great potential equalizer in most male-female relationships.

Yet despite the potential for birth control in promoting equality between the sexes, no external force can readily mandate or regulate marriages and the interpersonal relationships to assure that this potential is realized. As in politics, changes in interpersonal relationships depend upon shifts in the attitudes and behavior of the participants. These changes take time. While birth control has altered and expanded the number and type of relationships available to men and women, removing the opprobrium of casual sexual relationships, most people desire long-term intimate relationships at some point.

Birth control has been a catalyst for a variety of social changes which have made the exploration of both men and women for long-term intimate relationships easier. Yet simultaneously, some would argue that many of the associated changes have made the maintenance of a long-term relationship more difficult. Women are working in greater numbers and achieving greater economic independence. No longer solely dependent upon their husbands for economic support, women are more willing to divorce and leave an unsatisfying relationship. The ending of a marriage or long-term relationship is no longer the stigma that it was in the past, further contributing to increasing divorce rates. The greater number of unmarried adults in the population makes singlehood more attractive and satisfying. While birth control has created a potential for equalizing the roles in long-term relationships, it has also made leaving them easier.

One dilemma is that the potential created by birth control for greater equality in long-term intimate relationships is often not realized. Once in a potentially long-term intimate relationship, most people are guided by the past. They remember the sex-based division of labor in their own homes as children. For most people, this division was a traditional one, where the mother was less geographically mobile, more nurturing, and more risk averse than the father. Mothers frequently did not work outside the home, did almost all of the work in the home, and had the prime responsibility for raising children. Part of the current dilemma introduced by birth control, compounded by the feminist movement and the policy changes it achieved, is the difficulty of developing new nongender-based roles within the context of the home. Juxtaposed with the great new potential created by birth control for the abolition of traditional gender-based roles are mental maps from the past of appropriate behavior and prior socialization.

While birth control has increased the control women have over childbearing, it has not eliminated the necessity for it. Some couples in society must continue to have children to assure perpetuation of the species. Many wish—some strongly—to have children. For those couples, modern birth control usually makes it possible to achieve the desired number and spacing of children, while allowing the woman to pursue other career objectives.

The ability to delay childbearing through birth control technology, however, does not always result in the desired ideal family, since some proportion of couples who delay childbearing experience undesired infertility. Often women are postponing childbearing until later ages when fertility problems are more common. New technologies to correct infertility are increasingly available, solving this dilemma for some but not all prospective parents.

A more important dilemma remains of who shall rear the children? The presence of children in a household creates more work and obligations for adults in the household. For the affluent, some of these obligations may be met through purchased services, such as day care, tutoring, and domestic help to clean, cook, and wash clothes. Many households, however, are not able to afford all of these services, leaving these chores to someone in the household. Even for affluent households, someone must make the purchasing arrangements. Despite the fact that birth control shatters the physiological basis for the sex-based stereotype of the female as the more nurturing, less geographically mobile, and more risk averse, in most households this someone carrying out these child-rearing chores is still the woman.

Nor can all duties associated with child care be purchased, even for the affluent. Since children are not robots or even pets, they require parental attention and interaction for mental and emotional well-being. For special events important to the children, there is no substitute for the presence of a proud parent. Similarly, consistent daily interaction, usually in the evening, is important to the emotional development of children.

CONCLUSIONS

Technology has the great potential to radically transform the quality of living for those it touches. As with any power, this potential may be used to improve the quality of life. As with any fundamental change, dislocations and paradoxes may occur, creating personal and societal dilemmas.

Political power is the ultimate means for the allocation of values within society. Birth control has provided women the flexibility in career and family planning to facilitate political involvement. One of the greatest paradoxes is that the acquisition of political power by women has not matched their gains in other areas. In a democratic society, the success of women in politics depends upon shifts in mass attitudes. These shifts cannot be legislated or mandated, and occur even more slowly than shifts in the attitudes of elites.

As with birth control, work technologies have the potential for providing greater and more fulfilling career choices for women. As with birth control, other factors besides technology impinge upon the realization of this potential. Throughout history, work technologies have never succeeded in fundamentally altering the basic gender-based stereotypes that men are more geographically mobile, less nurturing, and risk-takers, while women are less geographically mobile, more nurturing, and risk averse. The computer age is no exception to this trend.

Work technologies may result in marginal improvements in the status of women, within the confines of the basic stereotype established by the prevailing reproductive technologies. If public attitudes toward women have not shifted in society generally to reflect the increasing irrelevance of the gender-based stereotypes of men and women due to birth control, improvements in work technologies will not necessarily improve the status of women. Legislation and regulation can promote sex equality in the work environment, but only if there are pools of female applicants with the requisite training and skills. If traditional gender-based stereotypes remain, despite the fact that they are no longer grounded in physiological reality, women will continue to be guided into less abstract, mathematical, and scientific areas of study which will limit their career options and success.

While birth control has removed most of the physiological basis for gender-based stereotypes, equality in interpersonal relationships cannot be easily legislated or regulated, any more than it can be in politics. Dilemmas for improvements in the status of women remain in interpersonal relationships, despite the significant impact of birth control. Birth control diminishes the double standard for sexual behavior of men and women, making it easier for women to find casual sexual partners and to have the same freedom as men to explore a variety of relationships. However, the dilemma of forming a long-term relationship, and of the roles of men and women within that relationship remain. The power of mental maps from the past is great. The difficulty for women of achieving equality of treatment within interpersonal relationships is compounded by children. This is a fundamental unresolved dilemma since societies must reproduce as well as produce to survive.

References

Abbey, Antonia. 1982. "Sex Differences in Attributions for Friendly Behavior: Do Males Misperceive Female Friendliness?" *Journal of Personality and Social Psychology*. 42:830–38.

Adams, Bert N. 1968. *Kinship in an Urban Setting*. Chicago: Markham.

Adams, Carolyn Teich, and Kathryn Teich Winston. 1980. *Mothers at Work: Public Policies in the United States, Sweden, and China*. New York: Longman.

Andersen, Margaret L. 1983. *Thinking About Women: Sociological and Feminist Perspectives*. New York: Macmillan.

Andrews, William D., and Deborah C. Andrews. 1974. "Technology and the Housewife in Nineteenth Century America." *Women's Studies*. 3: 309-28.

Association for Voluntary Sterilization. 1980. *Annual Report of Number of Sterilizations Performed in the United States through 1979*.

Aved, B.M. 1981. "Trends in Contraceptive Methods of Use by California Family Planning Clinic Clients Aged 10-55, 1976-1979." *American Journal of Public Health*. 71: 1162-64.

Bach, George R., and Peter Wyden. 1968. *The Intimate Enemy*. New York: William Morf.

Bainton, Roland H. 1973. *Women of the Reformation in France and England*. Minneapolis, Minnesota: Augsburg Publishing House.

Balles, Nancy J. 1978. *The Unenforced Law: Title IX Activity by Federal Agencies Other Than HEW*. Report of the National Advisory Council on Women's Educational Programs. Washington, D.C.: U.S. Government Printing Office.

Bandura, A., and R.H. Walters. 1963. *Social Learning and Personality Development*. New York: Holt, Rinehart & Winston.

Banner, Lois W. 1974. *Women in Modern America: A Brief History*. New York: Harcourt Brace Jovanovich.

Baxter, Sandra, and Marjorie Lansing. 1983. *Women and Politics: The Visible Majority*, rev. ed. Ann Arbor: University of Michigan Press.

Bensman, Joseph, and Robert Lilienfeld. 1979. "Friendship and Alienation." *Psychology Today*. 13 (October): 56-66, 114.

Bernard, Jessie. 1981. *The Female World*. New York: Free Press.

Bernard, Jessie. 1972. *The Future of Marriage*. New York: Bantam.

Bernstein, G.S. 1971. "Clinical Effectiveness of an Aerosol Contraceptive Foam." *Contraception*. 3: 37-43.

Berry, J.W. 1971. "Ecological and Cultural Factors in Spatial Perceptual Development." *Canadian Journal of Behavioral Science*. 3:324-36.

Bicchieri, M. 1972. *Hunters and Gatherers Today*.New York: Holt, Rinehart & Winston.

Binford, Sally R. 1968. "Early Upper Pleistocene Adaptations in Levent." *American Anthropologist*. 70.

Blumstein, Philip, and Pepper Schwartz. 1983. *American Couples: Money, Work, Sex*.New York: William Morrow.

Boles, Janet K. 1979. *The Politics of the Equal Rights Amendment: Conflict and the Decision Process*. New York: Longman.

Boulding, Elise. 1976. *The Underside of History: A View of Women Through Time*. Boulder: Westview Press.

Bronfenbrenner, Uri. 1974. Testimony Before the Senate Subcommittee on Children and Youth. In *American Families: Trends and Pressures*. Washington, D.C.: U.S. Government Printing Office.

Brownmiller, Susan. 1976. *Against Our Will*. New York: Bantam.

Buckley, J.E. 1975. "Equal Pay in America." *Equal Pay for Women: Progress and Problems in Seven Countries*, edited by Barrie O. Pettman. West Yorkshire, England: MCB Books.

Buhle, Mari Jo, and Paul Buhle, editors. 1978. *The Concise History of Woman Suffrage*. Urbana: University of Illinois Press.

Bullough, Vern L. 1979. "Female Physiology, Technology, and Women's Liberation." *Dynamos and Virgins Revisited: Women and Technological Change in History*, edited by Martha Moore Trescott. Metuchen: Scarecrow Press, Inc.

Bureau of the Census. 1981a. *Current Population Reports, Household and Family Characteristics: March 1980*. Washington, D.C.: U.S. Department of Commerce.

Bureau of the Census. 1981b. *Current Population Reports, Marital Status and Living Arrangements: March 1980*. Washington, D.C.: U.S. Department of Commerce.

Bushnell, L.F. 1965. "Aerosol Foam: A Practical and Effective Method of Contraception." *Pacific Medicine and Surgery*. 73: 353-55.

Campbell, Angus, Philip E. Converse, Warren E. Miller, and Donald E. Stokes. 1960. *The American Voter*. New York: Wiley.

Cannon, K.L., and R. Long. 1971. "Premarital Sexual Behavior in the Sixties." *Journal of Marriage and the Family*. 33: 36-49.

Cappiello, J.D., and M. Grainger-Harrison. 1981. "The Rebirth of the Cervical Cap." *Journal of Nurse Midwifery*. 26 (September-October): 13-18.

Casanova, J. De Seingalt. No Date. *Memoires*. . . . . Paris: Libraire Garnier Freres. 6 Volumes.

Catt, Carrie Chapman, and Nettie Rogers Schuler. 1926. *Woman Suffrage and Politics: The Inner Story of the Suffrage Movement*. New York: Charles Scribner's Sons.

Chafe, William H. 1972. *The American Woman: Her Changing Social, Economic, and Political Roles, 1920–1970*. London: Oxford University Press.

Chafetz, Janet S. 1974. *Masculine/Feminine or Human? An Overview of the Sociology of Sex Roles*. Itasca: F.E. Peacock.

Chapman, Jane Roberts. 1976. "Sex Discrimination in Credit: The Backlash of Economic Dependency." *Economic Independence for Women*, edited by Jane Roberts Chapman. Beverly Hills: Sage Publications.

Chesler, Phyllis. 1971. "Women as Psychiatric and Psychotherapeutic Patients." *Journal of Marriage and the Family*. 33: 746-59.

Chodorow, Nancy. 1978. *The Reproduction of Mothering*. Berkeley: University of California Press.

Clark, Alice. 1919. *Working Life for Women in the Seventeenth Century*. London: Routledge.

Clark, Terry M, editor. 1969. *On Communication and Social Influence.* Chicago: University of Chicago Press.

Coates, B., E.P. Anderson, and W.W. Hartup. 1972. "Interrelations in the Attachment of Human Infants." *Development Psychology.* 6: 218-30.

Connell, E.B. 1982. "Vaginal Contraception." *Advances in Fertility Research Volume I,* edited by D.R. Mishell, Jr. New York: Raven Press.

Cooley, Thomas Horton. 1909. *Social Organizations: A Study of the Larger Mind.* New York: Charles Scribner's Sons.

Coolidge, Olivia. 1966. *Women's Rights: The Suffrage Movement in America, 1848-1920.* New York: Dutton

Costain, Anne N. 1981. "Representing Women: The Transition from Social Movement to Interest Group." *Western Political Quarterly.* 34: 100-13.

Cowan, Ruth Schwartz. 1979. "From Virginia Dare to Virginia Slims: Women and Technology in American Life." *Technology and Culture.* 20: 51-63.

Cowan, Ruth Schwartz. 1977. "Women and Technology in American Life." *Technology at the Turning Point,* edited by William B. Pickett. San Francisco: San Francisco Press.

Cowan, Ruth Schwartz. 1976a. "The 'Industrial Revolution' in the Home: Household Technology and Social Change in the Twentieth Century." *Technology and Culture.* 17: 1-23.

Cowan, Ruth Schwartz. 1976b. "Two Washes in the Morning and a Bridge Party at Night: The American Housewife between the Wars." *Women's Studies.* 3: 147-72.

Cowan, Ruth Schwartz. 1974. "A Case Study of Technological and Social Change: The Washing Machine and the Working Wife." *Clio's Consciousness Raised,* edited by Mary Hartman and Lois W. Banter. New York: Harper Torch Books.

Davies, Margery W. 1983. *Woman's Place Is at the Typewriter: Office Work and Office Workers, 1870-1930.* Philadelphia: Temple University Press.

Davis, Hugh J. 1971. *Intrauterine Devices for Contraception.*Baltimore: Williams and Wilkins.

Davis, Keith E. 1985. "Near and Dear: Friendship and Love Compared." *Psychology Today.* 19 (February): 22-30.

DeLucia, L.A. 1963. "The Toy Preference Test: A Measure of Sex Role Identification." *Child Development.* 34: 107-17.

Diamond, Irene. 1977. *Sex Roles in the Statehouse.* New Haven: Yale University Press.

Dickinson, Robert L., and Louise Stevens Bryant. 1931. *Control of Conception: An Illustrated Medical Manual.* Baltimore: Williams and Wilkins.

Dienes, C. Thomas. 1972. *Law, Politics, and Birth Control.* Urbana: University of Illinois Press.

Dixon, G.W., J.J. Schlesselman, H.W. Ory, and R.P. Blye. 1980. "Ethinyl Estradiol and Conjugated Estrogens as Post Coital Contraceptives." *Journal of the American Medical Association.* 244: 1336-39.

Doan, Michael, and Patricia A. Avery. 1985. "New Women Politicians: Tested, Tougher, Wiser." *U.S. News and World Report.* 8 (March 4): 76-77.

Dubois, Ellen Carol. 1978. *Feminism and Suffrage: The Emergence of an Independent Women's Movement in America: 1848–1869*. Ithaca: Cornell University Press.

Durden-Smith, Jo, and Diane deSimone. 1983. *Sex and the Brain*. New York: Arbor House.

Duvall, Evelyn M. 1977. *Family Development*. 5th ed. Philadelphia: Lippincott.

Eisenstein, Z., editor. 1979. *Socialist Feminism and the Case for Capitalist Patriarchy*. New York: Monthly Review Press.

Elliot, Mabel A., and Francis E. Merrill. 1941. *Social Disorganization*. Rev. ed. New York: Harper & Row.

Elshstain, J.B. 1974. "Moral Woman and Immoral Man." *Politics and Society*. 453-73.

Epstein, Cynthia Fuchs. 1981. "Women and Power: The Role of Women in Politics in the United States." *Access to Power: Cross-National Studies of Women and Elites*, edited by Cynthia Fuchs Epstein and Rose Laub Coser. London: George Allen and Unwin.

Ernest, J. 1976. "Mathematics and Sex." *American Mathematical Monthly*. 83: 595-614.

Feinstein, Karen Wolk. 1979. "Directions for Daycare." *Working Women and Families*, edited by Karen Wolk Feinstein. Beverly Hills: Sage Publications.

Feldberg, Roslyn L., and Evelyn Nakano Glenn. 1983. "Technology and Work Degradation: Effects of Office Automation on Women Clerical Workers." *Machina Ex Dea: Feminist Perspectives on Technology*. Elmsford, N.Y.: Pergamon Press.

Ferree, Myra Marks. 1974. "A Woman for President? Changing Responses 1958-1972." Public Opinion Quarterly. 37: 390-99.

Ferrell, Mary Z., William L. Tolone, and Robert H. Walsh. 1977. "Maturational and Societal Changes in the Sexual Double Standard: A Panel Analysis." *Journal of Marriage and the Family*. 39: 255-71.

Filene, Peter Gabriel. 1974. *Him Her Self: Sex Roles in Modern America*. New York: New American Library.

Firestone, Shulamith. 1970. *The Dialectic of Sex: The Case for Feminist Revolution*. New York: William Morrow.

Flexner, Eleanor. 1959. *Century of Struggle*. Cambridge, Mass.: Harvard University Press.

Folsom, Joseph K. 1943. *The Family and Democratic Society*. New York: Wiley.

Fox, L.H., E. Fennema, and J. Sherman, editors. 1977. *Women and Mathematics: Research Perspectives for Change*. Washington, D.C.: National Institute of Education.

Freeman, Jo. 1975. *The Politics of Women's Liberation*. New York: McKay.

Freeman, Jo. 1973. "The Origins of the Women's Liberation Movement." *American Journal of Sociology*. 78: 30-49.

Freud. Sigmund. 1974. "Three Essays on Sexuality." Translated by J. Strachey. Reprinted in *Women and Analysis*, edited by J. Strouse. New York: Viking.

Friedan, Betty. 1963. *The Feminine Mystique*. New York: Norton.

Frieze. I., J. Parsons, P. Johnson, D. N. Ruble, and G. Zellman, editors. 1978. *Women and Sex Roles*. New York: Norton.

Frisch, Rose E. 1978. "Population, Food Intake, and Fertility." *Science*. 199: 22-30.

Frohock, Fred M. 1983. *Abortion: A Case Study in Law and Morals*. Westport, Conn.: Greenwood Press.

Gagnon, John H. 1977. *Human Sexualities*. Glenview, Illinois: Scott Foresman.

Gelb, Joyce, and Marian Lief Palley. 1982. *Women and Public Policies*. Princeton: Princeton University Press.

Gerbner, George. 1978. "The Dynamics of Cultural Resistance." In *Hearth and Home: Images of Women in the Mass Media*, edited by Gaye Tuchman, Arlene Kaplan Daniels, and James Benet. New York: Oxford University Press.

Glazer-Malbin, Nona. 1976. "Housework." *Signs*. 1: 905-22.

Glick, P.C., and A.J. Norton. 1977. "Marrying, Divorcing, and Living Together in the U.S. Today." *Population Bulletin*. 32: 2-38.

Gluck, Sherna, editor. 1976. *From Parlor to Prison: Five American Suffragists Talk About Their Lives*. New York: Octagon Books.

Gold, Michael Evan. 1983. *A Dialog on Comparable Worth*. Ithaca: ILR press.

Goldberg, Steven. 1973. *The Inevitability of Patriarchy*. New York: William Morrow.

Goldberg, S., and M. Lewis. 1969. "Play Behavior in the Year Old Infant: Early Sex Differences." *Child Development*.40: 21-31.

Goldstein, L. 1979. *The Constitutional Rights of Women*. New York: Longman.

Goode, William J. 1959. "The Theoretical Importance of Love." *American Sociological Review*. 24: 38-47.

Gordon, Michael, and M. Charles Bernstein. 1970. "Mate Choice and Domestic Life in the Nineteenth Century Marriage Manual." *Journal of Marriage and the Family*. 32: 665-74.

Gordon, Michael, and Penelope J. Shankweiler. 1971. "Different Equals Less: Female Sexuality in Recent Marriage Manuals." *Journal of Marriage and the Family*. 33: 459-66.

Gove, W.R., and G.R. Carpenter. 1982. *The Fundamental Connection between Nature and Nurture*. Lexington, Mass.: Lexington Books.

Goy, R.W., and B.S. McEwen. 1980. *Sexual Differentiation of the Brain*. Cambridge, Mass.: MIT Press.

Grossman, Allyson Sherman. 1980. "Women in Domestic Work: Yesterday and Today." *Monthly Labor Review*. 103: 17-21.

Guttentag, Marcia, and Helen Bray. 1977. "Teachers as Mediators of Sex Role Standards." *Beyond Sex Roles*, edited by Alice Sargent. St. Paul, Minn.: West Publishing Co.

Guttentag, Marcia, and Paul F. Secord. 1983. *Too Many Women? The Sex Ratio Question*. Beverly Hills: Sage Publishers.

Hapgood, Fred. 1979. *Why Males Exist: An Inquiry into the Evolution of Sex*.New York: New American Library.

Harding, S. 1981. "What is the Real Material Base of Patriarchy and Capital?" *Women and Revolution*, edited by L. Sargent. Boston: South End Press.

Hartley, Ruth E. 1964. "A Developmental View of Female Sex Roles Definition and Identification." *Merrill–Palmer Quarterly*. 10:3-16.

Hartley, Ruth E., and F.P. Hardesty. 1964. "Children's Perceptions of Sex Roles in Childhood." *Journal of Genetic Psychology*. 105: 43-151.

Hartmann, H. 1981. "The Family as the Locus of Gender, Class, and Political Struggle: The Example of Housework." *Signs*. 6: 366-94.

Hastings-Tolsma, M.T. 1982. "The Cervical Cap: A Barrier Contraceptive." *American Journal of Maternal Child Nursing.* 7: 382-86.

Hatcher, Robert A., Gary K. Stewart, Felicia Stewart, Felicia Guest, Nancy Josephs, and Janet Dale. 1982. *Contraceptive Technology, 1982-83,* 11th rev. ed. New York: Irvington.

Hedblom, Milda K. 1983. *Women and American Political Organizations and Institutions.* Washington, D.C.: American Political Science Association.

Heer, David M., and Amyra Grossbard-Shechtman. 1981. "The Impact of the Female Marriage Squeeze and the Contraceptive Revolution on Sex Roles and the Women's Liberation Movement in the United States, 1960 to 1975." *Journal of Marriage and the Family.* 43: 49-65.

Helfgott, Roy B. 1966. "EPD and the Office Work Force." *Industrial and Labor Relations Review.* 19: 503-16.

Himes, Norman E. 1970. *Medical History of Contraception.* New York: Schocken Books.

Hite, Shere. 1981. *The Hite Report on Male Sexuality.* New York: Ballentine Books.

Horney, Karen. 1926. "The Flight From Womanhood." *International Journal of Psychoanalysis.* 7: 324-39.

Howe, Louise Kapp. 1977. *Pink Collar Workers: Inside the World of Women's Work.* New York: Avon Books.

Hoyenga, K.B., and K. Hoyenga. 1979. *The Question of Sex Differences: Psychological, Cultural, and Biological Issues.* Boston: Little, Brown.

Huber, Joan. 1976. "Toward a Sociotechnological Theory of the Women's Movement." *Social Problems.* 23: 371-88.

Huber, S.C. 1975. "IUDs Reassessed." *Population Reports.* Series B. No. 2, January. Washington, D.C.: The George Washington University Medical Center.

Irwin, Inez Haynes. 1971. *The Story of the Women's Party.* New York: reprinted by Kraus Reprint Co.

"IUD Users May Have Higher Risks of Contracting PID, Studies Find: Pill May Have Protective Effect." 1980. *Family Planning Perspectives.* 12: 206-08.

Jacklin, C.N., E.E. Maccoby, and A.E. Dick. 1973. "Barrier Behavior and Toy Preference: Sex Differences (And Their Absence) in the Year Old Child." *Child Development.* 44: 196-200.

Jackson, M., G.S. Burger, and L.G. Keith, editors. 1981. *Vaginal Contraception.* Boston: G.K. Hall.

Jaggar, A., and P.R. Struhl. 1978. *Feminist Frameworks: Alternative Theoretical Accounts of the Relations between Women and Men.* New York: McGraw-Hill.

Jennings, M. Kent., and Barbara G. Farah. 1981. "Social Roles and Political Resources: An Overtime Study of Men and Women in Party Elites." *American Journal of Political Science.* 25: 462-82.

Johannes, John R. 1984. "Women as Congressional Staffers: Does It Make a Difference?" *Women and Politics.* 4: 69-81.

Joint Economic Committee, Subcommittee on Priorities and Economy in Government, U.S. Congress. 1978. *Hearings: The Role of Women in the Military.* Washington, D.C.: U.S. Government Printing Office.

Jones, E.F., J.R. Beniger, and C.F. Westoff. 1980. "Pill and IUD Discontinuation in the U.S., 1970-75: The Influence of the Media." *Family Planning Perspectives.* 12: 293-300.

Kagan, J. 1958. "The Concept of Identification." *Psychological Review.* 65: 296-305.

Kahn, Wendy, and Joy Ann Grune. 1982. "Pay Equity: Beyond Equal Pay for Equal Work." *Women, Power, and Policy,* edited by Ellen Boneparth. New York: Pergamon Press.

Kamerman, Sheila B., Alfred J. Kahn, and Paul Kingston. 1983. *Maternity Policies and Working Women.* New York: Columbia University Press.

Kanin, Eugene J., and Stanley R. Parcell. 1981. "Sexual Aggression: A Second Look at the Offended Female." *Women and Crime in America,* edited by Lee H. Bowker. New York: Macmillan.

Kantner, J.F., and M. Zelnick. 1972. "Sexual Experience of Young Unmarried Women in the United States." *Family Planning Perspectives.* 4: 9-18.

Keith, L.G., G.S. Burger, and M.A. Jackson. 1982. "Effective Use of Vaginal Contraception: A Method for the 1980s." *Contemporary Ob/Gyn.* 19: 64-85.

King, Karl, Jack O. Balswick, and Ira E. Robinson. 1977. "The Continuing Premarital Sexual Revolution Among College Females." *Journal of Marriage and the Family.* 39: 455-59.

Kinsbourne, M., editor. 1978. *Asymmetrical Functions of the Brain.* Cambridge, England: Cambridge University Press.

Kinsey, Alfred, Wardell B. Pomeroy, and Clyde E. Martin. 1948. *Sexual Behavior in the Human Male.* Philadelphia: W.B. Saunders.

Kinsey, Alfred, Wardell B. Pomeroy, Clyde E. Martin, and Paul H. Gebhard. 1953. *Sexual Behavior in the Human Female.* Philadelphia: W.B. Saunders.

Kirpatrick, Clifford, and Eugene J. Kanin. 1957. "Male Sex Aggression on a University Campus." *American Sociological Review.* 22: 52-58.

Kluckhohn, C. 1962. *Culture and Behavior.* New York: Free Press.

Koedt, A. 1973. "The Myth of the Vaginal Orgasm." *Radical Feminism,* edited by A. Koedt, E. Levine, and A. Rapine. New York: Quadrangle.

Kohlberg, Lawrence. 1966. "A Cognitive-Developmental Analysis of Children's Sex-Role Concepts and Attitudes." *The Development of Sex Differences,* edited by E.E. Maccoby. Stanford: Stanford University Press.

Kohn, Mel. 1969. *Class and Conformity.* Homewood, Ill.: Dorsey Press.

Komarovsky, M. 1953. *Women in the Modern World.* Boston: Little, Brown.

Kraditor, Aileen S. 1965. *The Ideas of the Woman Suffrage Movement, 1890—1920.* New York: Columbia University Press.

Kruez, Leo, and Robert Rose. 1971. "Assessment of Aggressive Behavior in a Young Animal Population." *Psychiatric Spectator.* 7: 15-16.

Landis, Judson T., and Mary G. Landis. 1977. *Building a Successful Marriage.* 7th ed. Englewood Cliffs: Prentice-Hall.

Lane, M.E., R. Arceo, and A.J. Sobrero. 1976. "Successful Use of the Diaphragm and Jelly by a Young Population: Report of a Clinical Study."*Family Planning Perspectives.* 8: 81-86.

Laslett, Peter. 1965. *The World We Have Lost.* London: Methuen.

Laws, Judith Long. 1979. *The Second Sex: Sex Role and Social Role.* New York: Elsevier.

Layde, P.M., V. Beral, and C.R. Kay. 1981. "Further Analyses of Mortality in Oral Contraceptive Users." *Lancet*. 1:541–46.

Leacock, Eleanor. 1983. "Ideologies of Male Dominance as Divide and Rule Politics: An Anthropologist's View." *Woman's Nature: Rationalizations of Inequality*, edited by Marian Lowe and Ruth Hubbard. New York: Pergamon Press.

Lee, Richard B., and Irven De Vore, editors. 1968. *Man the Hunter*. Chicago: Aldine.

Le Masters, E.E. 1974. *Parents in Modern America*. Homewood: Dorsey Press.

Lemons, J. Stanley. 1973. *The Woman Citizen: Social Feminism in the 1920s*. Urbana: University of Illinois Press.

Leonard, Jonathan Norton. 1973. *The First Farmers*. New York: Time-Life Books.

Lever, Janet. 1976. "Sex Differences in the Games Children Play." *Social Problems*. 23:478–87.

Lichtheim, George. 1961. *Marxism*. New York: Praeger.

Lipman-Blumen, Jean. 1984. *Gender Roles and Power*. Englewood Cliffs: Prentice-Hall.

Lipman-Blumen, Jean. 1976. "The Implications for Family Structure of Changing Sex Roles." *Social Casework*. 57: 67–69.

Long, Clarence D. 1958. *The Labor Force Under Changing Income and Employment*. Princeton: Princeton University Press.

Lott, Bernice, Mary Ellen Riley, and Dale R. Howard. 1982. "Sexual Assault and Harassment: A Campus Community Case Study." *Signs*. 296–319.

Lowe, Marian, and Ruth Hubbard. 1983. *Woman's Nature: Rationalizations of Inequality*. New York: Pergamon Press.

Lowenthal, Marjorie, Majda Thurner, and David Chiriboga. 1975. *Four Stages of Life*. San Francisco: Jossey-Bass.

Lynd, Robert, and Helen Lynd. 1937. *Middletown in Transition*. New York: Harcourt Brace Jovanovich.

Lynd, Robert, and Helen Lynd. 1929. *Middletown*. New York: Harcourt Brace Jovanovich.

Maccoby, E.E. 1966. *The Development of Sex Differences*. Stanford: Stanford University Press.

Maccoby, E.E., and C. N. Jacklin. 1974. *The Psychology of Sex Differences*. Stanford: Stanford University Press.

Mace, David R. 1976. "Marital Intimacy and the Deadly Love-Anger Cycle." *Journal of Marriage and Family Counseling*. 2:131–37.

McGuiness, D. 1976. "Away from a Unisex Psychology: Individual Differences in Visual, Sensory, and Perceptual Processes." *Perception*. 5:279–94.

Marzano, William A. 1983. "Sex and the Single Standard." *Psychology Today*. 17 (September): 76.

Mastalli, Grace L. 1977. *Sex Bias: Education Legislation and Regulations*. Report of the National Advisory Council on Women's Educational Programs. Washington, D.C.: U.S. Government Printing Office.

Masters, W.H., and V.E. Johnson. 1966. *Human Sexual Response*. Boston: Little, Brown.

Mathews, Donald K., and Edward L. Fox. 1976. *The Physiological Basis of Physical Education and Athletics*, 2nd ed. Philadelphia: W.B. Saunders.

Mead, George Herbert. 1934. *Mind, Self, and Society*, edited by Charles W. Morris. Chicago: University of Chicago Press.

Mead, Margaret. 1969. *Sex and Temperament in Three Primitive Societies*. New York: Dell.

Meissner, N., Elizabeth W. Humphreys, Scott M. Meis, and William J. Scheu. 1975. "No Exit for Wives: Sexual Division of Labour and the Cumulation of Household Demands." *Canadian Review of Sociology and Anthropology.* 12:424–39.

Mezy, Susan Gluck. 1978. "Does Sex Make a Difference? A Case Study of Women in Politics." *Western Political Quarterly.* 31:492–501.

Miller, Brent C. 1975. "Studying the Quality of Marriage Cross-Sectionally." *Journal of Marriages and the Family.* 37:11–12.

Mitchell, J. 1971. *Woman's Estate*. New York: Pantheon.

Morris, J.M. 1973."Mechanisms Involved in Progesterone Contraception and Estrogen Interception." *American Journal of Obstetrics and Gynecology.* 117:167–76.

Morris, J.M., and G. Van Waganen. 1967. "Post-Coital Oral Contraception." *Proceedings of the Eighth International Conference of the International Planned Parenthood Federation*. Santiago, Chile, April 9–15, edited by R.K.B. Hankinson, R.L. Kleinman, P. Eckstein, and H. Romero. London: International Planned Parenthood Federation.

Mosher, William D. 1982. "Fertility and Family Planning in the 1970s: The National Survey of Family Growth." *Family Planning Perspectives.* 14:314–20.

Mosher, William D. 1981. *Contraceptive Utilization, United States, 1976*. Vital and Health Statistics Series 23. Data from the National Survey of Family Growth, No. 7. Washington, D.C.: National Center for Health Statistics.

Moulds, Elizabeth Fry. 1982. "Women's Crime, Women's Justice." *Women, Power, and Policy*, edited by Ellen Boneparth. New York: Pergamon Press.

Mowrer, Ernest R. 1927. *Family Disorganization*. Chicago: University of Chicago Press.

National Advisory Council on Women's Educational Programs. 1982. *Educational Equity: A Continuing Quest*. Washington, D.C.: U.S. Government Printing Office.

National Advisory Council on Women's Educational Programs. 1981. *Women's Education: The Challenge of the Eighties*. Washington, D.C.: U.S. Government Printing Office.

National Advisory Council on Women's Educational Programs. 1980. *Equity for the Eighties*. Washington, D.C.: U.S. Government Printing Office.

Nimkoff, Meyer F. 1947. *Marriage and the Family*. Boston: Houghton Mifflin.

Nimkoff, Meyer F. 1934. *The Family*. Boston: Houghton Mifflin.

Nimkoff, Meyer F., and William F. Ogburn. 1955. *Technology and the Changing Family*. Boston: Houghton Mifflin.

Norgren, Jill. 1982. "In Search of a National Child-Care Policy: Background and Prospects." *Women, Power, and Policy*, edited by Ellen Boneparth. New York: Pergamon Press.

Norwood, Janet Lippe. 1982. *The Female-Male Earnings Gap: A Review of Employment and Earnings Issues.* U.S. Department of Labor. Washington, D.C.: U.S. Government Printing Office.

"NSFG 1982: Sterilization Use Up, Pill Use Down Among Married Women." 1984. *Family Planning Perspectives.* 16:37–38.

Nye, F. Ivan, and Felix M. Berardo. 1973. *The Family: Its Structure and Interaction.* New York: Macmillan.

Nye, F. Ivan, and Felix M. Berardo. 1966. *Emerging Conceptual Frameworks in Family Analysis.* New York' Macmillan.

Oakley, Ann. 1972. *Sex, Gender, and Society.* New York: Harper Colophon.

Ogburn, William F. 1950. *Social Change with Respect to Culture and Original Nature,* rev. ed. New York: Viking.

Oliva, G., and J. Cobble. 1979. "A Reappraisal of the Use and Effectiveness of the Diaphragm: An Appropriate Modern Contraceptive." *Advances in Planned Parenthood.* 14:27–32.

Oliver, John W. 1956. *History of American Technology.* New York: Ronald Press.

O'Neill, William L. 1969. *Everyone Was Brave.* Chicago: Quadrangle Press.

Oppenheimer, Valerie K. 1970. *The Female Labor Force in the United States.* Berkeley: University of California Press.

Parsons, J.E., editor. 1980. *The Psychobiology of Sex Differences and Sex Roles.* Washington, D.C.: Hemisphere.

Petchesky, Rosalyn Pollack. 1984. *Abortion and Women's Choice: The State, Sexuality, and Reproductive Freedom.* New York: Longman.

Petitti, D.B., J. Wingard, F. Pellegrin, and S. Ramcharan. 1979. "Risk of Vascular Disease in Women: Smoking, Oral Contraceptives, Noncontraceptive Estrogens, and Other Factors." *Journal of the American Medical Association.* 242:1150–54.

Phillips, Jordan M., Donald Keith, Joroslov Hulka, Barbara Hulka, and Louis Keith. 1976. "Gynecological Laparoscopy." *Journal of Reproductive Medicine.* 16:105–17.

Phillips, Jordan M., Jososlov Hulka, Donald Keith, Barbara Hulka, and Louis Keith. 1975. "Laparoscopic Procedures: A National Survey for 1975." *Journal of Reproductive Medicine.* 18:219–26.

Pleck, J.H. 1979. "Men's Family Work: Three Perspectives and Some New Data." Wellesley: Wellesley College Center for Research on Women.

Pogrebin, Letty Cottin. 1972. "Down With Sexist Upbringing." *Ms.* Spring: 18, 20, 25–30.

Powell, Lynda Watts, Clifford W. Brown, and Roman B. Hedges. 1981. "Male and Female Differences in Elite Political Participation: An Examination of the Effects of Socio-Economic and Familial Variables." *Western Political Quarterly.* 34:31–45.

Powers, Edward A., and Gorden L. Bultena. 1976. "Sex Differences in Intimate Friendships of Old Age." *Journal of Marriage and the Family.* 38:739–47.

Pyke, Magnus. 1967. *The Science Century.* New York: Walker and Co.

Rabban, M. 1950. "Sex Role Identification in Young Children in Two Diverse Social Groups." *Genetic Psychology Monograph.* 42:81–158.

Reich, Robert B. 1983. *The Next American Frontier*. New York: Times Books.

Reiss, Ira L. 1967. *The Social Context of Premarital Sexual Permissiveness*. New York: Holt, Rinehart & Winston.

Reiss, Ira L. 1960a. *Premarital Sexual Standards In America*. New York: Free Press.

Reiss, Ira L. 1960b. "Toward a Sociology of the Heterosexual Love Relationship." *Marriage and Family Living*. 22: 139–145.

Richards, Eric. 1974. "Women in the British Economy Since About 1700: An Interpretation." *History*. 59:337–57.

Richardson, L.W. 1981. *The Dynamics of Sex and Gender*. Boston: Houghton Mifflin.

Robinson, Ira., and Davor Jedlicka. 1982. *Journal of Marriage and the Family*. 44: 237–40.

Rohrbaugh, Joanna Bunker. 1979. "Femininity on the Line." *Psychology Today*. 13: 33–42.

Rollins, Boyd C., and Harold Feldman. 1970. "Marital Satisfaction Over the Family Life Cycle." *Journal of Marriage and the Family*." 32: 20–28.

Roper Organization, Inc. 1980. *The 1980 Virginia Slims American Women's Opinion Poll*. Storrs: The Roper Center.

Rosaldo, M.Z., and Lamphere, L., editors. 1974. *Women, Culture, and Society*. Stanford: Stanford University Press.

Rosenberg, B.G., and B. Sutton-Smith. 1968. "Family Interaction Effects on Masculinity-Femininity." *Journal of Personality and Social Psychology*. 8: 117–20.

Ross, Susan Deller, and Ann Barcher. 1983. *The Rights of Women: The Basic ACLU Guide to a Woman's Rights*, rev. ed. New York: Bantam.

Rossi, Alice S. 1984. "Gender and Parenthood." *American Sociological Review*. 49: 1–19.

Rothberg, Herman J. 1969. "A Study of the Impact of Office Automation in the IRS." *Monthly Labor Review*. 92: 26–30.

Rothschild, Joan, editor. 1983a. *Machina ex Dea: Feminist Perspectives on Technology*. Elmsford: Pergamon Press.

Rothschild, Joan. 1983b. "Technology, Housework, and Women's Liberation: A Theoretical Analysis." *Machina Ex Dea: Feminist Perspectives on Technology*. Elmsford: Pergamon Press.

Rothschild, M.A. 1979. "White Women Volunteers in the Freedom Summers." *Feminist Studies*. 5:466–95.

Royal College of General Practitioners. 1974. *Oral Contraceptives and Health: Report of Royal College of General Practitioners*. London: Pitman Medical.

Rubin, J.Z., F.J. Provenzano, and Z. Luria. 1974. "The Eye of the Beholder: Parents' Views on Sex of Newborns." *American Journal of Orthopsychiatry*. 44: 512–19.

Rubinstein, Carin. 1983. "The Modern Art of Courtly Love." *Psychology Today*. 17 (July): 43–49.

Rusche, Georg, and Otto Kirchheimer. 1968. *Punishment and Social Structure*. New York: Russell and Russell.

Ryder, N.B. 1973. "Contraceptive Failure in the United States." *Family Planning Perspectives*. 5:133–42.

Ryder, N.B., and C.F. Westoff. 1971. *Production in the United States 1965*. Princeton: Princeton University Press.

Safilios-Rothschild, Constantina. 1977. *Love, Sex, and Sex Roles*. Englewood Cliffs: Prentice-Hall.

Sandler, Bernice R. 1984. "The Quiet Revolution on Campus: How Sex Discrimination Has Changed." *The Chronicle of Higher Education*. February 29: 72.

Sapiro, Virginia. 1983a. *The Political Integration of Women: Roles, Socialization, and Politics*. Urbana: University of Illinois Press.

Sapiro, Virginia. 1983b. *Women Political Action and Political Participation*. Washington, D.C.: American Political Science Association.

Schirm, A.L., J. Trussell, J. Menken, and W.R. Grady. 1982. "Contraceptive Failure in the United States: The Impact of Social, Economic, and Demographic Factors." *Family Planning Perspectives*. 14:68–75.

Schoen, Robert. 1975. "California Divorce Rates by Age at Marriage and Duration of First Marriage." *Journal of Marriage and the Family*. 37: 548–55.

Schur, Edwin M. 1984. *Labeling Women Deviant: Gender, Stigma, and Social Control*. New York: Random House.

Scrimshaw, Susan C.M. 1981. "Women and the Pill: From Panacea to Catalyst." *Family Planning Perspectives*. 13: 254–62.

Serbin, L.A., K.D. O'Leary, R.N. Kent, and I.J. Tonick. 1973. "A Comparison of Teacher Response to the Pre-Academic and Problem Behavior of Boys and Girls." *Child Development*. 44:796–804.

Sheehy, Gail. 1974. *Passages: Predictable Crises of Adult Life*. New York: Dutton.

Sherris, Jacqueline D., Sidney H. Moore, and Gordon Fox. 1984. "New Developments in Vaginal Contraception." *Population Reports*. Series H. No. 7. (January-February).

Skolnick, A. 1978. *The Intimate Environment*. Boston: Little, Brown.

Smith-Rosenberg, Carroll. 1975. "The Female World of Love and Ritual: Relations between Women in Nineteenth Century America." *Signs*. 1: 1–29.

Smuts, Robert W. 1959. *Women and Work in America*. New York: Columbia University Press.

Solomon, Robert C. 1981. "The Love Lost in Cliches." *Psychology Today*: 15 (October): 83–94.

Speroff, L., R.H. Glass, and N.G. Kase. 1978. *Clinical Gynecologic Endocrinology and Infertility*, 2nd ed. Baltimore: Williams and Wilkins.

Squire, J.J., G.S. Burger, and L. Keith. 1979. "A Retrospective Clinical Study of a Vaginal Contraceptive Suppository." *Journal of Reproductive Medicine*. 22: 319–23.

Stephan, G. Edward, and Douglas R. McMullin. 1982. "Tolerance of Sexual Nonconformity: City Size as a Situational and Early Learning Determinant." *American Sociological Review*. 47:411–15.

Sternglanz, S.H., and L.A. Serbin. 1974. "Sex Role Stereotyping in Children's Television Programs." *Developmental Psychology*. 10: 710–15.

Stiehm, Judith Hicks. 1982. "Women, Men, and Military Service: Is Protection Necessarily a Racket?" *Women, Power, and Policy*, edited by Ellen Boneparth. New York: Pergamon Press.

Straus, Murray A. 1974. "Leveling, Civility, and Violence in the Family." *Journal of Marriage and the Family*. 36: 13–30.

Sulloway, Alvah W. 1959. *Birth Control and Catholic Doctrine*. Boston: Beacon Press.

Tarde, Gabriel. 1912. *Penal Philosophy*, translated by Rapelje Howell. Boston: Little, Brown.

Tarvis, Carole, and Carol Offir. 1977. *The Longest War: Sex Differences in Perspective*. New York: Harcourt Brace Jovanovich.

Tatum, H.J., and E.B. Connell-Tatum. 1981. "Barrier Contraception: A Comprehensive Overview." *Fertility and Sterility*. 36: 1–12.

Tea, N.T., M. Castanier, M. Roger, and R. Scholler. 1975. "Simultaneous Radio-Immunoassay of Plasma Progesterone and 17 Hydroxyprogesterone in Men and Women Throughout the Menstrual Cycle and in Early Pregnancy." *Journal of Steroid Biochemistry*. 6: 1509–16.

Thrall, Charles A. 1982. "The Conservative Use of Modern Household Technology." *Technology and Culture*. 23: 175–94.

Tilly, Louise, and Joan Scott. 1978. *Women, Work, and Family*. New York: Holt, Rinehart & Winston.

Tobias, Sheila. 1982. "Sexist Equations." *Psychology Today*. 16 (January): 14–17.

Toffler, Alvin. 1980. *The Third Wave*. New York: William Morrow.

Trescott, Martha Moore, editor. 1979. *Dynamos and Virgins Revisited: Women and Technological Change in History*. Metuchen: Scarecrow Press.

Tuchman, Gaye. 1978. "The Symbolic Annihilation of Women by the Mass Media." *Hearth and Home: Images of Women in the Mass Media*, edited by Gaye Tuchman, Arlene Kaplan Daniels, and James Benet. New York: Oxford University Press.

Turner, Daniel. 1717. *Syphilis: A Practial Dissertation on Venereal Disease*. London.

Twentieth Century Fund Task Force on Women and Employment. 1975. *Exploitation from 9 to 5*. Lexington, Mass.: Lexington Books.

U.S. Commission on Civil Rights. 1982. *Sexual Harassment on the Job*. Washington, D.C.: U.S. Government Printing Office.

U.S. Department of Commerce. 1980. *Statistical Abstracts of the United States*. Washington, D.C.: U.S. Government Printing Office.

U.S. Department of Labor, Bureau of Labor Statistics. 1982. *1981 Weekly Earnings of Men and Women Compared in 100 Occupations*. Washington, D.C.: U.S. Government Printing Office.

Vanek, Joann. 1980. "Work, Leisure, and Family Roles: Farm Households in the United States, 1920–1955." *Journal of Family History*. 5: 422–31.

Vanek, Joann. 1978a. "Household Technology and Social Status: Rising Living Standards and Status and Residence Differences in Housework." *Technology and Culture*. 19: 361–75.

Vanek, Joann. 1978b. "Housewives as Workers." *Women Working*, edited by A.H. Stromberg and S. Harkess. Palo Alto: Mayfield.

Vessey, M., M. Lawless, and D. Yeates. 1982. "Efficacy of Different Contraceptive Methods." *Lancet*. 1 (April 10): 841–42.

Walum, Laurel. 1977. *The Dynamics of Sex and Gender: A Sociological Perspective*. Chicago: Rand McNally.

Weinberg, Martin S., and Sue Kiefer Hammersmith. 1983. "Sexual Autonomy and the Status of Women: Models of Female Sexuality in U.S. Sex Manuals from 1950 to 1980." *Social Problems*. 30: 312–24.

Welch, Susan, and Albert K. Karnig. 1979. "Correlates of Female Office Holding in City Politics." *Journal of Politics*. 41:478–91.

Welch, Susan, and Lee Sigelman. 1982. "Changes in Public Attitudes Toward Women and Politics." *Social Science Quarterly*. 63: 312–22.

Wells, J. Gipson. 1984. *Choices in Marriage and Family*. Jackson, Miss.: Piedmont Press.

Westoff, C.F. 1972. "The Modernization of U.S. Contraceptive Practice." *Family Planning Perspectives*. 4 (July): 9–12.

Wexler, Sandra. 1982. "Battered Women and Public Policy." *Women, Power, and Policy*, edited by Ellen Boneparth. New York: Pergamon Press.

Williams, Trevor I., editor. 1978. *A History of Technology, Volume VI, Part I, and Volume VII, Part II*. Oxford, England: Clarendon Press.

Wilmore, Jack H. 1975. "Inferiority of Female Athletes, Myth or Reality?" *Journal of Sports Medicine*. 3:1–6.

Wilmore, Jack H. 1974. "Alterations in Strength, Body Composition, and Anthropometric Measurements Consequent to a Ten Week Weight Training Program." *Medicine and Science in Sports*. 6:133–38.

Woody, Thomas. 1929. *A History of Women's Education in the United States 1*. New York: Science Press.

Wrigley, E.A. 1969. *Population and History*. New York: McGraw-Hill.

Zelnick, Melvin, and John F. Kantner. 1980. "Sexual Activity, Contraceptive Use, and Pregnancy Among Metropolitan-Area Teenagers: 1971–1979." *Family Planning Perspectives*. 12:230–37.

Zelnick, Melvin, and John F. Kantner. 1977. "Sexual and Contraceptive Experience of Young Unmarried Women in the United States, 1976 and 1971." *Family Planning Perspectives*. 9:55–71.

Author Index

Subject Index

About the Authors

MARCIA LYNN WHICKER

Marcia Lynn Whicker is an associate professor at the University of South Carolina, teaching in the Department of Government and International Studies. Prior to 1978, she was on the faculties at Temple University in Philadelphia and Wayne State University in Detroit. She has worked for a variety of government agencies, including the Tennessee Valley Authority; the Department of Health, Education, and Welfare; the U.S. Comptroller in the Treasury Department; the Pennsylvania State Legislature, and the U.S. Congress.

Dr. Whicker has published in the areas of American politics, public administration, and public policy. Her articles have appeared in *Journal of Policy Studies, American Sociological Review,* and *Legislative Studies Quarterly.* She coedited *Perspectives on Taxing and Spending Limits in the United States,* and has coauthored with Dr. Kronenfeld, *U.S. National Health Policy: An Analysis of the Federal Role* (Praeger 1984).

Dr. Whicker holds a B.A. in political science and economics from the University of North Carolina, Chapel Hill; an M.P.A. in public administration from the University of Tennessee, Knoxville; and an M.S. in economics and an M.A. and Ph.D. in political science from the University of Kentucky, Lexington. She currently studies electronic engineering technology at Midlands Technical College in Columbia.

JENNIE JACOBS KRONENFELD

Jennie Jacobs Kronenfeld is a professor at the University of South Carolina, Columbia, S.C. She teaches in the Department of Health Administration, School of Public Health. Until 1980, she was on the faculty at the University of Alabama in Birmingham.

Dr. Kronenfeld has published widely in the areas of public policy, public health, and medical sociology. Her articles have appeared in the *Journal of Health and Social Behavior, Social Science and Medicine,* and the *American Journal of Public Health.* She has coauthored *Social and Economic Impacts of Coronary Artery Disease,* and, with Dr. Whicker, *U.S. National Health Policy.*

Dr. Kronenfeld holds a B.A. in history and sociology from the University of North Carolina, Chapel Hill; and an M.A. and Ph.D. in sociology from Brown University, Providence, Rhode Island. She frequently exhibits "superwoman" energy levels, combining the roles of wife and mother of two boys while being one of the youngest women to achieve the rank of full professor at USC. She has taught courses in sex roles, and has long been an ardent feminist. As a proponent of women's rights, she welcomed the opportunity to write this book as a way of reexaming equality for women.